PENGUIN AFRICAN LIBRARY
Edited by Ronald Segal

Which Way Africa?

Basil Davidson is a writer and historian of Africa whose
books have appeared in twenty languages. His work on
Africa includes *Report on Southern Africa* (1952); *The
African Awakening* (1955, dealing mainly with the Belgian
Congo and Angola); *The Liberation of Guiné* (Portuguese
West Africa) published in 1969 in the Penguin African
Library; and, on the historical side, *Old Africa
Rediscovered* (U.S. title, *The Lost Cities of Africa*) 1959;
Black Mother (1961); *The African Past* (1964, also in the
Penguin African Library); and *The Africans* (U.S. title,
The African Genius) 1969, an introduction to African social
and cultural history, as well as other books and articles
devoted to historical and contemporary topics. His latest
book is *Discovering our African Heritage* (1971).

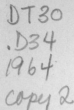
Penguin Books Ltd, Harmondsworth, Middlesex, England
Penguin Books Inc., 7110 Ambassador Road, Baltimore, Maryland 21207, U.S.A.
Penguin Books Australia Ltd, Ringwood,
Victoria, Australia

First published 1964
Second edition 1967
Third edition 1971
Reprinted 1973

Copyright © Basil Davidson 1964, 1967, 1971

Made and printed in Great Britain by C. Nicholls & Company Ltd
Set in Monotype Plantin

BASIL DAVIDSON

Which Way Africa?

The Search for a New Society

Third Edition

Penguin Books

It is now such a time that every man stands under the eaves of his own hat, and sings what he pleases.
Ben Jonson

Contents

Map   8–9

1 A Time of Great Change   11

2 The African Groundwork   19

3 The Foreign Contribution   34

4 Key Ideas   49

5 Political Springboards   55
African Nationalism
Pan-Africanism
The African Personality

6 The Real Colonial Crisis   83

7 The Problem of Transition   94

8 Early Approaches   108
The One-Party State
African Socialism
Neutralism
Neo-Colonialism
A New Model

9 Stumbling Blocks   134

10 After 1965: Independence in Travail   147

11 A Neo-Imperialism? Menace and Resistance   203

12 Which Way Africa? The Challenge of the 1970s   214

On the Record: The Charter of Unity   222

References   241

Index   251

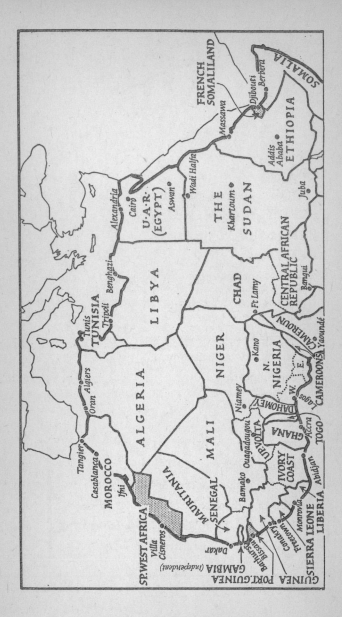

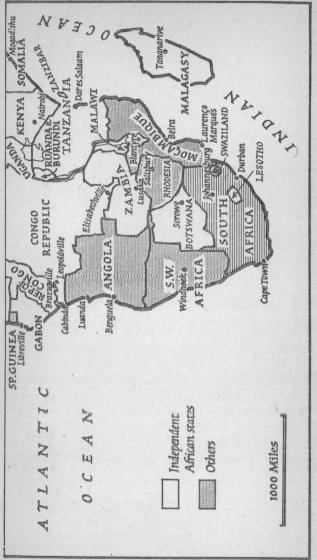

1 A Time of Great Change

There are brief climactic periods in history when the destiny of whole peoples seems to resolve itself for better or for worse. The old gives way to the new; and the new goes forward with a force that is sudden and mysterious.

Afterwards, peering back into moods and memories, historians explain this suddenness and mystery as an illusion, as the mere surface shift from deep-down currents of social and collective change. But those who were there at the time, who watched or played a part themselves, are none the less likely to recall their wonder and delight – or, according to their condition, their trouble and dismay – as though these emotions had really been the product of a kind of miracle. This is how it appears to have happened to people at all times of great upheaval. And this is undoubtedly how it has happened to millions of people in Africa these past years.

But even if the suddenness and mystery are an illusion, concealing the long and deep growth of a new independence, the insistent fact of *change*, and therefore the persistent fact of *choice*, are pressingly real. Africa today may be in many ways remarkably the same as it was twenty years ago: given the general groundwork of technological poverty, nothing else could be expected. Potentially, though, everything of importance in Africa has changed; and it has done so in a sense that may be called irreversible. It has changed so far that everything now seems possible where little or nothing seemed possible before. And people of the most various kinds and loyalties up and down the continent, from the peasants of war-shattered Algeria in the far north to the harried populations of the distant south, and all the way between, are repeatedly confronted with the questions of a great and often passionate debate, the questions of *change* and *choice*: what happens now? where do we go from here? and by which means?

These questions were much in the African atmosphere of 1963, when the earliest edition of this book was written. They were still there four years later, when there was need for a revised edition. In 1970, again up-dating and extending the analysis, one finds the same questions of change and choice more urgent even than before. This is partly because of independent Africa's frustration. Still more, it is because of independent Africa's development.

To grasp the nature of these questions, one needs to keep in mind the mood – often enough desperate – of Africa in the 1960s. No fewer than three colonial wars are being fought on African soil as I write these words. South Africa has long since embarked on a calamitous racial clash, while in Rhodesia the White rebellion of 1965 has further poisoned the air. As oppression tightens in the far south so does the tragedy of everyday life become more squalid, but also sometimes more heroic. The most ordinary men and women may say and do things which become decisive, not only for themselves but also for their whole community, and beyond it, for the world.

I take the following small but characteristic sample of behaviour from *Fighting Talk*, one of the many South African periodicals that have lately been suppressed. Not so many years ago this organ of the Congress resistance movement numbered among its harassed but voluntary distribution agents a young man called Mr E. Musi. His 'area' was among the forests and hills of Pondoland in the east of the Cape Province, one of those places in South Africa with a front of beauty and romance. Neither quality is much present, however, in the story of Mr Musi.

He realized one day that he was wanted by the police. Not, this time, for some usual offence such as carrying the wrong pass or telephoning from the wrong kiosk; but for something more serious. For something, apparently, connected with his efforts at getting *Fighting Talk* into circulation. He was ordered to call at the local forester's office for a parcel of newspapers.

Mr Musi was in trouble. If he did as ordered, he might well be inviting his own arrest. If he did not, he would be leaving his copies of *Fighting Talk* in the hands of a man who would certainly never let them go any further. How should he behave? He went to the forester's office and collected his parcel.

But his fears were confirmed when he found that the covers were broken.

Just as I thought [he wrote some time later from Basutoland, the British Protectorate to which he had managed to escape]. When I left the office carrying my parcel I nearly crashed with a police van, in which were two policemen, a C.I.D. in uniform and the Public Prosecutor from Mount Ayliff. They had stopped the van at a road-turn near the office, and were standing outside. Just at the time they saw me, they quickly climbed into the van and were driving towards me when I hid the parcel under a block of wood lying near the forest. . . . This is how I left Ndindindi.

The evening I left they were blocking the road near the forest, thinking they would see me coming out of the forest to my room in the workers' quarters. I left them as they were. The following morning they checked at bus stops between Kokstad and Mount Ayliff. I were watching their vans from the mountains. . .[1]

History does not tell what happened after that, though Mr Musi thought that he would soon be able to slip out from where he was and rescue the papers from under their block of wood. Very largely, Mr Musi's story is South Africa's now. The battle is joined.

Elsewhere, of course, the atmosphere is anything but one of fear and violence. Yet even where it is most peaceful, it is filled with furious argument, not only in the cities and capitals where politicians and intellectuals can be found but also, and perhaps even more, in the little towns and dusty villages where most Africans reside. Anyone who travels much in Africa can bear this out, provided, of course, that the travel is among Africans.

One day in November 1962 I drove some miles off an inland road in order to visit an Iron Age site on the distant slopes of Ngorongoro in northern Tanzania. Masai elders were settling cases in the shade of a tall tree, much as they must have settled them for untold decades of the past; but not far away, prodding a veil of noonday heat, the familiar flag of TANU, sign and symbol of the Tanzania African National Union, hung above an office of mud and thatch. A case of mere decoration? Not at all: this village office of TANU was manned. If its staff were not exactly rushed off their feet, they were certainly there.

Pushing on to Mbulu a couple of days later, I found the area commissioner, Mr Shamshama, deep in conference with village delegates of TANU: so deep, indeed, that they kept him up until the small hours of the night because they held, as he explained to me over breakfast next day, that a wrong appointment had been made of a man who 'did not understand his way', who 'could not be trusted as responsible'. The man was an official appointee, and so Mr Shamshama, in his character of government representative in Mbulu Area, loyally defended him. The compromise reached was not without interest. The government saved face by getting the man reappointed as chairman of the committee in question; but the village delegates carried their point by immediately voting him off it again.

'And that stands – what they've done?'

'That stands,' replied Mr Shamshama, nodding a thoughtful head.

But what is true of villagers in Tanzania is also true of villagers elsewhere. A large debate on the present and the future, on the ways and means of reaching a different kind of life, goes on all over this continent today, and among all sorts and conditions of people.

I mention this mainly to guard against a possible misapprehension from what follows. This book is an attempt to explain and discuss some leading African ideas on political and economic development. In these chapters, inevitably, we shall be largely considering the opinions and decisions of more or less prominent persons: politicians and writers and others who are much in the public eye. But it would be a serious misunderstanding of the real situation to imagine these leaders and would-be leaders as debating merely with each other, before an audience whose minds are so many simple tablets ready for the first emphatic imprint. The leaders of Africa today are in the same basic position as leaders in other countries: their actions and decisions reflect or react to particular scenes and situations, but the common element, in Africa as elsewhere, is the fact of public opinion.

The familiar belief that there is no such thing in Africa as public opinion – *African* public opinion – is another myth of the period now drawing to a close. Whether or not there was such a thing in the distant past – and historical evidence would show that there was – nobody need doubt that African public opinion, in the full meaning of the term, exists today. This view may not be accepted by such rulers as the Portuguese, who explain all nationalist manifestations in their territories as the work of 'communist agitators from outside'; but the evasions of the Portuguese rulers, we may think, do not merit serious attention. Those Europeans in the Rhodesias and Nyasaland who argued, twenty or fewer years ago, that African opposition to British plans for Central African Federation came merely from a 'few subversives', and that 'ninety per cent of the Africans know nothing about it at all',[2] have since had good reason to understand how wrong they were.

In what follows we shall review a mass of slogans, solutions, arguments, debates, decisions, and types of political behaviour. Behind them all it will be well to keep in mind the unseen audience, the village audience weighing and deciding for itself, often moved this way or that by audacious oratory or skilful manoeuvre, but still preserving, if sometimes awkwardly and sometimes curiously, a firm and final notion of what is good for ordinary folk and what is not. Even when most apparently abused by the failings of newly independent government, these are the people who will count for most in defining the limits of the possible. It could even be argued that they will count for more than they have usually counted for elsewhere, if only because their ties with leaders and representatives have remained, precisely, close and ever-present.

Such, then, is the company involved: a vast and vividly diverse audience split into a million meetings. Their matter for argument and counter-argument is practically as wide as life itself. Their debate has gone on from one end of the continent to the other, whether in vast organizations such as the Union des Populations Camerounaises, with its 3,000 *comités de village*, or in tiny ones like the 'old boys' of the Frafra Youngsters' Union and the Mouvement Autonome de Casamance, or in trade unions which have sometimes formed – as in Zambia and Kenya – a crucial means of political pressure.[3]

Many are still outside the debate. But those who have remained outside, in surviving isolation, are many fewer than ten years ago, fewer still than five years ago, fewer again than one year ago. For this has become a continent in the full ferment of deciding, of trying to decide, of believing that it *can* decide and thinking that it *must* decide, its course into the different years ahead.

It is not difficult to see why this should be so.

Within little more than a decade, two-thirds of Africa had emerged from more or less complete subjection to foreigners – less complete with the British and the French, more with the Belgians – and set out again upon its own.

Viewed across the skylines of history, the colonial period has been little more than an episode, even a brief one; but the skylines of history are distant, and to Africans those fifty or sixty years of foreign domination have been tremendous and traumatic. As we shall see, the impact of those years was always massive, and often terribly destructive. It left Africa with everything to build or rebuild. Many fragments of the 'old society' remained. But all too clearly they could never be put together again. Few people thought they should be. What was needed was a new society, a new pattern of daily life, a modern Africa equipped to join the modern world.

Before their political withdrawal some colonial powers, notably the British and the French in their different ways, tried to take a hand in this shaping of a new Africa. They promoted *élites* or 'middle classes', explicitly hoping that their ex-colonies would model themselves on French or British types of political and economic life; and in due course we shall take a look at the outcome of these efforts. What we must note here is that all these colonies, on becoming independent, were at once faced (whether or not they clearly recognized the fact) by difficult and fundamental problems of post-colonial reorganization.

This is the factor of choice. The liberated cannot go on in the old way, for their old masters have departed. They have to find a new way. This new way may be merely a shadowing of their one-time rulers; or it may be merely an exploration of fresh terrain. Or it may be one of many intermediate solutions, ranging from the mere letting-things-slide, at one extreme, to the other extreme of trying to change everything overnight. Africa has lately offered examples at both extremes, as well as of many variants in between.

Faced with this pressing need for reorganization, African politicians and thinkers have embarked on the task of defining what people should want and how they should get it. In doing this they have been led, repeatedly, into reviewing the solutions which other peoples have found or sought. They have had to discover, in so far as that is possible (and it is not so easy as it may sound), what the capitalist countries really mean by free enterprise and what the communist countries really mean by socialism – as well, of course, as investigating the credentials of a large and clamant family of other concepts and ideas. More than this, though – and here again we touch on a central theme in the African awakening – they have been led into thinking back to pre-colonial modes of thought and action; into considering what may be worth trying to conserve or recover from their own traditions of government and ideology; and, increasingly, into attempting a compromise between these major strands of thought and social organization, African and non-African.

In the space of this book I can hope to show only where the main lines of argument and action lead and spread, and to analyse a few probably decisive situations and examples. At this stage of the debate, however, a summary view may perhaps prove more useful than a comprehensive one, at least in promoting the kind of thought and fertile controversy which leads to resolution. We shall certainly miss some interesting details – for which I enter an early apology – yet discussions about African problems have suffered a great deal in the past, or so it seems to me, from minute inspection of the details at the expense of achieving any real idea of the underlying pattern.

New ideas act and react with old ideas. Out of this confused but necessary process a different structure of life increasingly takes shape.

First of all then, if briefly, what were the old ideas?

2 The African Groundwork

The peoples beyond the Sahara, an Italian traveller was reporting in the year 1447 from the oasis of Tuat, 'breed greatly, for a woman bears up to five at a birth'. Since then a great deal more nonsense has been written and believed about Africans. No doubt it could never have been otherwise. To the mariners and merchants of Europe, discoverers by land and sea, these 'natives' appeared as strange and unpredictable as they themselves undoubtedly seemed to the peoples whom they encountered. What is surprising is that much good sense none the less found its way into print. Along with the superstitious and, later, pseudo-scientific rubbish that was fed for centuries to European (and in due course North American) readers, the records reveal a deep vein of 'objective reporting'.

This was true even at the height of the oversea slave trade. Devaluation of African humanity then sank to a depth unequalled in history until South Africa's present rulers came to power. In defence of their practice of wrenching captives out of Africa, a group of Liverpool merchants declared in 1792: 'Africans being the most lascivious of human beings, may it not be imagined that the cries they let forth, at being torn from their wives, proceed from the dread that they will never have the opportunity of indulging their passions in the country to which they are embarking?'

Such attitudes allowed no respect either for the victims or for the peoples from whom they came. To those who condemned the trade, British governments of the day replied that it was far too profitable to be stopped. 'We cannot,' said Lord Dartmouth, Secretary of State for the Colonies in 1775, 'allow the Colonies to check or to discourage in any degree a traffic so beneficial to the nation.' The argument was persuasive: just how much so we ourselves are well placed to understand today. Nearly two centuries after Lord Dartmouth had enunciated his views on the indispensable benefits of the slave trade, another Conservative British government returned almost exactly the same reply to critics who condemned the sale of arms to the Republic of South Africa. The sale might have its unfortunate side; it was far too profitable to be stopped.

Yet even during the darkest years of the slave trade there were Englishmen and other Europeans in Africa who had begun to adopt a new attitude to the 'natives'. Their writings – one thinks, for example, of Dr Thomas Winterbottom, physician to the colony of Sierra Leone at the end of the eighteenth century – struck a new note of factual and even scientific inquiry. These investigators formed the slender pioneering column of all those later men and women who have laboured in the field of understanding Africa. And if today it remains true that a great deal of nonsense is still being written about Africans, it is also true that many of the sillier myths are being swept away. The verdict of modern scholarship is that the past of Africa is both long and interesting and contains the record of a continuous and in some significant ways highly successful development over several thousand years. This development gives no ground for any assumption of natural inferiority or even – quite surprisingly often – of any comparative failure in achievement.

Much of that development belongs to an Iron Age which is known to have begun about two thousand years ago, and to have involved, in the words of two British historians, 'a considerable fund of common political ideas'.[4]

What were these political ideas?

This is not the place to inquire deeply into the growth of pre-colonial cultures and civilizations in Africa. The point to notice here is that Africa's political and social history is neither new nor simple. On the contrary, a wide range of its underlying ideology undoubtedly goes back into a remote and complex past.

Any comprehensive history of Africa that may be written in

the future – and it cannot be written yet – will have to set Ancient Egypt, for example, near the centre of its picture, both because Egypt was a transmitter of ideas from Axia and, probably more important in the long run, because Egypt was the exploiter and developer of social and economic trends already indigenous to Africa. Moreover, as an outstanding French Egyptologist has lately observed, 'perhaps the greatest service Egyptology can offer is to furnish, as no other branch of study can, precious chronological points of departure for the ancient history of Africa'.[5]

But all this would provide only the beginning to the story of Africa's political development. Partly growing out of it, partly evolving new forms by reaction with pressures inside Africa and with other pressures from outside Africa, later history has produced a multiplicity of political and social patterns (and, of course, economic, religious, and artistic patterns as well): a multiplicity, indeed, as great as the varied and challenging nature of African experience and environment.

Anthropologists and historians have grappled with the task of sorting out these patterns into a manageably small number of leading types and categories. Not surprisingly, they have trouble with their terms. What, for instance, is a tribe? My *Pocket Oxford Dictionary* (but the longer versions merely elaborate) explains that a tribe is a 'group of people in a primitive or barbarous stage of development acknowledging the authority of a chief and usually regarding themselves as having a common ancestor'. This is well enough as far as it goes; but it does not go very far. The Yoruba of Western Nigeria are often called a tribe, at least by Europeans. Certainly they acknowledge the authority of their chiefs and generally regard themselves as having common ancestors: can we really believe that they are therefore 'primitive and barbarous'? Nobody who knows them will say so.

Of course it is true that the word 'tribe' has generally been used as a term of abuse. This is now unfashionable. 'Anyone who wants to use it [tribe] as a technical term, and not a term of abuse,' warns Dr Lucy Mair, 'should be clear that it simply means an independent political division of a population with a common culture.'[6] Like the Lowland Scots, perhaps, in the United Kingdom?

Mair, of course, was thinking of Africa, and specifically of East Africa. But Huntingford, thinking of the same region, goes further. A tribe in East Africa, he argues, 'is a group united by a common name in which the members take a pride, by a common language, by a common territory, and by a feeling that all who do not share this name are outsiders, "enemies" in fact'.[7] If this is true, as it appears to be, then why is a 'tribe' any different from a 'nation'? Isn't it mere mystification to describe a typical European people, with all their xenophobia, group-ambition, and sense of exclusivist pride, as a *nation*, while reserving the word *tribe* ('primitive and barbarous' being understood) for a people like the Yoruba? Such mystification, one cannot help feeling, is in no small part the fault of anthropologists who have generally cultivated a habit, when writing about African societies, of creeping in at the back door of political reality instead of marching boldly up the front steps.

The matter of names is not without importance, for it connects with the larger question of what actually happened. The usual picture of pre-colonial Africa – except for the Muslim states of the north, though even these were generally reduced in reputation to 'nests of piratical fanatics' – was presented in our standard works, at least until a few years ago, as one of unrelieved and hopeless . chaos or stagnation. Such primitive segments of the human race, it was understandably concluded, could not possibly have possessed a *political* history of their own. Or none, at any rate, that was worth talking about.

No serious historian has any such conviction nowadays. The last ten or twenty years have completely revised the standard view of African society, whether past or present, and with this revision there has come a need for a new terminology. So far, it must be said, new terms to describe the specific social and political systems of Africa are largely lacking, and we are obliged, for want of better, to make do with what we have from other lands.

Some familiar terms are clearly fitting. It is now agreed that a very large number of African peoples moved out of truly primitive forms of organization (during an Iron Age which began some two thousand years ago) into forms that can be called *states* and *empires*. Some of these remained at a simple stage of inner complexity; others moved into far from simple patterns of bureaucratic authority. Many based their means of government – and their central revenues – on types of loyalty and tribute which resemble feudalism. Quite a few British scholars reject this particular term, though on grounds which appear at the very least controversial; meanwhile they seem to find it difficult to suggest anything better, and accordingly take refuge in circumambient explanations which tend to finish where they begin.[8]

But whatever one may think of the credentials of African feudalism, there remains the fact, agreed by all whose opinions are of weight, that many African peoples formed themselves into states; and that some of these states grew into recognizably imperial solutions of the central 'question of power' – the question, that is to say, of *who* are to be the rulers and *whom* they are to rule. This process of 'state-forming', moreover, began a long time ago. It began most clearly of all in those regions where easy movement by man and horse made military and political enclosure possible and worthwhile: in North Africa, in the wide grasslands of the Sudan, and, not long after that (though seldom with the horse), in the forest fringe of Guinea and, later again (but never with the horse), in the vast woods and prairies of the centre and the south.

Two well-known medieval sources indicate what outsiders may have thought of such developments in Africa. An Arab of the Hejaz travelled down the East African coast somewhat more than a thousand years ago, gathered information from sailors and merchants, and afterwards wrote a memorable book which he entitled, not without a conscious touch of romance, *The Meadows of Gold and Mines of Gems*. He described a large African state near the mouths of the Zambezi River. This state was governed by a king whose authority rested on election, for he was chosen 'to govern the people with equity', and reached over the heads of many lesser kings in the neighbourhood. Al Mas'udi explained in his book that this 'king of kings' could none the less be deposed if he abused his power of government or failed to use it wisely. Altogether al Mas'udi appears to be describing a very typical chieftainship or kingship among a wide range of African peoples. There might well have been applied to this south-east African monarch of a thousand years ago the same traditional standards as those which Rattray recorded for the chiefs of Ashanti in 1929. These were 'enstooled' to the tune of the following public admonitions:

> Tell him that
> We do not wish for greediness
> We do not wish that he should curse us
> We do not wish that his ears should be hard of hearing
> We do not wish that he should call people fools
> We do not wish that he should act on his own initiative
> We do not wish things done as in Kumasi
> We do not wish that it should ever be said
>   'I have no time. I have no time.'
> We do not wish personal abuse
> We do not wish personal violence.[9]

West Africa, or at least the Western Sudan, was nearer to the Muslim states of the Mediterranean, and their scholars were better informed about it than they were about remote East Africa. In 1067, just a year after William of Normandy had won the Battle of Hastings, an Andalusian Arab named al Bakri published an account of political organization in the Western Sudan. Drawing on much evidence from travellers and soldiers who had been there (Morocco had lately invaded the Western Sudan in force), al Bakri showed that a considerable segment of the West African grasslands had long lain within the power of a single state, and that this empire could be reckoned as a notable enemy or ally.

'Ghana is the title of the kings of that people,' he wrote, 'and the name of their country is Aoukar. Their present king is called Tunka Manin. He came to the throne in [1062] ... and is the master of a large empire and of a formidable power....' Having described Tunka Manin's court and courtiers, al Bakri went on to illustrate the nature of his political organization. Using this account with other Arab sources, one may see that

Ghana's power rested partly on a strong central organization which could raise military levies of a feudal type, and partly on an intelligent exploitation of the gold and salt trade.

Salt was vital to the people of these torrid grasslands, as it still is; but in those days the best deposits of salt lay northward on the fringe of the Sahara. From there, too, Western Sudanese peoples had their copper. But gold came from the south, from the fringe of the forest belt or the forest belt itself. What the lords of Ghana essentially achieved – and in this they were followed by other imperial rulers later on – was to win political control over the means of sending out gold to the north and, at the same time, over the means of bringing in salt to the south. Thus they could and did draw revenues both from the import of salt and copper and the goods of North Africa, and from the export of gold and ivory. 'The king,' notes al Bakri in a key passage, 'imposes a tax of a dinar of gold on every donkey-load of salt that enters his country, and of two dinars on every load that leaves. A load of copper pays him five *mitcals*' (perhaps five-eighths of an ounce of gold, though the *mitcal* varied wildly in weight), 'and a load of miscellaneous goods pays him ten.'

Not only that. The king also saw to it that he monopolized the trade in gold, at least near its source. 'All pieces of gold found in the mines of the empire' – the gold will have come, in fact, mainly from alluvial deposits – 'belong to the king, but he lets the public have the dust which is everywhere familiar. Without this restriction, gold would become so abundant as practically to lose its value.' The kings of Ghana well understood their business. West African gold lay at the root of their revenues. It would remain so for their successors. Three hundred years after al Bakri an English king began importing West African gold for the new currency he meant to strike. And 'guinea' is still a word we use.

Thus in their *capacity* to raise revenues, responding to their *need* to finance the workings of an empire, the rulers of Ghana had clearly reached a stable pattern of political sophistication. They were not, of course, modern dictators: behind the bare record of their doings one must imagine a kind of royal authority resting on governors and chiefs and military henchmen, sub-chiefs and tributary peoples, all of these being enmeshed in their turn in a more or less coherent order of society. This system, together with its notable successor states and empires, occupies a complex and important place in the West African record. All this, by the same token, is part of the groundwork of Africa today.

Political history may be variously defined. My own definition would agree with those who hold that political history consists in analysing and illustrating how social authority was organized, distributed, and applied at any given place and time: of seeing how, in short, the central 'question of power' was actually settled by a given people or peoples.

But if this is a reasonable statement of what we are about, clearly we cannot rest content with looking only at societies and structures which achieved kingship. The fact is that many peoples reacted to the problems of their development and environment by evolving simple or embryonic forms of government, and that these systems served them well enough to endure for centuries. These primitive systems of government – primitive in the sense that they made do with rudimentary means of organizing, distributing, and applying social authority – are also part of the record. They cannot be ignored without serious distortion.

It may be said, broadly, that the origins of political history in this continent belong to the beginnings of the Iron Age, to the period of early settlement in an often hostile physical environment. New techniques of migration and cultivation, based on the iron spear and probably on the iron hoe, married with new methods of social organization and led on to the growth, wherever circumstances proved favourable, of large political systems such as Ghana. Here and there, however, the centralizing process whereby peoples came together within the tightening zone of a king's authority was partly lacking or was largely muted. Often enough, it remained altogether absent.

Of the latter cases, some of the most interesting (or, at any rate, the best studied) have occurred in the waterlogged lands of the Upper Nile, not far from the northern borders of Uganda, where such peoples as the Nuer and the Dinka have their home. Other cases may of course be found elsewhere: in parts of East Africa and West Africa, and, though on a different level of social growth, among the Pygmies and Bushmen of central and southern Africa.

These peoples have governed themselves in a great variety of ways. But most of them have been alike in living without any form of strong central rule, without states (much less empires), and often without any obvious or formal means of maintaining law and order and of prosecuting war and trade. It has been none the less abundantly shown that such people have generally possessed a workable and durable system for ensuring individual and even collective security, although their systems have seldom comprised any of the recognizable hierarchies of political power that make and enforce social rules and judgements. 'Among the Nuer,' according to Mair, 'no individual anywhere has authority to say whether fighting is permissible or to command that it should cease.'[10] This does not mean that the Nuer are satisfied with 'savage anarchy'. On the contrary, they have worked out and learned how to apply a great many useful rules about the conduct and control of society, though they have done so by means of an absolute minimum of delegated authority.

This apparent 'simplicity of tribal life' has misled many observers into supposing that people like the Nuer have lived with 'no rules at all'. It is now seen, by contrast, that Nuer government (if we may use the word for an authority so little and loosely formulated) is in fact a distinctive *system* of society, and that this system is the product of a long and difficult self-adjustment to a highly specialized land and climate. Technically at a primitive level of life, the Nuer are organizationally at a point that is anything but primitive.

For how do you live and survive if your land is under water half the year? What do you do if your environment contains neither metals nor stone, or none that you can get at? Where do you look for help if your neighbours live in the same way, or, far across the skyline, offer you no friendly hand? Lost in their enormous swamps and sodden grasslands, dwelling in scattered homesteads, the Nuer and their neighbours have not been discouraged. They have found a point of balance between the waters and the scorching sun on one hand, and the demands of cattle and a little cultivation on the other. The trouble with the Nuer, if it is a trouble, is that they have succeeded so well in attaining a stability which calls within itself for no change at all.

Contemplating their regular and so gently poised adjustment, one may better understand why many so-called primitive tribes have contented themselves with their own culture. Obedience to an accepted pattern of behaviour, the sanctioned product of long trial and error, was the condition of life itself: deviation could only bring disaster. This seemed and often was so true that men and women could implicitly believe it, and could see in social change nothing but foolishness or danger. Here, of course, one may comprehend why 'tribal life' required and applied such strict and all-embracing patterns of moral sanction on the behaviour of the individual. The stagnation of the Nuer, if that is what it is, precisely illustrates the *political* success of their development.

It is easy to exaggerate the apparent stagnation of 'tribal Africa'. These societies were the outcome of much and varied adjustment to a difficult environment. Emerging from a remote past, they went on growing or shifting in power and efficiency, changing their habits, meeting new challenges, evolving new patterns. Those that were successful – those that have survived – have revealed a marked capacity for adapting to new situations and for adopting new ideas. Much of the story of the African Iron Age is one of perpetual movement across the vast land mass of inner Africa by peoples who went through zone after zone of contrasting climate, soil, vegetation, and therefore means of livelihood. Stability and change play an underlying counterpoint in the African song.

Peopling their continent, the Africans brought in cereals and began cultivating them, learned how to raise cattle, adapted metal tools and weapons to their own use, undertook mining and smelting and forging on a continental scale, borrowed crops from other lands, introduced soil conservation and terrace agriculture where hillsides needed these, discovered the medicinal value of a host of herbs and plants, and worked out their own explanations of mankind and the universe. All this had taken place long before the first ships set forth from Europe.

But then and afterwards the slow and often painful processes of change continued. With new challenges – in the form of muskets, to take one important example – some of the older systems of 'minimal government' could not suffice. They had to be modified, made over into other systems nearer to or identical with those we recognize as states and empires. This occurred at all levels of political organization. At one end of the spectrum there were changes of imperial structure in the Western Sudan or the plateau lands of what is now Rhodesia; at the other, at the extreme of 'minimal government', new conditions encouraged simple village headmen to become 'kings and nobles', the better to wield their power but also, no doubt, the better to defend their people.

The examples are legion. One may trace the force of political change in every corner of the continent, and among peoples large or small. Thus the little Anuak clans of the west Ethiopian borderlands, obtaining muskets from their neighbours, developed an aristocracy. The chiefless peoples of the Tanzanian plains, facing a time of troubles, acquired chiefs. The numerous and enterprising clans of the Ashanti, persecuted by their neighbours, came together in a union made indissoluble by a ritual object – the famous Golden Stool – invented for the purpose. Menaced by the slave trade, the scattered peoples of the Niger delta founded city states and engaged in that curious trade themselves. Harried by Zulu regiments, the clans of the Drakensberg foothills formed themselves into the Basuto nation. And it was the same with the arts of peace. New technologies passed from people to people. Social norms expanded or contracted according to the pressure of the times.

All this, really, is only a way of saying that Africa's wide diversity of experience and environment has found a full reflection in the political and economic structures of daily life. Here in this capacious continental home there has been room for many contrasting phases of social growth to exist at one and the same time. There has been tolerance for many exceptions to the broadest rule of group behaviour. A few Stone-Age peoples still live alongside neighbours who entered the Iron Age fifteen or twenty centuries back. Chiefless peoples still border on others who have kings and 'kings of kings'. 'Minimal government' still goes on side by side with 'maximal government'.

Nothing in all this, surely, can leave room for thinking that peoples who have stayed content with primitive forms of government are therefore of lesser talent or intelligence than their hierarchical neighbours. I emphasize this point because there has sometimes been a tendency to suppose that this or that people, according to the sheer complexity of its political and social system, is really 'superior' to folk who have never seen the point of having chiefs and policemen. To think like this would be to adopt, in Anene's words, 'an out-of-date assumption that a moral hierarchy exists as regards centralized political organizations and what are usually described as segmented societies'.[11]

If historians of Africa have tended to emphasize the states-and-empires side of the story, this is partly because they have had to meet the bland assumption of European culture that no such states and empires ever existed, that Africans have therefore had no history worth the name and so no historical identity – and therefore, reaching at last the bottom of this line of thought, no claim to an inherent equality with Europeans. But the true study of history has reference only to experience and environment. Had all the peoples in the world developed in the same environment and under the same conditions of experience, no doubt they would all have developed in the same way: as it is, they have developed in a myriad different ways in response to as many different circumstances, and this is what history is about.

The diversity of African politics in the past, however, is only half the picture. The other half is not much less important. It consists of an underlying unity. Most of the populations of sub-Saharan Africa (and it may well have been true of North Africa before the Arab invasions of the eighth century) have shared close relationships to a single body of cultural beliefs and modes of behaviour. This is the reason why a purely regional study of the African past can never hope to yield the true keys to an understanding of Africa, nor reveal the richness of experience that lies within a pattern and social process continental in their scope.

In point of language, for example – the figure of 800 languages, according to Fortune, is a conservative one[12] – it now appears that the diversity is based on a unity provided by three basic groups. That in itself might seem to be saying little enough, but the statement wears a different aspect when one considers that the largest of these three groups is evidently parent to 'nearly all the languages of west and central Africa, east and south Africa'.[13] That again might seem to exclude large segments of the continent from the common cultural foundations to which I have alluded. Yet this, too, wears a different garb as soon as one remembers that many of the forms of kingship and religion that grew powerful in central and southern Africa were forms known and used by peoples of the far north, whether in the Nile Valley or along the fertile grasslands of the Saharan fringe. The familiar division of Africa into 'south and north of the Sahara' may be wonderfully convenient, but it can also be misleading. If the Sahara was undoubtedly a daunting obstacle to movement back and forth across its plains, it was seldom or never a true dividing line.

It seems clear that a number of common factors have profoundly influenced and worked on the majority of populations in the continent. Their basic ethnic and linguistic unities, now becoming ever more apparent, have had the firm cement of cultural unities as well. These have been economic, political, and ideological. Without attempting to develop this line of thought in any detail, I should like to suggest where it runs and leads.

The root problem, as we have seen, was to survive and if possible prosper in circumstances that were often very hostile. To an initially poor range of foodstuffs, there were added the edible banana some two thousand years ago (probably from south-east Asia) and much later, with the coming of the Portuguese, a number of valuable crops from South America. This economy could seldom or never be intensive outside the Nile

Valley and a few other favoured spots. But it seems to have been stable. It seems to have produced a regular overspill of population from the north-central areas into the centre and the south. Whenever this happened, families or clans or groups of clans moved in search of fresh land. And so the whole central and southern region of the continent, a vast and varied region of forest and marsh and grassland, was gradually peopled by folk of the same ethnic and linguistic stock. These populations split into a multitude of recognizably different peoples; and in this way there arose, across the gap and gulf of time, the many hundred variants of the Bantu language family.

This process, greatly simplified in this short explanation, likewise produced what Dr Audrey Richards has called 'the common features of Bantu political organization'.[14] These features – and they are not in fact limited to the Bantu language group – may be subsumed as: a family unit that is 'extended', encompassing many degrees of relationship besides those of husband–wife and parents–children; a strong emphasis of descent through family group and clan group; an almost universal tendency to make political authority dependent on family and lineage; and a loyalty to chieftainship that is linked to spiritual as well as temporal power.

And this in turn explains another set of common features: those that emphasize a basic unity of social behaviour and religious belief. Much of traditional African law illustrates the point. 'I conceive that land,' a Nigerian chief told the West African Lands Committee in 1912, 'belongs to a vast family of which many are dead, few are living, and countless members are unborn'. This idea is familiar in many regions of Africa. 'The universality of this concept throughout both Sudanese and Bantu Africa,' Elias writes, 'has been confirmed again and again wherever indigenous societies have been studied.'[15] Only last year a group of Ugandan students in London began publishing a discussion journal dedicated to 'the dead, the living, and the unborn'.[16]

Far from 'bowing down to wood and stone', as the old cliché had it, Africans are now understood to have long possessed religions and metaphysical systems – many of them (perhaps most) more or less clearly related to one another – worthy of serious attention. Man and the world were created at the behest of a Supreme God by the agency of lesser gods, and all these and other spiritual powers are worshipped or respected or implored by sacrifice and prayer. Beneath the gods are lesser powers, often evil, sometimes benign, occasionally both, who may be conjured by magical procedures much in the manner of traditional Europe – much in the manner, no doubt, of all pre-scientific societies. Long regarded by Europeans as squalid if not altogether contemptible, many African religions are now understood to have been – indeed, often still to be – as valid and respectable, within the terms of a non-materialist explanation of life and death, as any other in the world. Even the ghastly witch-doctor, so long a figure of gruesome terror to the European eye, turns out on closer acquaintance to be little different in his intentions from the family doctor round the corner.

All these 'factors of underlying unity', as they may reasonably be called, have their bearing on the political growth of modern Africa. They are as vital to the 'native background' as the diversity they support, or as the 'foreign contribution' we shall now consider.

3 The Foreign Contribution

A giraffe arriving at the Chinese court in 1415, together with ambassadors from the East African city-state of 'Ma-lin', was understandably received with some attention. The emperor himself agreed to welcome it with stately ceremonial. Accompanied by a 'celestial horse', which was probably a zebra, and a 'celestial stag', which was possibly an oryx, this unlikely beast from the uttermost ends of the western sea was felt to be a singular though not surprising token of worldwide respect. Besides, its safe arrival was something of a triumph. Its arduous journey had taken it across the Indian Ocean to Ceylon or southern India and thence, by trans-shipment, onward to China.

This giraffe in any case deserves a place in history, for the ceremonial obligation to accompany ambassadors from distant countries home was among the reasons why the renowned Admiral Cheng-Ho sailed for 'Ma-lin' in 1417, and thus made China's first attested landfall on Africa. Chinese-African trade had previously gone through many intermediaries; now for a few brief years there was direct if rare intercourse. I mention the fact as a comment on the frequent assertion that continental Africa possessed no knowledge of the outside world until the arrival of Europeans. The element of isolation was undoubtedly a real one, especially in central and southern Africa; but the isolation was never complete.

East Africa and the Eastern world were long involved in a two-way traffic of much value to both, as also were West Africa and the Muslim North from Morocco to Egypt. The more we learn of the past, the more clearly we may recognize that these inter-penetrating influences were many and important. Of those that came from outside, Islam was among the greatest. It won the loyalty of a number of West African leaders and some of their peoples at least from the eleventh century A.D.: fine tombstones of Spanish marble more than 900 years old, found near Gao on the Middle Niger and carrying Muslim inscriptions in Arabic, bear witness to this. Other disciples of Muhammad converted the little towns and trading settlements of coastal East Africa; in time the peoples of these places built a notable Muslim civilization of their own. Operating radically in the political field, Islam helped to reduce ethnic separatism and to form new states.

All such influences and ideas and techniques from outside Africa, entering the continent over many centuries through its peripheral borderlands in east and north, were additions to the stock of African thought and behaviour. These additions could be absorbed and used, and often were, without destroying the general fabric of traditional society. They modified the fabric, introduced new strands and colours and patterns, provoked new forms and fashions; yet the overall effect was almost always one of reinforcement and renewal, not of destruction. The European colonial impact, however, was not like this. Its impact, generally, was altogether different both in kind and in degree. Nothing like it had been seen or known before; and nothing afterwards could ever be at all the same again. The reasons are various. They lay partly in the sheer destructiveness of the methods employed. Yet there was something in this conquest that was even more ruinous of existing society than forced labour, firearms, and the rest could ever be by themselves. This new factor was the expansive nature of European civilization.

It can be shown without much difficulty that the leading states of Africa and Europe were divided in medieval times, five or six hundred years ago, by no 'cultural gap' of any great significance. Law and order in the Western Sudan were probably superior under the earlier emperors of Mali than in contemporary France and England, while the scholarship of Timbuktu and Djenne could possibly have given points to that of Oxford or Paris. But the 'cultural gap' between Africa and Europe at the beginning of the colonial period, a hundred years ago, was so wide that many Europeans found it genuinely difficult to believe that Africans were altogether human. No doubt the gap in 1860 was really less enormous than it seemed to European travellers of the time, few of whom were men of learning or reflection. All the same, it was a gap which spanned, for Europe, the displacement of superstition by science, of handicraft manufacture by industrialism, of feudal politics by modern politics, and of primitive trading by the skills of a highly ingenious capitalism.

Thus the Europe which invaded Africa was an entirely different Europe from medieval times, while Africa, if by no means unchanged within itself, was still in the age before machines and industrialism. To ask why Europe should have advanced so far ahead of others would open an unending detour: the Chinese, one may note in passing, had led the world in technological achievement until the fifteenth century only to come to a long halt for reasons which scholars still discuss without agreement. The point to remember here is that this differential between an invading Europe and an invaded Africa proved crushing to traditional society.

This is where the 'foreign contribution' becomes for the first time absolutely decisive. Yet if the colonial period was in a large sense revolutionary, its revolution was a strange one. Its contribution was not to build or even lay foundations for the new society that Africa needed; what it did was to open the way for the new by undermining the old. Contrary to the claims of its prophets, colonial rule did not 'civilize' Africa, or modernize Africa in any meaningful sense of the word, much less leave Africans with the mere job of taking over the prepared positions of a new social structure. Philanthropic individuals and institutions may have worked hard for the good of Africans; their saving labours, though often brave and even generous, could never be more than palliative and peripheral. For while colonial rule built a few roads and railways and opened a few mines and plantations (though for its own convenience and enrichment), dropping here and there a few crumbs of educational and social enlightenment, its central effect was one of dismantlement. Within its new frontiers, it took apart; it did not put together again.

But this central effect of dismantlement, though generally negative, has been none the less decisive. In the wake of colonial rule, an independent Africa can no longer continue in anything resembling its pre-colonial condition. It will now either suffer a new subjection or it will 'catch up' and live fully in the modern world. It will either start to build a new society, or it will collapse into chaos.

We can divide Africa's experience of Europe into five main phases.

First there was mutual discovery. In this the Portuguese of the fifteenth century were the true pioneers, leading the rest of sea-going Europe down the long west coast and far beyond. These early encounters were few and far between. They were accompanied by much raiding and piracy from European ships, but gradually settled to an often peaceful trading partnership.

This partnership in commerce lasted in one way or another for nearly four centuries. Concerned at first with African gold and ivory and peppers, and with European cottons and metalware, the trade soon deviated into a wholesale transport of African captives for enslavement in Europe's new mines and plantations of Brazil, the Caribbean, Central and North America.

For Africa, this traffic was destructive, even disastrous. But for Europe it became a considerable source of wealth. During this second phase of contact with Africa (and partly thanks to it), England and France began their industrial revolution. Europeans also started to explore inner Africa. Apart from a few lone wanderers, like Park in the Western Sudan and Bruce in Ethiopia and along the Upper Nile, discovery was concentrated for West and South Africa in the decades of about 1820 to 1860, and somewhat later for the eastern and central regions. There was still no conquest but for a few forays by the Portuguese, whether in Angola and Moçambique or along the middle reaches of the Zambezi, and the slow spread of Boer and afterwards British penetration from the Cape of Good Hope.

A third phase of closer European involvement, arising from the ending of the second, came with the abolition of the oversea slave trade, the growth of European imperialism and its internecine rivalries, the use of quinine against malaria, and, on the whole, a new capacity (whether military, economic, or political) for effective conquest. All these and other factors began to mature soon after the middle of the nineteenth century. They set the scene for colonial invasion and partition, which began, with a fourth phase, some seventy or eighty years ago.

Today another phase opens with the rise of African independence and a relationship, at last, of mutual respect. But here and now we are concerned with the years between about 1880 (though colonial rule had in fact already begun at a few points along the coast) and 1960, the year that crowned Africa's modern assumption of responsibility for her own affairs.

All these phases, setting off chains of action and reaction of the most diverse kinds, properly belong to 'the foreign contribution'. They became generally decisive for political and economic change, however, only with the fourth phase: that of conquest, annexation, and partition.

The dismantlement of traditional society occurred in different ways, military, political, social, and economic. Most painful, though perhaps least influential on the course of history, was the purely physical destruction. This varied with time and place and person; not infrequently it was severe. Nobody knows how severe it really was, because vital statistics are missing, as are many of the records. 'They can have my Congo,' King Leopold remarked in 1908, when the Belgian Parliament took over responsibility for the Congo Free State, 'but they've no right to know what I've done there'; and he proceeded to a great bonfire of documents.[17] Yet many documents survived. In 1919 Belgium's official Commission for the Protection of the Natives could estimate that the population of the Congo might have been as much as *halved* since the beginning of European occupation some forty years earlier.

Of course the degree of violence and destruction greatly varied. Often enough there was little or none, and sometimes the colonial conquest was the means of bringing peace to ravaged lands. European accounts have naturally tended to emphasize the pacific side of the process; Africans, reacting the other way, have tended to ignore it. On the whole, the violence would seem to have been more frequent than Europeans have lately cared to remember. Men like Carl Peters, the imperial German agent in East Africa, were certainly exceptional. Replying to overtures for peace from the ruler of the Gogo, Peters replied (and so recorded in his memoirs): 'The Sultan shall have peace.... Plunder the village, set fire to the houses, and smash everything to pieces that will not burn!' He was as good as his word, and not only on that occasion. 'Everywhere the spectacle was repeated. After a short resistance the Gogo fled in all directions; burning brands were thrown into the houses, and the axes did their work in hewing the pieces which could not be burnt.'[18] Yet such conduct, though unusual, was by no means unique.

When we come to the French and British, the case grows rather more complex. Initially, their impact was often little less severe than that of the Germans in East or South West Africa. We shall never know how much damage was done to the South African Bantu-speaking peoples by those 'kaffir Wars' that filled so much of the nineteenth century; while the military expeditions of the French from Senegal eastwards were seldom conducted with much respect for 'the rules of war'. In their equatorial territories the French likewise applied the same frantic system of exploitation by concession companies that had made such havoc in Leopold's Congo. Returning in 1905 to the countries he had helped to win for France, the explorer de Brazza observed in bitter disillusionment that 'ruin and terror have been visited on this unhappy colony'.

Yet physical destruction was not the underlying long-range factor in social dislocation. Africa had yielded millions of captives for slave labour in the Americas, but traditional systems of government had largely held firm through all the period of 'human export', or else adjusted themselves to circumstances they could no longer hope to control. Africa's traditional systems might have survived the colonial blood-letting as well, and even the political impact of colonial rule in itself, since colonial rulers (or the less short-sighted among them) were often well enough pleased to compound with willing chiefs and elders. What swept away the means of such survival (even though the appearance of survival might often still persist) was the economic intervention of the invaders.

With this, too, the impact greatly varied. In territories of white settlement there was an immediate drive to enclose vast regions of land within which Africans could no longer farm or live except as labourers. South Africa and Southern Rhodesia have become the outstanding examples, though Kenya and Algeria have run them close. By 1951, for example, the amount of land 'scheduled for African occupation' in South Africa was no more than 9·6 per cent of the whole country; today, with a few additions forced by the sheer pressure of rural overcrowding, it is still less than 12 per cent, the rest being kept for Europeans. When several million peasants are stuffed away like this, the consequences can only be disastrous, both for their land and for themselves. A White Paper of 1936 remarked of the South African 'Native Reserves' that 'speaking generally', they were 'congested, denuded, overstocked, eroded, and for the most part in a deplorable condition';[19] and yet this was the way in which rural Africa was supposed to survive.

At the other end of Africa, Algeria has offered another spectacle of 'ruin by enclosure'. Here again the real cause of destruction lay not so much in the greed of individuals as in the system they promoted. Before its intensive occupation by the French, the fertile coastwise uplands of Algeria had been profitable producers of food for home consumption, notably cereals and mutton. But French settlers had no interest in growing food for the local market and turned, almost from the first, to the production of wine for export. The area under vines rose from a mere 4,000 acres in 1830 to no fewer than 750,000 acres in 1953.

Algerians began feeling a new hunger. For while the production of cereals had remained at about the same level since the 1880s, the population (thanks largely to modern medicine) had almost tripled in the same period. It has been calculated that the average Algerian had five quintals of grain a year in 1871, four in 1900, but only 2½ in 1940. The situation on the eve of the great insurrection of 1954 was that fewer than one thousand European landowners possessed about one-seventh of all cultivable land outside the barren southern regions, while more than half a million peasant *families* had no land at all.

Yet land was useless without labour, and so were mining

concessions. The enclosure of land and the opening of mines went hand-in-hand with pressure on rural Africans to leave their homes and work for European wages, or rather, since wages were altogether inadequate, for European employers. It is here that we arrive at what was probably the most destructive element in the economic system of the invaders.

Directly forced labour was used in all colonies, though seldom in a massive way except in the Congo Free State and the early years of the Belgian Congo, in the French equatorial territories, and in the Portuguese colonies. Of course there are exceptions to this statement (as there are to every generalization about Africa): the Boer farmers of the south were (and still are) accustomed to regard Africans as natural slaves, while the toll of forced labour exacted by European colonial administrators of all nationalities, up and down the continent, defies reasonable estimate. But generally it remains true that the British and the French early came to prefer *indirect* methods of forcing Africans to work for Europeans. Their approach was simple. They applied a money tax to peasants who lived without money. Either the peasants earned the money to pay the tax, which meant going to work for Europeans – or the police seized them for 'punishment', which meant, of course, the same thing. Out of this system, and the evasions and resistances that it evoked, a conviction arose among Europeans that Africans were feckless, idle, and incapable of responsible work.*

It is hard to exaggerate the extent and the effects of this imposition of the need to work for Europeans on countless millions of subsistence farmers and their dependents. It went on everywhere, and it went on recklessly. Large areas were denuded of their 'fit adult males' for long periods of time. Huge populations

*King Leopold provides the characteristic comment on forced labour – direct or indirect – as on so many other aspects of early colonial practice. Refusing in 1905 to stop forcing Congolese to collect rubber for him, he said that the coercive system might be changed 'when the Negro has generally shaken off his idleness and become ready to work for the lure of wages alone'. Meanwhile, though Leopold omitted to say so, rubber-collecting remained as cheap for the agents of the Congo Free State as it was costly in health and even life for the Congolese who were forced to do the work. For Leopold's further attitudes, see Professor Jean Stengers's penetrating analysis of relations between the Belgian Parliament and their 'King of the Congo': *Belgique et Congo: L'Elaboration de la Charte Coloniale*, Brussels, 1963.

adjusted to colonial rule by taking it increasingly for granted that their men would annually leave home and 'migrate' to the towns and mines and white plantations. The resultant impoverishment of rural life – and we shall return to this central point – was often calamitous. Thick volumes of evidence emphasize this fact. Here a couple of examples will have to suffice.

What the effect of migrant labour could be on a previously stable society was indicated by an official report for Nyasaland in 1935, by which time the system had been in operation for many years. 'The whole fabric of the old order of society,' commented this grave though cautious report, 'is undermined when 30 to 60 per cent of the able-bodied men are absent at one time' – as was the case in Nyasaland by then. 'Emigration [on this scale], which destroys the old, offers nothing to take its place, and the family–community is threatened with complete dissolution.'[20]

The gross effect, one may repeat, was serious and continuous dismantlement of the pattern and structure of social life. And this was compensated by no corresponding gain in understanding and advancement by the men who went away to industrial work. For they went to the mines of the Rand or the Rhodesian Copperbelt, and there they worked as unskilled labourers beneath a colour bar of white enforcement. And this bar for long denied them access to any real participation in the new world of industry they were supposed to have entered.

Nyasaland may be regarded as having existed at one extreme of the migrant-labour pressure and experience, for this was a colony of relatively benign and gentle rule. At another extreme there lie the Portuguese colonies. According to the report of a senior Portuguese Inspector of Colonies in 1947, the situation in Angola 'is in some ways worse than simple slavery. Under slavery, after all, the native is bought as an animal: his owner prefers him to remain as fit as a horse or an ox. Yet here [in Angola] the native is not bought – he is hired from the State, although he is called a free man. And his employer cares little if he sickens or dies, once he is working, because when he sickens or dies his employer will simply ask for another.'[21] One could pile on the evidence; abstracted from its emotive context, the effect was always one of widespread and continuous under-mining of traditional life and welfare.

The colonial period may itself be divided into a number of sub-periods. *Invasion* was one of these. *Pacification*, as it was called, was another: a protracted period, this one, to the point that Belgian Congo archives, for example, can reveal no fewer than thirty 'armed operations' against Africans for a year as late as 1915. After pacification, which was generally complete by about 1920, there followed the main central phase of the colonial period – *stagnation*. It engulfed all the colonial rulers, French, British, Belgian, Portuguese, Italian, and Spanish (for the Germans were out of the game by now). The 'period between the wars', 1919–39, was more often than not one of complete stand-still except for a generally improved rate of profit on foreign mining operations. The colonial governments were left to live as best they could off the product of their own taxation; and this was so small that nothing but the bare minimum of administration could be paid for. Dismantlement continued.

The Second World War and its aftermath brought consider-able change. With full employment in the western world, raw material prices boomed. Economic stagnation gave way to economic development; political repression began to retreat before the rise of a new nationalism. The continent began to heave and shift within itself. The 'sleepy giant', in Langston Hughes's affectionate phrase, was waking up at last.

In this sub-period after 1945 – the period of *struggle* – it is possible to argue that dismantlement stopped and reconstruc-tion began. Perhaps so: yet one should be cautious at this point. As we shall see, the period of liberation inherited a major social crisis, and many of the elements in this crisis owed their origins, or at least their aggravation, to the years after 1945.

On the credit side there was notably a large expansion in the number of Africans who were able to win access to higher education. After 1945 'the new and significant development is the enormous increase in the number of students [who went from Africa to Western Europe]. . . . Whereas their number is estimated to have been between 500 and 600 in 1939 [British colonies only], this had doubled by 1945, and had quadrupled by 1946. This sharp upward trend has continued, and on 1 January 1955, there were 10,000 colonial students in Britain, of whom 3,500 had arrived during 1954.'[22] French colonies experienced much the same growth.

But other colonies did not. The Portuguese (and Spanish) are once again at an extreme of negation. Only a few hundred non-whites from the Portuguese African colonies have managed to climb into the university bracket during the last hundred years or so, and the position today is not significantly better (indeed, in some ways it is worse) than half a century ago. Nor is the situation significantly different at lower levels of education: the number of children at primary school in Angola and Moçambique is generally believed (in default of any reliable statistics) to constitute less than 1 per cent of the population, while the proportion at secondary school remains virtually invisible.

It could have been expected that a wealthy and industrially advanced country like Belgium would adopt a different approach. Yet, at the level of secondary and university education, the Belgian record is no better than the Portuguese, and may possibly be worse. Primary schooling (though with a heavy religious bias) reached a relatively high level in the Belgian Congo; semi-skilled and even skilled jobs were likewise open to African labourers. But even during their last years in the Congo the Belgians held firm to their earlier conviction that it would be wrong, because dangerous, to allow Africans to acquire any real knowledge of the outside world. Higher education in the Belgian Congo had produced fewer than a score of African graduates by the year in which the Belgians retired; in this vast country of peasant-farmers, there was only one Congolese graduate in agriculture.

This might have mattered less if higher education in Europe had been allowed to produce more. But the Belgian rulers took great care, and they were very careful people, to ensure that it should produce none at all. 'We have seen,' remarked a Belgian Minister of Colonies in 1954, 'that those natives who have been shown Europe, and given a very advanced education, do not always return to their homelands in a spirit favourable to civilization and to the Mother Country in particular.'[23]

It is accordingly not easy to perceive the constructive side of the Belgian colonial effort, even in the boom years after 1945. Its conductors could rightly claim to have ended the Arab-Swahili slave trade from the East Coast, together with the wretched internecine wars that had gone with it. Unfortunately, this useful achievement appears to have been at the cost, for other reasons, of no small proportion of the peoples concerned. Belgian rule had likewise opened roads, railways, and river communications; promoted mining industries, plantations, and even (latterly) a little manufacturing industry; and introduced millions of Africans to the spectacle of modern enterprise. Unhappily, though, the millions were all too often debarred from any real participation in the enterprise itself. The keynote of Belgian rule was paternalism; yet it was a kind of paternalism that seemed more than a little unwilling to see its 'children' on the road to maturity. None of this, needless to say, argues for a moment that Belgium was without her men of conscience and her administrators of high merit. But they were enmeshed in a system which could survive, it seemed, only in the absence of any genuine social, political, and economic advancement by the peoples of the country itself.

None of this, equally, argues that the Belgians were essentially much more wasteful or neglectful of human talent in Africa than their neighbours, the British and the French. Any Englishman who believes that the efforts of his countrymen have resolutely laid foundations for a new and modern society in Africa should consider the figures for primary and secondary education, no mean test of the rate of change and improvement in any society, African or not. Tanganyika passed under British authority in 1919. Forty years later, in 1959, its population had risen to nearly ten millions. And in 1959 the total number of secondary-school enrolments for Standard 12 (the last in the four-year secondary course) was 318, while the total number of School Certificates gained was 245. Kenya did a little better. Out of a population of some eight millions, 799 African boys and girls took School Certificate, and 654 achieved it. In Uganda, with a population of about six millions, as many as 860 African pupils won School Certificates in 1960. But adding these figures together, what do they reveal? That some 24 million people in British East Africa, after several decades of colonial rule, could together achieve an annual total of fewer than 2,000 School Certificates: less than one for every 12,000 of the population. It may be added that the university college of Makerere had 878 students in 1959, while the Royal College in Nairobi had 290; and even some of these came from outside East Africa.

Shortage of money? If this were a conclusive argument one would expect to see Northern Rhodesia, with enormous copper earnings every year, equipped with many secondary schools and even a university college. Yet in 1958 Northern Rhodesia, with more than two million Africans, possessed only one secondary school offering a complete course to the Senior Cambridge Certificate level. In Southern Rhodesia, likewise not lacking in revenue, figures for the same year of 1958 show that 12,148 African boys and girls entered school at the very bottom of the scale, in sub-standard A, but that those who reached the very top of the scale, standard 12, *numbered only thirteen.*[24]

Thus, while it is certainly true that in some respects (though not, it will be seen, in others) the process of dismantlement of traditional society slowed down after 1945, it is also true that the work of reconstruction scarcely began in the 'advanced colonies', and did not begin at all in the others.

In the wake of all this, with emotional judgements still reverberating through the whole firmament of debate, it is far from easy to summarize the outcome. There is no doubt that colonialism signalled a major upheaval in African life. And maybe the curious and contradictory nature of this upheaval can best be approached through a comparison with the industrial revolution of late-eighteenth- and early-nineteenth-century Britain. There, too, the change from one way of life to another took place through the violent and often blind destruction of traditional life and welfare, promoting great poverty and unprecedented rates of death and disease before producing, however slowly and reluctantly, a gentler and more expansive civilization, with re-awakened social responsibility and, in the twentieth century, the beginnings of community development.

The colonial hurricane may be likened to that industrial transition. Both were the product of new pressures in world society with which the old ways were unable to coexist. Both were dedicated to an ideology of worldly individualist ambition. Both were hugely wasteful of human life and happiness. Both carried men away on a flood of dreams and nightmares, real enough at the time though reading strangely to us now. There is little point in lengthy moralizing. But just as it is clear today that the child labour and starvation of the English industrial revolution, with all the other horrors it entailed, were deplorably wasteful of human life and talent, so also may one now perceive that the colonial system, executing its work of dismantlement, was guilty of the same kind of waste and destruction.

There is another level of comparison as well. The whole outcome in Africa clearly turned, as it had turned in England, on the degree in which the victims of the system could get to understand their situation, band together, and find ways of remoulding it to their advantage, thus generalizing the benefits previously available only to the ruling few. British efforts in that direction make up Britain's social history for the last hundred years or more. In Africa, a similar attempt dates from soon after the end of the Second World War.

Not that Africa's movement of emancipation and self-enlargement, any more than Britain's, was without its long period of ideological and political preparation. The African awakening began with the plans and projects of men who had understood the 'colonial situation' – and its challenge – not only in the stagnating years of the twenties and thirties, but even before that 'situation' had fully taken shape.

There is no space here to examine how far this understanding drew on memories of pre-colonial independence, and how far on liberal or radical ideas arriving from the outside world. It seems probable, for one, that the ideas animating the French revolution had more influence on certain parts of coastal Africa than has been generally allowed. 'They have made,' wrote an angry William Wilberforce in 1801 of the democratically obstructive colonists of Sierra Leone, 'the worst possible subjects, as thorough Jacobins as if they had been trained and educated in

Paris.'[25] But the memories of an older independence were always potent. They echo firmly from the words of pioneering thinkers like Horton, Blyden, and Hayford; and it is with these that any serious study of the ideas animating the movements for African independence, nationalist or not, has to begin.

4 Key Ideas

Many strands have gone into weaving the fabric of African nationalism, whether from native history or foreign example, devotion to high ideals or personal careerism, peace or war, hope or despair. We have glanced at some of them. Certainly, the list of 'foreign names' is long. The martyrs of Christianity are there; so are Rousseau and the Jacobins. Tom Paine is there; and Marx; Mazzini, and many lesser men.

Ideas of emancipation were transmitted and transposed in many ways and through many channels, most of them obscure. Egalitarian convictions reached by African troops on service outside their own countries during the two world wars are often said to have stood high on the list of pressures making for political change. Between 1914 and 1918, for example, more than 3,000 men of the Gold Coast Regiment served elsewhere. 'If they were good enough to fight and die in the Empire's cause,' declared the *Gold Coast Independent* in the wake of that war, 'they were good enough . . . to have a share in the government of their countries.'[26]

It remains true, however, that the fabric was and is African, and that the dominating colours come from within the continent. One can see this even in the way in which general ideas discussed in other countries have acquired their African character.

Africa, in ages past, was the nursery of science and literature; from thence they were taught in Greece and Rome, so that it was said that the ancient Greeks represented their favourite goddess of Wisdom – Minerva – as an African princess . . . Many eminent writers and historians agree that these ancient Ethiopians were Negroes . . . And why should not the same race who governed Egypt . . . who had her churches, her universities, and her repositories of learning and

49

science, once more stand on their legs and endeavour to raise their characters in the scale of the civilized world?[27]

These words of a Sierra Leonean doctor, J. Africanus Horton, written in *A Vindication of the African Race* published nearly a century ago, may or may not be good history: they strike in any case a very modern note. They sound the depth of modern African attitudes. And it is certainly true, in so far as it may matter in this context, that Herodotus was suggesting in the fifth century B.C. that the Egyptians were dark in colour and woolly of hair; that the Kushites (Horton's 'ancient Ethiopians') had invented their own alphabet, and were widely using it, by about 200 B.C., and that subsequent African peoples evolved highly literate variants of Islamic culture; while African forms of religion now appear, on less prejudiced inquiry, to be as spiritually respectable as other large systems of belief. So, in Horton's thinking – at the roots of African nationalism – old ideas combine with new, and unfamiliar thoughts with others which seem obvious.

The ideas of the African renaissance have a long and mixed pedigree. And a recognition of this is necessary to any consideration of the scope and nature of the slogans and programmes with which Africans have sought and found their political independence. It appears worth emphasizing that African nationalism is very far from being the sudden consequence of argument and action by what a former Chairman of the British South Africa Company described, in 1959, as 'a hard core of agitators and self-appointed leaders'. The 'hard core' theory can be argued only by those who are dishonest or politically inexperienced, for it is simply *not* how politics work. 'Agitators and self-appointed leaders' get nowhere unless they till well-prepared soil: let anyone who doubts this try pushing (no matter how 'hard') a Labour policy from door to door in a middle-class suburb, or, of course, the reverse.

The point is worth insisting on, perhaps, because many people still appear to think that African nationalism has been, and possibly still is, a minority phenomenon. Some people who think this do so in good faith: they tend in all honesty to interpret the actions and words of African leaders simply in reference to personal ambition, individual prejudice, or mere quirks of character. All these influences play their part, no doubt, but none of them matters beside the primary influence: the persistent pressure of popular opinion. Merely 'personal' interpretations of the African scene will obscure more than they reveal.

Others, it should be said, only pretend to believe that African nationalism has been the work of handfuls of agitators or self-appointed leaders. It is doubtful if the present rulers of South Africa actually hope that any reasonable person will accept their view of African nationalism as 'a communist plot'. Still, it does seem that many Europeans in Africa carefully harbour that illusion. Explaining how white civilization may yet be saved in Southern Rhodesia, a recent writer in that country urged that 'immediate action must be taken to counteract the virulent propaganda emanating from certain radio stations, notably Cairo. The mental poisoning pouring from these stations, if not countered, can have only disastrous effects.'[28] Countered, that is, not by social reforms calculated to remove grievances, but by radio-jamming and other censorship.

This line of thought, if that is what it can be called, is still followed by the Salazarist regime in Portugal, where a Foreign Minister has lately claimed that the Portuguese colonies are 'confronted by the greatest conspiracy ever fabricated against any country'.[29] It may be that this politician actually believed what he wrote: the Portuguese rulers, after all, have dealt in conspiratorial politics for more than forty years. But that is no good reason for anyone else to believe it.

The key ideas of African nationalism are in fact neither new nor poor in parentage. Some of them are political in origin; others are religious. They all need to be kept in mind, however vaguely, when approaching the storms and battles of the past few years. 'Poor Resident,' wrote a Nyasaland African pastor *half a century* before Sir Roy Welensky and his associates were busy explaining the essentially 'communist' (and therefore, in Central Africa, quite new) nature of nationalism, 'he thinks too much of his skin and not of his heart. What is the difference between a white man and a black man? Are we not of the same blood and all from Adam? This startles me much – is Europe still Christian or

Heathen? ... If we had power enough to communicate ourselves to Europe we would advise them not to call themselves "Christendom" but "Europeandom". Therefore the life of the three combined bodies [Missionaries, Government, Companies] is altogether too cheaty, too thefty, too mockery. Instead of "Give" they say "Take away from".'[30]

There is one other preliminary point which seems important. Aderibigbe, a Nigerian historian, has lately complained that European writers have tended to overlook African resistance to the imposition of colonial rule, whereas for Africans, he says, the fact of resistance has been and still remains of great psychological significance.[31] And it is true that one can easily gain, from several recent historians, the impression that the colonial system was introduced more or less from one year to the next, or one decade to the next, with little more than 'local trouble' and, generally, to a great sigh of relief all round. Yet if others have tended to forget what really happened, Africans have evidently not. Even if they do not always or often know many of the facts, they know the stories of resistance; and the stories speak of long and exhausting struggle against invaders who came with fair words and stayed with foul. This memory of resistance adds its special flavour to African nationalism, giving it here and there an edge of bitterness that is otherwise attractively absent.

Not many documents have survived to record the African view of that struggle. But those which have invariably sound a note of pride and repudiation that also has its place in the genesis of current ideas. 'I have listened to your words,' an East African chief wrote in Swahili (the letter is fortunately preserved) to the German invader, von Wissmann, 'but can find no reason why I should obey you.... If it should be friendship that you desire, then I am ready for it, today and always; but to be your subject, that I cannot be ...'[32]

This particular chief, as it happened, was also a slaver. No doubt it was right that his regime should go, as, in the course of fierce battles with the Germans, it eventually did. But the argument that the colonial regime occasionally imposed a better system on a worse is one that African nationalists have never found persuasive – a reluctance to see good in foreign domination that will surprise rather few people in the world today. And they have found it all the less persuasive because they have remembered their resistance. They have kept alive the names of many a hero who, like the brave Horatius admired so much by English schoolboys, died 'facing fearful odds, for the ashes of his fathers and the temples of his gods'. This attitude is likely, it seems, to persist. The more the colonial invasion recedes into the past, the more will Africans resurrect the epic of their struggles to resist it. In this, once again, they will of course be behaving, for better or for worse, like other peoples in other lands.

With these 'points of background' out of the way, we may now at last get down to considering what aspirations and intentions have moved the nationalism of Africa, and, after that, what success there has been in realizing them. Finally, it may then be possible to embark on some cautious prophecy about the future. If our approach has been rather slow and indirect, what follows will prove, I hope, all the more meaningful.

My first plan was to work to a regional scheme, for it is true that the key ideas of nationalism have a regional history and impact that are various and important. What happened in British West Africa was not the same as what happened in East Africa. The course of emancipation in the Congo was different from the growth of resistance in French territories. The Portuguese colonies remain, if less than in the past, in a daunting isolation of their own. . . . But the more I considered this plan of approach, the less satisfactory it promised to be. For it is also true that the ideas of African nationalism have acquired a continental validity (if within differing forms and fashions); that a regional approach would involve much irritating repetition; and that the influence of one region upon another constitutes a crucial aspect of the whole unfolding of events and programmes.

At some risk in over-simplification – but how avoid this, anyway? – I propose to look at recent African experience under a few general headings. These cover the more important of the root-ideas that have been in play and have framed the situations of the 1960s. There is first a cluster of ideas which may be grouped as 'cultural and political': *nationalism* itself, *Pan-*

Africanism, neutralism, the last being linked in turn to notions of African particularity or to interpretation of broad political concepts. Then there is another group which may be labelled 'economic and developmental': *African socialism* and *neocolonialism* are typical of these.

They are the concepts that define or point to the aspirations or intentions of most of the men and women who were active in the independence movements of the 1950s and rose to national leadership early in the 1960s. Sometimes they are concepts with little or no real content in terms of practical action. At other times they have had a very real content, only to be submerged in floods of heady verbalism or ideological confusion as men strove to keep afloat in the turmoil of the times. At other times again, these ideas or concepts have taken shape in forms very different from their ideal projections during the 'heroic period' of pre-independence struggle. Like other peoples in an era of testing change, or the need for change, Africans have found reality a tough material to work on. The fact remains that they have worked on it: Africa in 1970 is a vastly different continent, so far as human opportunities and social structures are concerned, than the Africa of twenty or even of ten years earlier. Demagogy, dishonesty, occasional failures may have stood in the way: they have not prevented forward movement. In measuring this forward movement, an examination of root-ideas can tell us much.

5 Political Springboards

In Europe, at any rate, the word 'nationalism' has lately got itself – and how understandably! – a very bad name. It has generally come to represent a narrow-minded and backward-looking chauvinism: xenophobic, jealous, and at odds with the proper destiny of man. Yet this was not always so. This was not how nationalism appeared to the standard-bearers of Europe's 'submerged nationalities' a century ago. What they were fighting for was not the 'right to dominate' but the 'right to be free'. *This we swear, this we swear,* declaimed Hungary's great poet of the revolutionary year 1848, *slaves we will no longer be!*[33]

It may be, of course, that the nationalism of Africa will follow the same dismal road as the 'tribal nationalism' – to borrow Miss Hannah Arendt's telling phrase – of recent European history. That is one of the great unanswered questions of Africa's tomorrow. But for Africa today the dominant ideas of nationalism have been closer to those of the anti-imperialist movements of nineteenth-century Europe.

African Nationalism

The simple and straightforward demand for equality of rights has been, and is, as strong a motivation here as it ever was in Europe: stronger, perhaps, because the provocation has been so much more considerable. It would be hard to believe that the Hungarians of 1848 were 'slaves' to the Austrian Emperor in anything like the sense that vast numbers of Africans have been – and still, here and there, remain – slaves to other imperial masters. The first and greatest sense of African nationalism has been, and indeed is now, the desire for personal emancipation.

An illuminating statement about this egalitarian meaning of nationalism has come from the long-imprisoned Rhodesian (Zimbabwe) writer, Ndabaningi Sithole.

He was arguing with a white South African writer, Stuart Cloete. 'Let us have no illusions,' Cloete had written. 'The black man hates the white. Above all he hates him for being white, because this is something he can never be.'[34]

Nothing, Sithole replied, could be further from the truth:

On a purely human basis the African accepts the white man. In the majority of cases it is the white man who does not accept the African. One of the reasons why the white man fears granting the African full independence is that the African may use against the white man the hateful methods he has seen the white man use against the African.

What the African hates in the white man is his unfair social, economic, political, and educational discriminatory practices¯which relegate the African to second- or third-rate citizenship in the land of his birth. The African hates the white man's arrogance, his mania for humiliating him in the land of his birth . . . Politically, the white man dominates the African; economically, he exploits him; socially, he degrades his human status . . . It is these things that the African hates, and not the white man himself.

It is no accident, of course, that this statement should come from an African of Southern Rhodesia, where the whole white effort – whether masquerading as 'partnership' or declaring itself honestly as the means to an otherwise impossibly high minority income – has been to 'prove' that the black man is in fact an inferior kind of human being without any reasonable claim to a natural equality with the white. This claim has been made more often and emphatically, as you would expect, precisely in those territories of permanent white settlement where discrimination takes an ever-present, inescapable form. But it is also present elsewhere, if in muted tones, and this is because the whole of colonial Africa, in west or east, south or centre, has felt the same discrimination, has heard the same insistent declaration of natural white superiority.

This, too, is an aspect of the matter that tends to be forgotten. The claim to a natural superiority – and therefore to a 'right to dominate' – has come not only from white Rhodesian bars and clubs and their like, nor has it always been couched in the jargon of racial hatred and contempt that is customarily encountered in such places. The most respectable authorities have made this claim. 'In early life,' opined an eminent British anthropologist some seventy years ago, setting the tone for much that was to follow, Africans

evince a degree of intelligence which, compared with that of the European child, appears precocious; and they acquire knowledge with facility till they arrive at the age of puberty, when the physical nature masters the intellect, and frequently deadens it. This peculiarity, which has been observed amongst others of what are termed the lower races [he might have added, the lower classes too!], has been attributed by some physiologists to the early closing of the sutures of the cranium... They can imitate, but they cannot invent, or even apply. They constantly fail to grasp and to generalize a notion.[35]

A famous Victorian traveller, Sir Richard Burton, put the same idea more crudely. Once an African has become adult, he explained, 'his mental development is arrested, and thenceforth he grows backwards instead of forwards'. Exploded myths, no doubt; yet long-lived...

Meeting this kind of argument in his book of 1959, Sithole comes down to cases. 'There is no word here for "Thank you",' Cloete had written, 'for the people are without the concept that requires its use.' On the contrary, Sithole replies; and he proceeds to offer a short list of terms for 'thank you' in Ndebele, Shona, Luganda, Hausa, Tswana, and Sotho.

'The African,' Cloete had explained, 'has been conditioned by centuries of savage competition to seize what he desires wherever he can find it.' Anyone who knows anything of European history in the last hundred years (not to speak of earlier times) may wryly smile at Cloete's belief that Africans could be thought peculiar in this respect. Sithole makes the point.

We do not deny this... What concerns us here is the context in which [Cloete] makes this statement. He wants to give the false impression that it is *only* the African who has been so conditioned. We could reverse his statement so that it is equally applicable to any race in this world: namely, the European has been conditioned by centuries of savage competitive life to seize what he desires wherever he can find it. The occupation of Asia, Africa, the Americas, Australasia, and other non-European lands by Europeans is an historically irrefutable piece of evidence [to this effect] . . .

There is no need to follow Sithole further. The case is clear: nationalism in Africa today is primarily a claim for equality of status and of rights, for personal dignity, self-respect, full participation in the things of the material world as well as in the things of the spirit: a consistent effort to rescue Africans from their condition of acquired inferiority to which they have been relegated through the years. And this is everywhere true. The only real difference between regions is that the claim was heard in these terms a good deal earlier in West Africa than elsewhere. Nearly sixty years ago a Gold Coast (Ghanaian) writer recalled – with a relaxed note of laughter somewhat characteristic of his country – how he had argued with a certain European mining expert.

After he had spoken of *native* bush-path, *native* canoe, *native* river, *native* mines and *native* gold [wrote Mensah Sarbah], I asked him to explain to the court, in what respects *native* gold and the other native things particularly differed from those found in other parts of the world, but he could not; for the absurdity of always describing in Africa everything non-European as *native* had dawned on him by that time.[36]

'Native,' as we know, has long become a word so loaded with contempt in any part of English-speaking Africa as to be, merely by itself, a badge of supposed inferiority, not to say downright shame. I remember discussing this with an enlightened white trade unionist in South Africa some nineteen years ago. As a young woman she had made a tour of Europe, including the Soviet Union. 'Even then,' she recalled, 'I still regarded the natives as being pretty well sub-human. I remember they asked me in Russia if I was a native of the Union of South Africa; and I replied indignantly: "No, I'm a white woman, can't you see?"' Well, but this kind of thing gets tedious in the course of time; and African intellectuals have abolished the word 'native' without feeling any further need for explanation.

Claims for equality of rights required clothing in political dress; and this soon took the necessary form of a demand for self-government. Here too, and for easily understood historical reasons, British West Africa led the way. (Early 'French African' claims were confused and therefore delayed by theories of assimilation and of French citizenship regardless of race, colour, or religion.) Not being colonies of settlement – differing sharply in this respect even from some of their French colonial neighbours – Nigeria, Ghana, and Sierra Leone (with Gambia adding a minor harmony in the background) had early acquired at least the embryonic institutions of representative government.

In 1844 a dozen Fanti chiefs in the Gold Coast had agreed in certain circumstances to recognize the authority of British criminal law, and this *Bond* became a symbol of the political autonomy of African chiefs within their range of authority – as well, of course, as a recognition of British rule. But 1852 brought the creation of a legislative assembly in the territory, and although this proved abortive, it set men thinking. The movement towards self-government was slow and uncertain, and was obstructed by British policy more often than it was encouraged; but 1888 none the less saw the nomination – democratic election being still far ahead – of an African to membership of the legislative council. In 1894 there came the establishment of three municipal councils; and gradually it became clear, as the years slowly succeeded each other, that representative government for the whole country could be permanently withheld only by force. Yet not until after 1945 did the threat of force begin to appear difficult and undesirable for Britain to apply. Developments in Lagos and the southerly parts of Nigeria followed much the same lines.

Nationalism, as such, appeared in full array during the First World War. There emerged the National Congress of British West Africa and other bodies to the same general effect. Names began to be heard that were soon famous. One of them was that of Joseph Ephraim Caseley Hayford. Speaking at Freetown in 1920, this Gold Coast journalist traced, for the whole of British West Africa, a programme whose wider meaning we can easily recognize today. 'We have passed the childhood stage,' Hayford declared on that occasion, 'and much as we appreciate the concern of our guardians, the time has come for us to take an intelligent active part in the guiding of our own national destiny; and that is the primary fact that has called into being the National Congress of British West Africa.'[37]

The terms seem old-fashioned and Uncle-Tom-like today; but when they were used they sounded subversive in many ears. The *national* note was firmly struck, if still in a vaguely regional context, and for reasons that were perfectly clear to the men of that time. To far-seeing men of colour these reasons had long been clear. 'The claims of no people,' an American Negro leader, Martin Delany, had argued as early as 1852, 'are respected by any nation until they are presented in a national capacity.'[38] This indeed may yet prove to have been Europe's major contribution to African politics: the conviction that progress and equality were possible only at the price of 'nationhood' – even though the concept of exclusivist nationalism was one which fitted the African situation even less hopefully than any other.

Become nations: or you cannot become free. In some such imperative as this the European message reached African ears, decade after decade, through a multitude of more or less sceptical exhortations. A people without nationalism was said to be a people without history, and a people without history could have no identity, and therefore no real claim on that dignity and self-respect which even the poorest European peoples had successfully acquired for themselves. The lesson was to be well learned.

So it came about that Africans, more and more, found themselves impelled to demand their freedom within ideological boundaries which seemed right and natural to their European rulers – the kind of boundaries within which the peoples of Europe had gained their own independence. The notion that freedom could be possible and even preferable within supranational boundaries or by means of supra-national or even continental institutions was impossibly far ahead at the time; and, as we well know, to a large extent still is so. Whether regionalist and 'unitarian' solutions are to remain impossible, however, is already a significant part of the ideological conflict in Africa at this moment, a point to which we shall return later.

Having posed their demands within a narrowly national framework – even though this often represented multi-national or supra-national realities, as notably in Nigeria – African leaders pressed them. The years of the late twenties and thirties – of what I have called the phase of stagnation – offered, however, only repression in return. Little was achieved. But the Second World War, fought most consciously against the ideology of racism represented by the German Nazis and Italian Fascists, proved a great liberator. Sithole has a wry and telling tale to this effect.

'Away with Hitler! Down with him!' said the British officer [appealing for Africans to fight against Hitler].
'What's wrong with Hitler?' asked the African.
'He wants to rule the whole world,' said the British officer.
'What's wrong with that?'
'He is German, you see,' said the British officer, trying to appeal subtly to the African's tribal consciousness.
'What's wrong with his being German?'
'You see,' said the British officer, trying to explain in terms that would be conceivable to the African mind, 'it is not good for one tribe to rule another. Each tribe must rule itself. That's only fair. A German must rule Germans, an Italian, Italians, and a Frenchman, French people.'[30]

The point was taken. African nationalism came of age during this war. By 1944 powerful new notes were sounding up and down the continent. The old Uncle-Tom-ism vanished from the scene. What was felt now was not 'appreciation for the concern of our guardians', but growing impatience with any claim that these guardians had ever played a useful purpose.

'We who live in this blessed country of Nigeria,' wrote Nnamdi Azikiwe, one of the outstanding pioneers of West African nationalism, just sixteen years before his country became independent, 'know that until we are in control of political power in our country we would continue to be the footstool of imperialist nations, who are interested selfishly in their economic prosperity and social prestige. . . . If there is any doubt about the yearnings of Nigerians for self-government, it should be dispelled forthwith. We are fed up with being governed as a

Crown Colony, which we are NOT. We are nauseated by the existence of an untrammelled bureaucracy which makes, administers, and interprets our laws, without our knowledge and consent. The idea of our paid civil servants ruling and lording it over us is a challenge to our manhood, both as a nation and as a race.'[40]

The blessed country of Nigeria, of course, contained several peoples whose right to consider themselves as nations, even within the narrowest meaning of the term, was obvious to anyone who had thought about the matter. But the need for a nationalist framework was understood even where peoples had generally lived without it, or without more than a primitive sense of it. 'National union is necessary,' ran a Congolese manifesto in 1956, 'because the whole population [of the Belgian Congo] must now accept a national character and the unity that flows from it. . . . We are convinced that it is perfectly possible for Catholics, Protestants, Salvation Army-ists, [*Salutistes*,] and Muslims to agree on a programme for their common good such as respects the principles of natural morality engraved in the hearts of all men worthy of the name . . .'[41]

Such arguments were widely accepted. When the French in 1959 and 1960 finally withdrew their political control from their West and Equatorial African dependencies, it appeared natural that the administrative units in question should become as many separate states. Besides, peoples long suppressed were eager to stand forth in the world with an acknowledged identity of their own. All the same, it is worth recalling in this connection that there were efforts to transpose the colonialist federal structures of French West Africa and Equatorial Africa (eight and four units respectively) into independent federal structures; and the full record, when it becomes available, may yet show that these efforts could have succeeded if governments in Paris had cared actively to help them.*

For even in the full surge of nationalism during the fifties there were not lacking men who said that *federal structures*, and not a maze of little separate states, ought to follow the colonial

---

*Ironically, it was the *Loi Cadre* of the Fourth Republic which, while opening the way to territorial independence, largely ruined the hope of territorial federation.

partition. Nigeria was fortunate in this respect. The eight territories of French West Africa might well have repeated Nigeria's
example. There were men in East Africa who already argued that
the road of 'balkanization' must quickly take them to disaster.
The same note was struck in the central-southern regions.

This underlying thought belonged to another of nationalist
Africa's basic group of ideas.

Pan-Africanism

It might have been expected that the ideas expressed by Pan-
Africanism would evaporate with the coming of political independence to most of Africa. For they were initially the ideas of
the Negro diaspora beyond the Atlantic. They spoke for the
dream of those many men and women of African descent who,
finding themselves in the midst of white American cultures
which rejected them, reacted by looking back across the ocean
for a new integration of their lives and hopes. 'Black Africa,' in
the well-known words of the Martinique poet, Aimé Césaire,
'is the mother of our West Indian civilization, and it is she who
will regenerate our energy and hope. . . .'

Another poet, Claud McKay, has put it this way:

> For the dim regions whence my fathers came
> My spirit, bondaged by the body, longs.
> Words felt, but never heard, my lips would frame;
> My soul would sing forgotten jungle songs.
> I would go back to darkness and to peace.
> But the great western world holds me in fee,
> And I may never hope for full release
> While to its alien gods I bend my knee . . .[42]

Not only that: there was also the belief that a free Africa could
help to liberate the Negroes overseas. 'It may be that the day is
not far off,' a Negro American had written in the *New York Age*
in 1923, 'when the new Negroes of Africa will be demanding
that their blood brothers in the United States be treated with
absolute fairness and justice.' An extravagant fancy when it was
written: yet in 1963 a conference of African students from
twenty-six countries expressed their solidarity 'with Negro

students fighting for equality in the United States of America'.[43]

At the root of these mainly transatlantic ideas about Pan-Africanism or Pan-Negroism, there lay the dual notion of Black rights and of 'Africa for the Africans'. How completely this was so may be seen in the first Pan-African Congress ever held. Organized in 1900 by a Trinidad barrister, H. Sylvester Williams, it gave a platform to another figure who would become much better known, W. E. B. DuBois. These men looked across to Africa with a bitter awareness of their own unity in disfranchisement: here in the New World all Africans had lost their separate ethnic loyalties, languages, cultures, sense of difference from one another;* and so it appeared natural to regard all Africans as belonging to the same great territorial unit, Africa, however much that unit might be divided within itself by 'the frontiers of foreign rule'. This visionary attitude induced an illumination that was to seem prophetic in later years, for it was during this first Pan-African Congress that DuBois threw down his famous challenge. 'The problem of the twentieth century,' he declared in the year of its birth, and with colonial conquest in full assault, 'is the problem of the colour line – the relation of the darker to the lighter races of men in Asia and Africa, in America and the islands of the sea.'

The Pan-Africanists were naturally ignored by the busy imperialist world. They were few, and they seemed to have no influence. But they went on hammering at their theme. American Black missionaries began exporting their ideas into the heart of Africa.[44] Political journalists began reflecting and developing them on the West Coast. In 1919 a second congress met, this time in Paris where the victorious Powers of the First World War were deciding how they should settle the peace. Fifty-seven delegates were present: 'Negroes in the trim uniform of American army officers,' an American newspaper reported at the time, 'coloured men in frock coats or business suits, polished French Negroes who hold public offices. . . .'[45]

The delegates boldly addressed themselves to the Powers.

---

*There were corners of the New World where the descendants of transported Africans had clung to some of their old ways and languages. But these cases were marginal; they do not affect the argument here.

They called on them to 'establish a code of law for the international protection of the natives of Africa, similar to the proposed international code for labour', and laid down a list of 'principles' by which 'the natives of Africa and the peoples of African descent' should henceforth be governed. We are still, it will be seen, at a relatively early stage of the argument: outright demands for self-government and independence seemed hopelessly premature, as indeed they undoubtedly would have been. The colonial Powers were still engaged in 'pacifying' their newly won subjects in Africa: the notion that they should now pack their bags and leave would have struck them, even if they had deigned to notice it, as absurd.

Yet these demands of the second congress pointed forward to a steady crystallization of new ideas. They were Pan-African, and they were libertarian. Moreover, and the influence of DuBois counted for much in this, they gave due weight to the customs and beliefs of pre-colonial Africa – to all that complex of tradition which had carried Africans through the years before conquest. They affirmed:

> The land and its natural resources should be held in trust for the natives.... The investment of capital and granting of concessions should be so regulated as to prevent the spoliation of the natives and the exhaustion of natural wealth.... Slavery and corporal punishment should be abolished and forced labour except in punishment of crime.... It should be the right of every native child to learn and write his own language, and the language of the trustee nation, at public expense.... And the natives of Africa should have the right to participate in government as fast as their development might permit....[46]

During and after the Second World War these ideas and others like them became common coinage among youthful nationalists in Africa; and now they were rephrased for a specifically African context. In this respect the sixth congress, held at Manchester in 1945, was crucial. Here for the first time the Old Guard from over the ocean was flanked by new men from the continent itself: obscure young men, for the most part, whom few in England (or anywhere else) had ever heard of – among them Kenyatta from Kenya, Nkrumah from the Gold Coast, Akintola from

Nigeria, Johnson from Sierra Leone. The old notion of 'European trusteeship' went neck and crop out of the window into the Manchester fog. 'We demand for Africa,' the delegates resolved, 'autonomy and independence, so far, and no further, than it is possible in this One World for groups and peoples to rule themselves subject to inevitable world unity and federation.'

The language was unambiguous in spite of a romantic bow in the direction of 'world unity'. It offered a new tune to the brief harmony of worldwide victory over racism. To grasp the hopes of that meeting one must recall the scene in India at the time, for India was then moving rapidly towards independence under pressure from the militant Congress movement, and the British Labour Party, just elected to power, was known to favour that cause. If India could be free, why not Africa? There was ground for a new hopefulness. Meanwhile the Pan-Africanists in Manchester restricted themselves to a threat of what might have to happen if Africa's legitimate ambitions should continue to be thrust aside. 'We are determined to be free,' they said, '(but) if the Western world is still determined to rule Mankind by force, then Africans, *as a last resort*, may have to appeal to force in the effort to achieve freedom. . . .' It was the first time that Africa's challenge would be posed in this form. Later years would see it realized in North Africa, in the Portuguese colonies, and elsewhere on the continent.

The ideas of Pan-Africanism, though budded outside Africa, were not allowed to wither with the coming of independence. So little were these ideas forgotten, indeed, that they may even be said to have presided over the 'great year of independence', 1960, when no fewer than sixteen African colonies won at least a measure of political sovereignty.

The historical facts are that a multitude of colonies became independent states; that constitutional declarations in favour of federal union went for little or nothing; that the one coherent effort at securing such a union – between the former colonies of Senegal and Soudan – fell apart almost at once;* and that unity movements soon took the merely diplomatic and tactical form

*The Federation of Mali, formed on 17 January 1959 and dissolved on 1 August 1960.

of 'bloc alliances' named after the capitals where they were formed, such as Casablanca, Monrovia, and Brazzaville. Yet it is also true that the ideal of continental unity was enshrined during this formative period as one of the guarantees, perhaps the fundamental guarantee, of true development and progress. With a startling impact on large numbers of men and women, there suddenly appeared the prospect of an African civilization into which all the many different streams of African thought, experience, and resource should flow, fortifying the belief that these peoples could thus achieve a place and weight in the world commensurate with their continent.

There was plenty of ground for scepticism. Africa remained full of more or less bitter internecine conflicts and potential frontier wars. The large capitals of the world flew a score and more of African flags on separate (and separately very costly) embassies and missions; and each of these represented a network of élitist interests and careers. The old sores of ethnic separatism began to reopen. A little country like Kenya, weighed down with poverty and unemployment, was expected to take its final steps to independence as a cluster of petty statelets loosely connected to a central government. Other newly independent states threatened to go the same way. Yet the ideas of unity stubbornly remained, and even now remain, near the centre of the picture. The vision still glitters, still beckons.

The astonishing persistence of the idea of a Congolese nation, in the face of every obstacle and provocation to the contrary, is perhaps the most convincing token of the power in that vision. As another token, here is a summary of resolutions passed by a conference of delegates from twenty-six African student unions in Europe and America when they met in London in April 1963. These resolutions are important not only for what they said but also for who composed them. Many crucial jobs were to be filled in Africa from the ranks of these delegates during the next few years:

Instruments giving expression to African Unity [should] be created as a matter of urgency.... A method of political coordination [should] be worked out in the consolidating of African Unity.... A Political Constitution applying throughout the continent [should] be formulated and accepted. . . . This Political Constitution should make provision for the establishment of a Pan-African Parliament, a Pan-African Executive and Public Service. . . . A Pan-African Army under joint high command [should] be created from national contingents in order to safeguard the integrity of the African continent. . . .

This Pan-African Army is urgently needed in order to defend Africa against continuing aggression in South Africa, Angola, Portuguese Guinea, Moçambique, and other areas temporarily under colonial subjection. . . .

Africa should be free of all foreign military bases, nuclear and atomic testing facilities, and foreign military missions or pacts. . . . The foreign policy of African countries should in any case be guided only by the principles of a most rigorous positive neutralism. . . . African countries must therefore free themselves from partnership in any foreign national groupings which are not compatible with African positive neutralism. . . .

That these were not isolated voices, mere student romantics rebelling against the established trend of orthodox opinion in their homelands, was shown by the African Unity Conference of thirty-two independent countries (all except two, Morocco and Togo, represented by their heads of state) which gathered at Addis Ababa in May 1963. There, a charter for African unity was drawn up and accepted. An Organization of African Unity was formed, providing for an assembly of heads of state or government to meet at least once a year, a council of ministers to meet at least twice a year, a secretariat (to be situated in Addis Ababa), and a commission for mediation, conciliation, and arbitration.* With this, an organic concept of political and economic unity in Africa was at least on the record.

Much of the drive behind the Addis conference was undoubtedly due to President Nkrumah of Ghana. The 'ideas of Manchester' had remained with him. He saluted Ghana's independence in 1957 by roundly declaring that the achievement would be meaningless unless it helped towards the liberation of the whole continent. With that in mind, Nkrumah early set about promoting unity of action. When French Guinea became independent in October 1958 he made available to President Sékou Touré a loan of £10 millions (other loans of £4 to £5

*See On the Record, p. 183.

millions each were later advanced to Mali and Upper Volta, as well as many lesser sums to nationalists up and down the continent) and, a month later, concluded a Ghana-Guinea 'union' which was intended 'to form a nucleus for a Union of African States'.[47] A month later again an All-African People's Conference at Accra gathered delegates from sixty-two nationalist organizations. In July 1959 Nkrumah went to Saniquellie, in Liberia, for unity discussions with Presidents Tubman and Touré; in December 1960, with Touré and President Kéita of Mali (now severed from Senegal), he formed a Ghana–Guinea–Mali Union. This was named 'the Union of African States and was to form a nucleus of the United States of Africa'.[48] In January 1961 these three states met at Casablanca with the leaders of Egypt, Morocco, and the Algerian Front de Libération Nationale (FLN), as well as a representative of the Libyan government, and established a consultative assembly together with other coordinating instruments.

None of this escaped sharp criticism and opposition from other African states. Nigeria led another grouping – known as the Monrovia Bloc after the Liberian capital where it first met – while many former French colonies had a separate 'organization' of their own, known as the Brazzaville Bloc, with President Houphouët-Boigny of the Ivory Coast in the lead.

Yet these various and often acutely opposed groupings all met at the Addis conference where they at least declared for progress towards unification of *overall* policy and objective. If much of the running continued to be made by Ghana, the final pace was set by Nigeria and like-minded 'moderates', including Liberia and Ethiopia, who all put forward detailed plans for varying methods of securing common action and agreement. It was the government of the Sudan, for instance, which pressed that Africa should become a zone free of nuclear weapons and foreign pacts. The conference was rightly hailed as a success. It had achieved more than the sceptics had believed possible. Though later frustrated, the OAU was in being.

It was certainly helped by finding a common enemy in the continued white domination of southern Africa – whether by the South African National Party under Dr Verwoerd or by the agents of the Portuguese dictator, Salazar, or by the settlers of Southern Rhodesia. Looking back, though, one can see that opinion had moved a long way since the eve of 'independence year', 1960. Reacting then to Ghanaian propaganda for unity, the Prime Minister of Nigeria, the late Sir Abubakar Tafawa Balewa, had voiced a widespread attitude when declaring, in January 1960: 'A United States of Africa? Oh, surely it is very premature to start talking about anything like that. Nigeria has not the slightest intention of surrendering her sovereignty, no sooner has she gained her independence, to anyone else, including other Western African countries.'[49]

In 1963 the idea of a full-blown United States of Africa, vigorously sponsored by Nkrumah, was evidently still 'very premature'; but the suspicion that such an idea was somehow part of a 'Ghanaian plot' had disappeared (or at any rate much faded), and several steps towards a supra-national organization of African states had actually been taken – with the Nigerian government's active sponsorship and participation. Moreover, programmes for regional unity looked then like making progress in British East Africa, where three former colonies, Tanganyika, Uganda, and Kenya (the last not yet quite independent) met in June 1963 to consider practical steps towards federal union.

The real lines of division had in fact significantly shifted. At the Addis conference these were no longer between 'Casablanca' and 'Monrovia', between the 'left-wing' states and the 'moderates'; and they had likewise moved from the familiar Ghana–Nigeria deadlock towards a new pattern. This new pattern tended, though latently as yet, to assemble the genuinely independent leaders (whether 'left-wing' or 'moderate') on one side, leaving the much-less-than-genuinely-independent spokesmen of the Brazzaville grouping on the other. Apart from the Ivory Coast and Madagascar, relatively large and rich, these 'Brazzaville' states were a scattering of little former French colonies whose dependence on France, whether directly through financial and other ties or indirectly through 'association' with the West European Common Market, was often described as 'semi-colonial'.

How far this description might be justified could be measured to some extent by the number of French troops stationed in the ex-colonies of West and Equatorial Africa and Madagascar: early in 1963 they still attained the remarkable total of 20,000. The presence of these French troops, together with French advisers and administrators, was in line with military agreements signed with France by all these territories except Guinea and Mali, agreements which provided for bilateral military planning and the installation of permanent French military establishments. They cost France £68 millions in 1963.

It was hard to see how such agreements could be compatible with a full development of local sovereignty. 'One of the key clauses in each of the agreements,' *West Africa* remarked on 24 August 1963, after the brief intervention and withdrawal of French troops in defence and then abandonment of Fulbert Youlou in Congo (Brazzaville), 'is that which allows African governments to appeal to French armed forces to assume the "maintenance of the organization of their own armies" .... In response to such an appeal, France may "intervene directly" in the African state.... France also has special agreements with most of her African ex-colonies to deal with the participation of French armed forces in the maintenance of public order.... Although these particular agreements remain secret, they appear to provide for the indigenous government to call upon French troops to intervene in case of a threat to peace and public order. The call may be refused, and must anyway be approved by a decision of the French cabinet.' Thus France retained much indirect and even direct political and military power in most of her former African territories. The distance between these French Community agreements and the British Commonwealth framework might be seen by comparing their impact and implications with what happened in Nigeria. There the mere acquisition of British military air-staging rights failed to withstand Nigerian opposition. In 1969 the French were at war in Chad.

It was clearly with these 'Brazzaville states' in mind, tied so closely and even exclusively to France and the West European Common Market, that Nkrumah at the Addis conference hammered home his theme that 'Africa must unite or perish'; called for 'common functional organs'; and argued that 'it should be possible to devise some constitutional structure which secures these objectives and yet preserves the sovereignty of each country joining the Union'. Only an Africa free to develop its vast potential without hampering restrictions by the old colonial Powers could properly advance the interests of its several parts. Only an Africa with a centralized political direction could successfully give effective material and moral support to Africans not yet free.

So many blessings must flow from our unity; so many disasters must follow on our continued disunity. . . .

It is said, of course, that we have no capital, no industrial skill, no communications and no internal markets, and that we cannot even agree among ourselves how best to utilize our resources. Yet all the stock exchanges of the world are preoccupied with Africa's gold, diamonds, uranium, platinum, copper, and iron ores. Our capital flows out in streams to irrigate the whole system of Western economy. Fifty-two per cent of the gold in Fort Knox at this moment, where the U.S. stores its bullion, is believed to have originated from our shores. . . .

Proposals for an African Common Market drew the same kind of arguments in its support. Not long after the Addis conference the United Africa Company (a dependent of Unilever) opened in Ghana a plant to manufacture 24,000 tons of soap a year, as well as toothpaste and related products. Speaking on this occasion, Nkrumah pointed out that the factory was no larger not because Unilever could not afford a much bigger one, but because there was an insufficiently large market. 'Many African states,' he went on, 'still impose customs duties and import restrictions originally designed to limit the trade of the colony in the interest of the manufacturing industries of the imperial power.' If they had factories, these were small, 'and the price of our manufactured goods is far higher than it need be if there was a larger market'. The foreign investor suffered no less. His 'vested interest in African unity is as great as that of any African today'.

Whatever his fellow-leaders at Addis may have thought of Nkrumah's words, the larger fact remained that the nationalism of a major part of Africa had at least made some turn – even in spite of separatist agreements linked to the 'protection area' of the West European Common Market – away from small-nation isolationism along familiar lines and towards the concept of continental integration. It is perfectly evident from the present scene that the difficulties in actually realizing this objective, or any serious aspect of it, are many, stubborn, and opaque. These difficulties may prevail in the 1970s. What we can note today is that a large number of African peoples, including some of the most dynamic and least poor, had become concerned with unity. This may still prove to be one of the most telling if least observed factors of the years ahead.

The reasons for this trend were complicated. Pan-Africanist propaganda could never have made headway against the fervent pressures of small-nation separatism unless its teachings had fallen on fertile ground. Part of this ground lay in the common formation of Africa's leaders. (Many of ex-French West Africa's leading intellectuals, for example, got to know each other, discussed the same ideas, and nursed the same hopes, at the William Ponty *lycée* in Dakar.) A larger part lay in the manifest truth that nearly all of Africa occupied the same political and economic position in relation to the rest of the world, and shared the same basic problems. But still another part, and not the least, lay in what may be called a growing sense of 'one-ness', of 'African-ness', of possessing the same fundamental scale of values and beliefs, a scale which formed an 'identity' that was specifically African, a 'personality' that should now, in the wake of colonial subjection, find its full and public expression.

The African Personality

If I went to heaven, and God said, 'Aggrey, I am going to send you back, would you like to go as a white man?' I should reply, 'No, send me back as a black man, yes, completely black.' And if God should ask, 'Why?' I would reply, 'Because I have a work to do as a black man that no white man can do. Please send me back as black as you can make me.' ... I am proud of my colour: whoever is not proud of his colour is not fit to live.[50]

That was fifty years ago, and the confidence for which Aggrey

73

spoke was part and parcel of the West African nationalist movement. But the characteristic writings of Négritude belong to the
poets of the Caribbean and their French-speaking African
friends in the Paris of the nineteen-forties and fifties, although it
was actually in 1939 that Césaire had 'founded the movement'
with his *Cahiers d'un retour au pays natal* (*Notes on Going Home*).
As with Pan-Africanism, Négritude with them was a means of
protest, a weapon in the struggle for equality of status, a challenge cast in the face of a world which appeared to worship mere
material achievement.

Romantic, 'political' only by implication, even metaphysical,
Négritude was the mantle of culture within which deprived and
despised peoples should now regain their birthright. 'Only
Africa,' in Césaire's words, 'can revitalize, repersonalize the
West Indies.' But Africa had first to 'repersonalize' herself,
move out from under the shadow of Europe and display her own
virtues to her own delight, show the world that she too was an
integral and inseparable part of humanity's achievement and
endeavour:

> For it is not true at all that the work of man is finished
> that we have nothing more to do in the world
> that it is enough that we should set ourselves in the steps
>   of the world
> but the work of man is only beginning . . .
> and no race possesses the monopoly of beauty intelligence
>   force
> and there is room for all of us at the rendezvous of
>   victory.[51]

These ideas excited the intellectuals of all those African
countries faced with European policies of cultural assimilation.
Many followed Césaire's trumpet call. Brilliant among them was
the young Léopold Senghor, now President of Senegal, whose
poetry most dramatically displays the schismic clash between
'becoming a Frenchman' and 'remaining an African', and
resolves it – at any rate in verse – in favour of the second.

Senghor strode the pavements of the white man's world and
sang their misery and solitude, longing for the 'joy and community' of his homeland, as in his poem *New York*, where white

Manhattan and black Harlem are compared with one another:

> No mother's breast, but only nylon legs. Legs and breasts
> 　　　　　　that have no sweat nor smell,
> No tender word for there are no lips, only artificial
> 　　　　　　hearts paid for in hard cash . . .
> Nights of insomnia or nights of Manhattan . . .
> Harlem! Harlem! Now I saw Harlem! A
> 　　　　　　green breeze of corn springs up from
> 　　　　　　the pavements ploughed by
> 　　　　　　the naked feet of dancers,
> Bottoms waves of silk and sword-blade breasts, water-lily
> 　　　　　　ballets and fabulous masks . . .[52]

The note was a new one from an African, but not unique. 'I feel ridiculous,' sang Léon Damas,

> in their shoes, in their dinner jackets
> in their stiff shirts, their paper collars,
> with their monocles and bowler hats
> I feel ridiculous
> with my toes that were not made
> to sweat from morning to evening
> in their swaddling clothes that weaken my limbs
> and deprive my body of its beauty.[53]

It passed from the French-speaking poets to those who wrote in English. 'Then I came back,' remembered Abioseh Nicol of Sierra Leone, 'sailing down the Guinea coast':

> Go up-country, they said,
> To see the real Africa.
> For whomsoever you may be,
> That is where you come from.
> Go for bush – inside the bush
> You will find your hidden heart,
> Your mute ancestral spirit.
>
> And so I went,
> Dancing on my way.[54]

It acquired a more clearly political accent, reaching out towards a conflict of cultures and policies and programmes, as in these lines by the Ghanaian Dei-Anang:

> Here we stand
> Poised between two civilizations
> Backward? To days of drum
> And festal dances in the shade
> Of sun-kist palms.
> Or forward?
> Forward!
> Toward?
> The slums, where man is dumped upon man? . . .[55]

It moved across the continent. It was heard and echoed back in remote places, as in this statement of defiant hope by the poet-statesman of Angola, Agostinho Neto:

> My mother (black mother whose sons depart)
> you taught me to wait and hope
> as you had learnt in bitter days
>
> But in me
> life killed that mystic hope
> I am not the one who waits
> but the one who is awaited
> And we are Hope
> your sons . . .
> searching for life.[56]

Négritude 'naturalized itself': in so doing, it lost much of its racialist undertone and stood forth as a statement about people, people who happened to be African. But all this – and the poetry of the African renaissance became a flood in these years of self-realization and self-questioning – struck at the artists with peculiar force. They were involved in national movements impatient of the traditional past, the past that had delivered them into colonial subjection; and yet the idiom of a new and different future seemed repeatedly to lead them back only to European forms and motives that spelt imitation – and therefore disaster for any true growth of the arts. Which path could they follow?

Beier has commented:

The Nigerian artist finds himself between two groups of people: enthusiastic Europeans, many of whom want him to be exotic and who want to recognize in his work clever adaptations of traditional motifs. On the other hand there is the Nigerian middle class, who are not very interested in his activities but who certainly do *not* want to be reminded in any way of traditional art, which is a world they feel they have left behind them, and in which they do not recognize any lasting values.[57]

The artistic dilemma is thus a real one, and will not soon be resolved. But it is variously posed. Very differently, for example, in South Africa. The protest and political inwardness of Négritude consisted precisely in its denial of assimilation – because assimilation meant acceptance of Africans (or West Indians) only at the price of becoming 'honorary whites'. But in South Africa Africans were offered 'acceptance' (the inverted commas are very necessary) only if they remained *outside* the pale of white civilization – which meant, in the circumstances of South Africa, denial of any real access to the modern world. Apartheid, 'separate development', promised nothing but a permanent deprivation of dignity and manhood.

Reacting against this, African writers in South Africa have proclaimed what may be called the indivisibility of culture. For them, Négritude and its accent on African-ness seemed only to be playing into the hands of white communities whose own policy was based on a reversal of the same conception. They have consequently tended to condemn Négritude as a kind of racialism, and in doing so they have found justification in the more extreme forms of Negro protest now appearing in the United States, among for instance the 'Black Moslems', who seem to have elevated the older 'Back to Africa' ideas of Marcus Garvey and others into a fanatical creed of racialist exclusivism. 'To us in multi-racial communities,' the South African Ezekiel Mphahlele has remarked in an illuminating commentary, 'Négritude is just so much intellectual talk, a cult.'[58]

Mphahlele believes that a new art in Africa will arise from the stuff of life itself, and not from any cult of particularity, separateness, or racial difference. At the back of his thought there lies the memory and knowledge of the way in which Africans of his own country, grappling with the squalid superficialities of white culture which are all that is 'allowed them', have none the less succeeded time after time in creating valid works of art, whether in music, painting, or literature. He is impatient with the solitary souls who try 'reintegration' in condescending Paris or London. 'The number of African artists and writers who have not been discovered, because they are locked up in their ghettoes in multi-racial communities, and who cannot speak to a world audience because of brutal white rule and racial prejudice, is much too large compared with the few who go abroad – too large for us to worry excessively about the latter.' It is one of the historical achievements of Africans in South Africa to have raised the ideal of non-racialist humanism above the muck and misery of apartheid. And one may well believe that it is one of Africa's major tragedies that these very Africans should be sealed off behind barricaded frontiers during the crucial years of continental search for a common future.

But Négritude, in 'naturalizing itself', became part of a larger and more emotive theme. 'My country groans,' in Azikiwe's words, 'under a system which makes it impossible for us to develop our personalities to the full.'[59] What did he really mean? In answering this question we encounter the ideological projection of the political and programmatic slogans of the past ten years and more. With the idea of 'the African personality', nationalist politics took a new and original turn. 'National liberation' became identified with 'African liberation'. The claims of Pan-Africanism acquired a philosophical justification.

The thought expressed in Azikiwe's words was given a continental framework. It was right to liberate the peoples of Africa because they could not otherwise enjoy their own separate identities – but also because they could not otherwise develop that special attitude and temperament by which Africa, within her multitude of variations, displays her inner unity, her 'personality' that is ultimately unique, distinct, and comprehensive.

To some extent this proclamation of 'an underlying African cultural unity' may be a mere response to the familiar European proposition – that nothing but colonial rule has ever united Africans. 'The only common factor in the heterogeneous tribes of Africa,' according to a recent and characteristic European statement of this sort, 'is the human form.'[60] This kind of attitude is considered profoundly offensive by educated Africans today not so much, it seems, for its splenetic condescension as for its denial of any cultural basis for unity. For if it were true that the many peoples of Africa are nothing more than a scatter of unrelated or even fundamentally opposed units, then clearly the fate of these units must lie in the slow crystallization of nation-states whose individual weakness or ambition can never hope to save them, at least for long into the future, from the tutelage of foreign masters, or else from wars of conquest such as the records of European nation-states have abundantly illustrated. But is the independence of Africa to be merely a prelude to anything as unpromising as that? The ideologists of Africa today have generally revolted against any such prospect. 'On the contrary,' they tend to reply, 'we shall build our future on the basis of an underlying cultural unity which, in fact, really does relate most of our peoples to the same body of ideas.'

What 'underlying cultural unity'? What 'body of ideas'? We shall take a look at the political answers – neutralism, African socialism, and the like – in a later chapter. Here I want only to enlarge a little on the philosophical answers. They may yet prove weightier than they seem to be at present. For a number of thinkers have begun to search for a social cement, if one may call it that, capable of giving the concept of African unity a strength derived from traditional custom and religion, both of which are powerful because effective and venerable factors in African social thought: in the thought, that is, of many Africans in many countries about the standards by which they have lived in the pre-colonial past and by which they ought to live in the post-colonial future.

We have already touched, in the final section of chapter two above, on some of the fundamental elements in this line of thought. Apart from being a natural reaction to the familiar colonial stereotype – that all in Africa was 'primitive, savage, and chaotic' before the coming of Europeans – this line of thought is also a product of Africa's having discovered itself in the past few years. The old colonial notion that 'Africans have no history worth the name' is now seen – and, by Africans, with an understandable enthusiasm – to be wide of the truth. But this new recognition of long and complex historical processes lying behind the materially simple fabric of African life has evoked (and partly been evoked by) a new interest in African thought. The best of modern European and North American anthropologists have altogether abandoned the old condescension: what they are now concerned with is to show why African society developed as it did, why it did not develop differently, and why, in general, its forms of development deserve respect.*

Their work has begun to throw a vivid light into previously dark places. Reading modern accounts of African philosophy and religion, indeed, one gains the impression that in no other field had non-African misunderstanding and belittlement of Africa gone so far. There now appears a consensus of agreement among scholars who have lately worked in this field that African approaches to the basic problems of creation and survival are to be regarded as no less meaningful and effective than other pre-scientific explanations, whether religious or merely metaphysical. West African religion, for example, was long thought of as a blind and furious fear of images – 'fetishes' – whose unpredictable behaviour only confirmed the general chaos and insecurity of life. 'But why isolate West Africa from the rest of the world?' Parrinder asks. 'This has been one of the most harmful effects of speaking about "fetishism". For there is not a single religious or magical practice in West Africa that cannot be paralleled in some other continent. Magical objects abound in Asia and in Europe, and for a scientific comparative study of religions it is quite useless to talk about "fetishism" any longer.'[61]

Briefly, the same approach now governs the analysis of Africa's philosophical systems. The pioneering work of men like Rattray, Griaule, Tempels, Evans-Pritchard, and Fortes has revealed that such systems have existed without any need for inverted commas or for pressing the evidence. But it has also revealed that these systems possess a close common relationship over a very wide region of the continent and a very wide spread of social situations and concepts. 'We have thought,' wrote Tempels in his justly famous book, *Bantu Philosophy*, 'that we were educating children, "grown-up children"; and that seemed easy enough. Now suddenly we understand that we are con-

*Discussed in detail in my *The Africans* (U.S. title *The African Genius*) 1970.

cerned with an adult humanity which is conscious of its own wisdom, moulded by its own universalist philosophy.'[62]

This is not the place to open an inquiry into what that philosophy may be. It required thirty days for Ogotommeli, sage of the Dogon of the Western Sudan, to explain his understanding of the Universe to Marcel Griaule; and Dogon philosophy is only one variant of many which reflect the basic ideas of dynamism, life-force, and *muntu* – mankind comprehending 'the dead, the living, and the yet unborn'. It would require many pages merely to summarize the general ideas whose poetic reflection is at least suggested in the following lines on the nature of death:

> The dead are not under the earth:
> they are in the fire that is dying,
> they are in the grasses that weep,
> they are in the whimpering rocks,
> they are in the forest, they are in the house,
> the dead are not dead . . .

It is another question how far such explanations can survive the scientific education which is now becoming available to at least a minority of Africans; though it may be thought that they will now, perhaps in a humanist garb, acquire a fresh lease of life. What matters to us here is that the universalist concepts of African philosophy (the metaphysical integument, as it were, of what used to be called 'animism' or 'fetishism') are now being interpreted, more and more, as the ideological foundations on which Africans may stand in claiming to possess a common culture of the general status and influence as other 'world systems' of belief – Christianity, Islam, Buddhism – uniting otherwise disunited peoples. Here, for example, is a current philosophical interpretation of the basis for African unity. It comes from a group of Ugandan intellectuals who have summarized what they believe to be fundamental African ideas in the word *Ntu-ism* – from *ntu*, generic Bantu root for man or mankind:

To us what is important is not the way the imperialists have classified us, rather it is our common attitude towards life, culture, and heritage. In choosing the name *Ntu*, we have taken it to represent a philosophy that runs throughout Africa . . . Most of the ideas which reflect the African way of life are embodied in the philosophy of *Ntu* . . . We would like to divorce ourselves from the European method of demographic classification of Africans into Negroes, Bantu, Hamites, Nilotes, etc. As far as we are concerned, these divisions are of little significance, because they are not based on any deep and thorough analysis of African philosophy. . . . [But] we do not intend to revive the past as it was. . . . We want to integrate into modern life only what seems valuable from the past. Our goal is neither the traditional African nor the black European, but the modern African. . . .'[63]

It will be observed that these Ugandans are using traditional ideas not as the groundwork for racialist obscurantism but as a means of preaching humanist unity.

Summing up, we may think that the slogan of the African Personality has had a dual content. It emphasizes African particularity over against the rest of the world (and therefore of African equality with other major human groupings), but it also affirms a basic unity within the countless diversities of African life. Of course, a slogan of such varied and widely attractive nature can take several destinies – from a black racialist reaction to white racialism (as with the 'Moslems' in the United States) at one extreme, to an internationalism or supra-nationalism which is now, as many believe, an indispensable condition of African self-realization. And obviously the slogan is flourished by all sorts of eager folk who bother little about its inner implications. The fact remains, in any case, that propaganda for the projection of 'an African personality' has widely come to seem a valid means of asserting the full humanity of all peoples in Africa, no matter what their situation. This being so, the ideas behind it can be expected to continue as an underlying influence on future ideological development.

6 The Real Colonial Crisis

Such have been the general ideas, or the more important of them, with which Africans have sprung into their years of emancipation. But what, really, was the situation to which the ideas applied? There had been much dismantlement of traditional society; but this was not the only consequence of foreign rule. To many colonies Europe had brought much, material and mental, that was new. Some of the new intrusions cancelled each other curiously out: fewer people fell victim to disease, because modern medical techniques protected them, but more people suffered from malnutrition, because larger harvests failed to accompany larger populations. Yet, in the overall accounting, these intrusions, industrial, commercial, ideological – and the list is long and interesting – had combined into a process of dislocation and disruption that was unprecedented in history.

Before considering what became of the hopeful slogans of the nineteen-fifties, we must take another look at the real situation in which they were applied. That is the subject of this and the following chapter.

While it is no safer to generalize about Africa than about any other large and contradictory subject, the situation in most colonies on the eve of independence – and therefore in the early years of self-rule – can none the less be summarized in one short phrase: acute and worsening poverty.

This was not, of course, the intention of the colonial powers: it was the result of a failure (in the circumstances, an inevitable failure) to reorganize traditional life on a new basis. Even in such comparatively favoured colonies as the Gold Coast, whose farmers produced most of the world's cocoa, there were regions of increasing poverty. 'There can be no doubt,' according to Dr

Margaret Field, 'that in spite of seasonal bursts of spending on luxuries, cocoa has lowered the basic standards of living and nutrition. It has diverted attention from subsistence farming: the habit of steady diligence has declined. . . .'[64]

Some of the general grounds for believing that most economies in Africa were involved in acute and worsening poverty have been noticed in an earlier chapter. The traditional subsistence economies of Africa had provided on the whole a sufficient diet for their populations, as may be seen from the historical fact that no major part of Africa ever appears to have suffered chronic famine in the past. By 1945, however, they were far gone in ruin. Devaluation of the rural economy, coupled with the migrant labour system and the enclosure of land by Europeans, had reached a point of continental crisis from which no colonial policy-maker could see a clear escape. Official records of the last colonial years are loud with lamentations of despair.

A full review of this culminating crisis in a system which had never achieved stability except in stagnation – and even then only between bouts of 'pacification' – would have to consider many factors. Not the least of these would be the impact of 'world terms-of-trade', which have regularly cancelled out higher African production (as well as loans and gifts from abroad) by raising the price of Africa's manufactured imports or lowering the price of her raw material exports. Moreover, the rate of impoverishment has greatly varied.

This rate of impoverishment has been greatest, it would seem, in territories of permanent white settlement, and smallest in some of the more fortunate West African countries. Yet even in Nigeria, where 'subsistence' economy has survived to some extent as a valid means of livelihood (married uneasily, here and there, with production for cash-markets), an official report of 1951 showed that 51 per cent of children in the Northern Region died before they were six, while 70 per cent of all children admitted to hospital in the Eastern Region were found to be suffering from malnutrition.[65] For the country as a whole more than 20 million people (perhaps half the population) were thought to be living on an everyday level of a very low order, with widespread hunger and disease. Yet this was still a long way from the catastrophe which had overtaken most of the rural African population of South Africa.

Within the last few years or so the government of South Africa has moved towards the creation of semi-autonomous African statelets, known as 'Bantustans'. In these, it is claimed, Africans will be able to develop in unhampered freedom 'along their own lines'. Leaving aside any other aspect, consider only the physical situation of these 'Bantustans'. They are, of course, the old Native Reserves under a new name – the ten or twelve per cent of the whole land surface of South Africa in which millions of rural people are supposed to live and prosper. The greater part of these Reserves was in ruinous condition more than thirty years ago.* In 1948, the year in which the Afrikaner Nationalists came to power, an assistant director of Native Agriculture observed of one of the more important of the Reserves, the Ciskei in the Eastern Cape, that 'over perhaps ten per cent of the total area, the incidence of soil erosion may be described as slight; over fifty per cent as bad; over the balance, as nothing less than terrifying'.[66] Writing at about the same time of the neighbouring and much larger Transkei – the first of the 'Bantustans' – two South African medical specialists, J. and T. Gillman, reported 'ample evidence that among a population malnourished for one or two generations, the adults already harbour such extensive lesions in many organs that chances of cure are at present remote. . . .'[67]

But what was true of the reserves in South Africa was also true, in more or less identical degree, of other reserves in colonies which practised the same system, such as Southern Rhodesia or Kenya, or those which practised a comparable system, such as Moçambique or Angola; although in all these cases it is difficult or impossible to find adequate statistical information, either because it was not collected or, if collected, not fully published. 'Throughout our inquiry,' noted the East Africa Royal Commission of 1955, 'we were impressed by the recurring evidence that particular areas were now carrying so large a population that agricultural production in them was being retarded, that the natural resources themselves were being

*See page 40 above.

destroyed, that families were unable to find access to new land, and that land which should have been lying fallow was being encroached upon. Such a situation ... implies that there must either be a change in the use of land or a reduction in the number of people whom the land has to sustain.'[68]

That was one aspect of the matter. There were others. One of these was the colonial emphasis on production for export instead of for local food consumption. We have seen what this meant in the case of Algeria.* (The earlier switch from food to cotton production in semi-colonial Egypt had provided a perhaps still more shattering example of rural disaster.) In the Gold Coast, much wealth was earned from exporting cocoa. But there were dwindling crops in other agricultural sectors: even in 1961, Ghana still had to spend some £26 millions (mainly from cocoa assets) on the import of food alone. Other countries, lacking Ghana's comparative wealth, needed the food but could not or would not buy it. Much good land in Southern Rhodesia went into the production of tobacco, a crop from which Africans could gain nothing except wages at a rate unusually low even for the southern regions of the continent. The Belgian Congo offered similar examples: large quantities of African land and labour were taken out of local food production for the benefit of export crops. Portuguese colonial policy has enforced cotton cultivation over substantial areas of Angola and Moçambique. Some of the results were described by the Bishop of Beira in 1950:

Whoever has frequent contact with certain of the cotton zones [of northern Moçambique] has no difficulty in recognizing that the principal effort of the native ... is absorbed by the cotton, and that there remains not much time or effort to grow food which is needed by him and by others. I know a region which used to be a granary for lands afflicted with hunger. After the cotton campaign was begun there, the fertile fields ceased to supply food for the neighbouring populations and the people of the region itself also began to feel hunger. There belongs to my diocese a region in which for six months the black spectre of hunger reaped the lives of the inhabitants ...[69]

None of this was denied by officials – or not, at any rate, in

*See page 40 above.

their moments of reflection. Many conscientious men of good will sought for solutions to a crisis whose existence all admitted. It is not a question, needless to say, of loading guilt on the shoulders of colonial administrators who were often, as individuals, admirable in their attempts to deal with a situation which was simply too much for them. But there is a great need to see this situation as it really was; and as, to a considerable extent, it still is.

Rural Africa was dying on its feet. But surely the compensation, the way out, lay in the new industries and economic options which colonial enterprise was bringing into the continent? Yet all these rested on African labour; and African labour, more often than not, was migrant labour. If ever there was an argument for the ultimate validity of Pan-African ideas, surely it lay here. Year after year, from one end of the continent to the other, countless hundreds and thousands of men could be found trudging on foot from territory to territory – unless their prospective employers, like the South African gold mines, had got the migrant system so well organized that they could provide lorries, trains, and even aeroplanes.

Borders and frontiers, closed or open, made no difference to this ceaseless movement of men in search of wages: the sheer need to earn money (initially to pay taxes, afterwards to ensure survival of their families) drove them across every obstacle. In an average year, for example, half the total force of able-bodied men in Basutoland is away working in South Africa. The proportion for Malawi has often been almost as high. Tanzania attracts 40,000 migrants every year from Ruanda, Urundi, and Moçambique. In West Africa the plantation economy of the Ivory Coast rests on labour from neighbouring Upper Volta; an even larger number of peasants from Upper Volta goes annually to Ghana. A map of all these annual migrations, sketched across Africa, would show a cobweb of trodden paths.

This many-sided movement, repeated year by year, has had profound social consequences; and none of them can be said to have been good. One has been to hasten the decline of rural areas where over-population had not been a cause of poverty. Traditional disciplines have disappeared with this steady drain of the very individuals who would otherwise best exercise them. 'The young people go off to the towns, life dies out in villages which are sad and comfortless, without sufficient food, where forced labour services pile up without any hope of a man's seeing an end to them, where sickness is widespread without the European's fighting against it . . .': such was the conclusion of a by no means radically minded Belgian observer in the Congo of 1946.[70] It would be easy to lay other such testimony alongside his. The 'economic options' of colonial enterprise proved powerless to solve the rural crisis; on the contrary, they only deepened it.

Then perhaps the way out, the one escape from the crisis, lay in the new African towns and cities? Steady urban employment for a living wage was undoubtedly the right solution; but urban employment was for the most part neither steady nor exchanged for a living wage. The round figures, true enough, are impressive. It may be that as many as nine or ten million Africans south of the Sahara, and some three millions to the north of it, were classifiable as wage-earning workers by the last years of the colonial period: perhaps six to eight per cent of the total population, compared with a very much smaller fraction ten or twenty years earlier. But the round figures tell little of the story.

To begin with, a considerable proportion of these workers were migrants 'on contract'. They were men who came to work in mines and plantations for their keep as well as for a small wage of which they could take home part (often a very small part) to their families at the end of periods of six or twelve months, or even longer. At best, these men could be said to be subsidizing rural poverty; at worst, they were merely surviving as individuals. Only rarely could they become components in a new industrial system that was integrated with the needs and capacities of their own people. Generally their labour was little more than a means of saving the colonial economic balance from complete upset. Thus Algerian migrant labour in France was the mere counterpart of rural poverty at home – a poverty which resulted from the production of wine for export, low wages and low peasant productivity, coupled with the life-saving mechanism of modern medicine. The same is true of many other African countries. Such primitive economic systems had no inherent expansive capabilities: they merely helped to tide men over from one lean year to the next.

There were other deplorable effects. The colonial records are full of complaints against a migrant-labour system which could offer men neither the stability of village life nor access to a new life in the towns. The case of South Africa is once again flagrant but only, one suspects, because so much more is known about South Africa than about other countries where conditions have been much the same. Here the truth was exposed in a memorable statement by a South African Secretary for Health eighteen years ago. Dr Gale pointed out that the 300,000 or so workers recruited for the South African mines were fit when they reached Johannesburg, since 'the mines recruit only physically fit persons'. The mine medical services exercised (and the position is no different today) great care in examining their recruits for tuberculosis. They treated incipient cases, but they turned away those over whom the disease had gained an evident hold.

'Sample surveys here and there,' Dr Gale reported, 'suggest that some seventy-five per cent of those who leave the mines with incipient T.B. are dead within two years ... [but] in the interval they have spread infection' in their villages. Venereal disease, carried initially by prostitutes who attracted the returning labourer after his period of bachelor barrack-life in the mining compounds, was another obvious menace. Even the labourer who contracts syphilis while working in the mines, according to Dr Gale's expert evidence, 'does not always get treatment that is adequate to protect him from long-term effects of the disease. The gross early manifestations of syphilis can easily be cleared up by a few injections, and the labourer rendered fit for work again. But unless treatment at weekly intervals is continued for twelve or twenty-four months the disease merely becomes latent. There are no obvious manifestations ... [but] if infection is acquired at the age of 20 or 25, the breakdown comes at 35 or 40 in the prime of working life. Before this stage the sufferer has been rejected by the recruiting agents; and the medical services are powerless to help him. The mines had him when he was an asset. The rural area has him when he is a liability. . . .'[71]

For industrial labour to offer any real alternative to a rural economy in crisis, moreover, it would be necessary for wage levels to permit the creation of an urban society in the full sense of the word: of one, that is, where men can live and prosper with their families, win a better standard of life, and embark upon the complex process of fitting themselves and their children for the modern world. Migrant labour has prevented this by preventing men from bringing their families to town. And even where migrant workers have been able to make this family transition, their wages have still been calculated, more often than not, on the needs of a single man.

This last point has been an important cause of *worsening* poverty. The general level of wages has been another. In very recent years, wages in secondary industry have considerably increased in some countries, notably South Africa, though this is not to say that they have kept up with the rising cost of living. But for the solid core of wage-earning workers, whether on white farms or mines, they have remained at a staggeringly low average. 'All in all, it is fair to say that the average African miner [in South African gold-mining] received in cash and in kind about 100s. a month in 1951, compared with 63s. a month in 1890.'[72] Given the fall in the purchasing power of the pound since 1890, it is obvious that the real wages earned by these hundreds of thousands of men fell steeply during the period. And this steep fall in wages, we may remark in passing, was accompanied by a corresponding reduction in the general working costs of the mining companies. 'In 1897, average working costs were 29s. 6d. per ton milled. Forty years later, in 1937, they were 18s. 11d.'[73] It is small wonder, then, that a radical African voice should complain in 1963 – after the Consolidated Gold Fields mining company in South Africa had announced a record annual profit of more than £7 millions – that 'the company is thriving upon cheap African labour inherent in the system of white domination in South Africa'.[74]

But South Africa, it may be objected, is a special case. Yet less so, apparently, than one may think. Like South Africa, Southern

Rhodesia has operated a system of cheap migrant labour as the basis of its economy. Arguing that movement of African workers from country to town could not be stopped, Sir Godfrey Huggins (later Lord Malvern) pointed out in 1944 that 'the Europeans insist on this drift to the towns. They insist on having this native labour. . . . We cannot exist for five minutes without the native today. He is absolutely essential to our wage structure if nothing else.'[75]

What was this structure? Sir Godfrey explained: 'If we went on a purely European basis with the present conditions of living and pay – I am not complaining about them but merely pointing out a fact – the country would be down and out in five minutes.' Perhaps it was not surprising in these circumstances that a British sociologist, writing on industrial efficiency and the urban African in the Southern Rhodesia of 1953, should have discovered that 'the average urban African is unhealthy, badly housed, uneducated, and he lacks any security in town even if he happens to be born there'.[76]

There was clearly a great and urgent need for the benefits which, it was promised, the Federation of the two Rhodesias and Nyasaland would bring in its train. But what benefits in fact did that Federation, formed in 1953 and dissolved ten years later, actually bring? A United Nations investigation of 1958 gives one telling answer. According to its statistics, which are as good as any that can be found, the prospective Federation's crucial mining industry paid out £1,400,000 in African wages during 1945 and made gross profits, after royalty payments, of £5,590,000. In 1956, three years after Federation and a fairly sharp rise in the cost of living, the industry paid out £6,400,000 in African wages, but made gross profits of just over £80,000,000.[77] The change is interesting. In 1945 African mineworkers received wages equal to about 25 per cent of the gross profits; in 1956 their share had dropped to about 8 per cent. Federation was evidently rather more beneficial to mining shareholders than to the African miners themselves.

It would be easy, though tedious, to journey from territory to territory and expose much the same situation in all of them. The Belgian Congo in the years after the Second World War was generally supposed to be enjoying a boom. Judged by the value of its mineral and other exports, this was certainly the case. Yet a UNESCO report of 1956 could none the less find that children in Leopoldville, greatest of all the cities of the Congo, were in a desperate condition. 'On a conservative estimate, the proportion of undernourished children was about half.'

And what is one to say of British East Africa? There the Royal Commission of 1955 found that 'cash earnings per head of the African population amounted to only £3 3s. as compared with £8 8s. in the Belgian Congo. . . .' The Mombasa riots of 1939, the Commission recalled, had been 'mainly caused by bad housing'. A Nairobi official report of 1948 showed that *employed* workers were sleeping 'under the verandas in River Road, in noisome and dangerous shacks in the swamp, in buses parked by the roadside, and fourteen to the room in Pumwani, two to a bed and the rest on the floor'. Indeed, the position was noticeably growing worse. 'A study of official reports and the evidence of witnesses with knowledge of urban matters convinces us that conditions of life for the poorer Asian and the majority of Africans in the towns have been *deteriorating over a considerable period.*'[78]

Low wages, once again, were high on the list of causes.

The wages of the majority of African workers are too low to enable them to obtain accommodation which is adequate to any standard. . . . The high cost of accommodation relative to wages is, in itself, a cause of overcrowding, because accommodation is shared in order to lighten the cost. This, together with the high cost of food in towns, makes family life impossible for the majority.

And why were these wages so low? The Commission explained this too. Wage rates in the past had been set for migrant workers who came to town *without* their families. 'Their wages were calculated on the needs of a single man'; and yet, even though many men now had their families with them, 'this has remained the basis on which wages are paid until the present day'. These wages 'are insufficient, not only to feed, house, and clothe their families, but even for their own needs'. And the Royal Commission went on to quote the astonishing statement made by a Committee on African Wages in Kenya which had reported in

1954, that '*approximately one half of the urban workers in Private Industry, and approximately one quarter of those in the Public Services, are in receipt of wages insufficient to provide for their basic, essential needs of health, decency, and working efficiency.*'[79]

With such evidence – and big deposits of it lie around in many and perhaps all colonial territories – it is hard to avoid the conclusion that the social and economic crisis of the forties and fifties must have erupted, if the colonial system had continued, into a *manifest* breakdown of the whole pattern of rule.

As it came about, the actual breakdown was largely concealed from the outside world. Colonial power withdrew before what seemed to be a purely political pressure, and the outside world tended accordingly to see the African drive for emancipation merely in political terms. It saw, more often than not, only the top seventh of the iceberg. But the bulk beneath the surface – the social and economic crisis – was none the less there. It was this that constituted the real colonial crisis, the heaviest burden left lying on the shoulders of Africa.

7 The Problem of Transition

This, then, was not so much a political crisis, as a social and economic one.

At the beginning of October 1952 a conscientious Belgian missionary in the steamy scrub country of the Lower Congo was making his 'usual tour in order to enregister children for the regional schools'. He came to a place called Makakulu Tseke, where a school served about twenty-five villages. Here he expected to find 147 boys whom he had convoked, through messages to their parents, because they were old enough to go to primary school. 'I was not a little surprised,' he recalled afterwards, 'to discover that of these 147 boys, thirty-four were away from home in Leopoldville, nearly a quarter of them. And not one of these boys was old enough to pay tax' – and therefore to be under fiscal pressure to leave home and earn the cash wherewith to meet it.[80]

What became of these small boys? History does not relate. But the UNESCO survey of Leopoldville, three years later, found that most children there were well fed until they were two or three, but that after this age 'many children know hunger very early', while 'on a conservative estimate, the proportion of undernourished schoolchildren is about half'. What the survey called 'hunger-training' started at the age of six 'in most poorer families'.

The probability in 1952 was that few of the thirty-four boys who had run away from Makakulu Tseke to the big city had got themselves into school there. Most would have sought out an uncle or a cousin and found some kind of job to do. With or without 'hunger-training', they would have made ends meet. But the ways in which they would have done this were many and various; and not a few of them testified to social chaos.

One aspect of this chaos was juvenile crime. Here again the sociological records are remarkably consistent in their avowal of a breakdown in social life affecting most of the larger towns and cities. This breakdown flowed largely from a more or less complete disruption, under very adverse urban conditions, 'of the practice of joint responsibility exercised by the extended family for the upbringing of younger relations'.[81] Looking into the social situation at the leading Gold Coast port of Sekondi in 1948, Busia found the courts much exercised with youthful crime. But 'for every juvenile who is put before the Court, there are probably four who are not apprehended'.

What kind of crime? Petty theft, of course; but here in Sekondi prostitutes also played a part in corrupting the young. Thus Busia came into touch with 150 'pilot boys': 'virtual or potential delinquents fending for themselves by stealing, gambling, acting as guides to sight-seers, or directing European sailors and soldiers to prostitutes', many of them with no settled home but sleeping 'in market stalls, on lorries, or on verandas'. Their favourite bar, Busia records, was called the *Love All Canteen*; the sentiment intended was evidently not Christian.

Prostitution had become a major problem. Busia thought that here, once more, the main cause lay in a breakdown of the traditional order, above all of the closely adjusted network of responsibilities in African family life. There was evident an over-riding conflict of cultural values at many levels, but 'most prominently and most obviously of all in increased crime, prostitution, juvenile delinquency, unbridled acquisitiveness, bribery, and corruption ... the symptoms of a maladjusted society'.

Such maladjustment was revealed by every serious survey of African urban life during these pre-independence years. All the surveys traced the line of cleavage between the old order and the new confusion which represented – or might one day crystallize into – a new order; and their findings are strongly reminiscent of those much earlier reports which had revealed the misery of European cities in the early days of mass industrialism. They did for Africa, though at a more scientific level, what Engels had done for the British working class in his famous report of 1844, or what Booth did later for the London poor. The total situations – of utter upheaval and the crude destruction of old values by new pressures – were no doubt pretty much the same.

In the African townships of Brazzaville, for example, Balandier found a notably low proportion of women to men. 'The result of this is that there is great competition for women, and about sixty per cent of legal cases concern adultery, divorce, the custody of children, claims for sexual services, and even incest.'[82] Grévisse had much the same to say of Elizabethville. Surveys made in South Africa and the Rhodesias reached conclusions that were little different. We have glanced at what the Royal Commission thought about East African housing: in Dar-es-Salaam, for example, it was calculated that 'the average number of persons living in a room sixteen feet by twenty feet is eight, and that in some rooms it is as much as twelve'. There could be only one outcome:

the evils associated with the absence of family life – drunkenness, prostitution, and venereal disease – are rife in the towns with large African populations. A large proportion of the women who come to towns to escape from customary marriages, earn their living by prostitution or enter into irregular unions. . . . The lack of family life means the majority of children in the towns grow up with little parental control.

There were protests and attempts at improvement. To see the colonial period as one of simple disintegration would be to travesty a highly complex process. There were many administrative efforts at tempering and reducing the misery of life. But while it is true that something was done, here and there, to alleviate individual distress, provide more housing, expand the intake of primary schools, and supply the more obvious needs of elementary welfare, it is also true that these efforts could never be more than marginal, for the basic problem, the problem of constructing a new social order, was beyond the capacity of the system. The East Africa Royal Commission saw this very well, though phrasing it rather differently.

In East Africa, the Commissioners pointed out, 'tribal units' shaken by the dislocation of traditional life and the widening vision of a modern kind of life, 'cannot revert to a past which offered to their members no prospect of material advancement nor ... can they go forward, or even stand still, under their present customary, legal, and economic organization of land, labour, and capital. To go back to the subsistence economy of the past, or even to stand still in the dawn between the old institutions which are dying and the new which are struggling to be born, would be to court economic disaster.'[83]

Yet how to go forward? Government might do a great deal, but 'it must be realized that only the members of a society themselves can create a community. This will only come about when people have been drawn together into social groups by a common level of education and wealth, irrespective of divisions of tribe or race....' Nothing worthwhile could be achieved 'unless all have equality of status as citizens'.[84] But equality of status meant equality of voting rights; and this in turn would mean an end to the colonial regime. All too clearly, 'creation of a community' would have to await the coming of independence.

It was at this point that the social and economic crisis spiralled into a political crisis as well. Very consciously in some cases, less so in others, the best of the nationalist leaders came to understand that the post-independence 'creation of a community' must depend not only on implanting a new social order in the towns, on resurrecting the villages and expanding the economy, but also and above all on the sure establishment of a new political order. And this last would have to have priority because only a new political order could provide the minimal conditions necessary for ensuring that the other objectives could be achieved. This is what Nkrumah meant when he proclaimed his well-known slogan: 'Seek first the political kingdom, and the rest shall be added unto you.' Others put it otherwise, but they all had the same thought in mind.

What was the extent of this political crisis? How far had the old political order gone to pieces? In parts of Africa, it seems, very far. A skilled observer in the rural Belgian Congo could decide as early as 1946 that 'nowhere any more, one can say, does the chief really administer his tribe; nowhere does the grouping remain intact', and that 'the ties which once united members of the same tribe, both to one another and to their common chief, are everywhere relaxed and often broken'.[85] This was an extreme case of the consequences of 'direct colonial rule', and perhaps it was an extreme judgement. The chaos that followed on Belgian withdrawal from the Congo in 1960 brought faithful evidence that tribal loyalties could still be crucial in deciding how men and women behaved. Yet even the stiff and costly 'tribal wars' in the Congo of 1960–61 were not, one suspects, quite what they seemed, but rather, perhaps, the desperate result of a seeking for some point of loyalty and cohesion when public security seemed altogether to have disappeared. This has probably been true even of Kenya, where 'tribalism' has sometimes appeared to have driven all before it.

'Don't be misled by all this talk of tribalism in Kenya,' an East African leader said to me at the end of 1962. 'It isn't the same as the old tribalism – the old system that really stood for a certain type of stability and even progress. This new tribalism is the consequence, quite a lot, of the parliamentary system you've imposed on Kenya. That system – what does it mean? It means jobs, handing out jobs to the clever few. But who are the clever few? Often enough they're bright boys on the make. So when they don't get what they want in Nairobi, they go back home and organize a gang of supporters – easy enough in rural Africa, you know – and they make a row, and you call it tribalism. But do you think the old chiefs would have stood for that kind of caper?'

Some Africans have clearly seen the hand of local Europeans in the Kenya 'tribalism', seeking to divide Kenya Africans so that European interests might be better protected.* And it was

*In a disturbing book about the Kenya Emergency (1953–60), for example, J. M. Kariuki, a Kikuyu 'detainee', admits the force of 'tribal fears' in Kenya but argues that the colonial government did much to aggravate these by its refusal to allow any countrywide, and therefore supra-tribal, political organization by Africans. The government likewise increased jealousy among African politicians 'by its refusal to recognize either that Kenyatta was the only possible generally acceptable leader, or if he was not, that nobody else could presume to usurp his place until he had rejected the offer and opportunity. So they delayed ... the settlement of the relative power positions of the various politicians', and 'split the country into two groups.' J. M. Kariuki, '*Mau Mau*' *Detainee*, Oxford, 1963, p. 166.

undoubtedly true that the constitutional plan which proposed in 1962 to 'balkanize' Kenya into a cluster of petty states owed much of its inspiration and argument to European politicians in Kenya. Something of the same kind seems to have happened in the Congo. Tshombe's party coalition in Katanga was called the Conakat. 'Who cemented this Union [Conakat]? We do not hesitate to say it: the European.' That was the judgement of a Belgian by no means unsympathetic to Tshombe and what he stood for.[86] Or 'take the case of the Baluba and the Lulua in Kasai', commented another observer. 'Their antagonism "flared", and was considerably more publicized than tribal fights normally are, when it was in the interests of Forminière [the Belgian diamond concern in Kasai] that these things should happen and be known to happen. When that ceased to be the case, the Lulua and the Baluba seemed to become gradually reconciled.'[87]

It is accordingly unwise to infer from such cases as the Congo and Kenya that 'tribalism' still counts for much with Africans – at least, when they are left to themselves. But even if it did count for much, the traditional political order could never be subtended into an efficient system of post-colonial rule. By 1953 – and I quote the Congo again because it was one of the few colonies with a good statistical service – nearly one quarter of all Africans were living *hors chefferie*, outside the areas of chiefly control, and the proportion was rising fast.

Much the same shift was taking place elsewhere. The chiefly order was doomed. Furthermore, people wanted to get into the modern world, and chiefly rule was identified precisely with the world of ignorance and subjection they were eager to quit. All too often chiefs had become mere stooges of the administration, and therefore opponents of all who wished to 'create a new community'; or else they had burgeoned under colonial benevolence (as in Northern Nigeria and Ruanda) into petty dictators whose authority far exceeded the norms of the pre-colonial past.* In any event the great majority of chiefs (though with

*In an authoritative comment in his autobiography, *My Life* (1962), the Sardauna of Sokoto, Sir Ahmadu Bello, was emphatic that 'the old Emirates [of Northern Nigeria] were originally much more democratic than they were when the British left them'.

reservations here and there) had come to stand squarely in the way of political change.

And again, whether this was really so or not, it was certainly believed to be so by a vast number of ordinary people, even in those regions of 'indirect rule' where traditional chiefs had cushioned the impact of colonial government. The case of the little East African country of Ruanda is instructive. At the end of 1959 the people forming the majority in Ruanda, the Hutu, took advantage of relaxed colonial authority to rise against their traditional overlords, the Tutsi. Constituting some four-fifths of the population, the Hutu considered that Tutsi rule had become oppressive and out-of-date. They desired to throw it off. And they were convinced that the Belgians, who had governed Ruanda as a mandated and afterwards trusteeship territory for forty years, had always sided with the Tutsi 'nobles' against themselves, the Hutu 'commoners'.

The Tutsi naturally denied this. Yet it would seem that the Hutu were largely in the right. As long ago as 1930 the Belgian Bishop of Ruanda, Monsignor Classe, speaking from a position of immense influence on government, had urged that 'the greatest disservice which the government could do to itself and to the state would be to eliminate the Tutsi caste. A revolution of that nature would lead the entire state directly into anarchy and to European-hating Communism. . . .'[88] This seems to have been the general Belgian point of view until the late fifties. By then, however, the Tutsi – representatives of the traditional ruling order – were regarded by the Hutu as part and parcel of the colonial regime: the one, they thought, should go with the other, and the sooner the better.

This kind of thing happened in other areas where chiefs retained some authority. Of course there were exceptions. Many chiefs in Yorubaland, for example, were active in the campaign for independence: to the point, indeed, that Western Nigeria today has made a consistent attempt to 'marry the old with the new' and 'make the chiefs feel they have a place in the new order'. With the creation of a House of Chiefs, there was an opportunity for these often able men to express their views, 'while ensuring that they will not be a stumbling block on the way of progress. At the local level the power to alienate land has been taken from the chiefs and brought back into the hands of the democratic councils. . . .'[89]

Some chiefs have made themselves the spearhead and symbol of political change, no matter at what cost to themselves. Best known among these, perhaps, is Chief Luthuli of the African National Congress of South Africa, who was awarded a Nobel Peace Prize in 1962 after his leadership of the passive-resistance campaign against the aggressions of apartheid. What non-whites in South Africa have generally thought about Luthuli was probably well expressed in *Flash*, roneotyped news-sheet of the African National Congress and Natal Indian Congress, as long ago as 1952. 'They might dismiss our chief. They might take the chief to the utmost ends of the earth, but his destination remains unchanged in the hearts of his people, who are both the heirs and the stewards of his matchless dreams and his matchless deeds.'[90] High-flown words, no doubt; but their readers, given the odds, will scarcely have thought them overdone. And the great point about Luthuli was precisely that he had stepped out of the 'old order' and was leading boldly towards a new.

Now and then, of course, chiefs tried to have it both ways. They made their peace with the colonial power, but they saw that the alliance would not work. In 1945 the illiterate Balum Naba of the Moshi was put up by the French administration and his fellow-chiefs to oppose the 'nationalist firebrand', Félix Houphouët-Boigny, President of the Ivory Coast today. The Balum Naba failed, much to his own relief. For 'whenever he was able to free himself from [official] supervision, he told people – "Vote for my friend Houphouët. . . . What will I do in that Paris, with my forty-four wives and at my age? I can't speak a blasted word of French."'[91] And what indeed would he have done?

All these factors and others of the same sort have played their part in reshaping, promoting, or retarding the practical realization of key political ideas in the drive for independence. They have also, as we shall see later, given rise to new sets of ideas, doctrines, 'myths'; and their influence on all of these is not yet spent. Social and economic disintegration, political confusion: these were part of the challenge to 'new Africa'. But over and beyond them lay another aspect of the challenge. What sort of new Africa did people want? Did they know what they wanted?

These questions, too, have conditioned the thoughts and hopes of every African who has sought to play a leading part in the transition from colonial rule to independence. They were questions that were far from easily answered. Often enough they were fobbed off by sheer power of oratory, lost to mind in demagogic fireworks. They insistently returned. An outside view has sometimes portrayed the drama that was now beginning to develop as mere play between a handful of skilful or un-scrupulous leaders and a vast following of 'simple village folk'. But this was seldom the case. Even when most cunning or least careful of the public weal, leaders have had to pay attention, even close attention, to what their followers expected.

In these preliminary years, the programmes were remarkably general. Just because the essence of African nationalism was a demand for equality and self-respect, they needed to be little else. 'Vote UNIP for an end to Federation,' ran one characteristic poster, on this occasion issued by the United National Independ-ence Party of Northern Rhodesia in October 1962: 'Economic stability and prosperity for all. More schools and better education. Decent housing and better hospitals. Democracy and security for all. Independence.'

On the trade-union front – an active part of the independence campaign in many British and French colonies – the *Zimbabwe Labour News* of Southern Rhodesia appealed in September 1961 for 'one national wage' – irrespective, that is, of race – and reminded readers that 'we are moving into a new Zimbabwe in which labour cannot be content to deal only with wages, hours, and conditions of work, but must have an increasing voice in determination of economic policies'.

'Freedom is our birthright, self-government our heritage as sons and daughters of the free men and women who inherited Africa for the Africans . . .' declared the Freedom Charter of PAFMECA (Pan-African Freedom Movement for East and

Central Africa, later extended to include Southern Africa as well). Even so politically conscious a leader as Nkrumah had been content, in 1947, to summarize the aim of 'the national liberation movement in the African colonies' as being 'to win freedom and independence'. The early declarations all followed these simple lines.

Often they concealed more complex thoughts. Some leaders came to the movement in reaction against personal discrimination: what they wanted, at the back of their minds, was to create the kind of community which should palely mirror the advanced societies they knew, in particular France, Britain, and the United States, but with themselves in control. A few came to it from Marxism, either as more or less loyal exponents of the Soviet interpretation or as men who had quarrelled with the Communists and evolved, like the West Indian George Padmore, a variant of their own. There was the usual quota of careerists who said whatever seemed convenient. But the rank-and-file, in so far as one can safely generalize, only knew that they wanted a life that should be different and better than before.

The emphasis was on material change. More and bigger – and the flashier the better! All the same, as those tumultuous months and years rushed by, another note began to make itself heard: mostly, to begin with, from poets and writers whom nobody read, or nobody in Africa. Life in African cities began to seem ugly and unpleasant, and not only for reasons of poverty. Social values had turned into money-values; and it appeared that little else remained. 'Everything,' deplored a Congolese writer over ten years ago, 'is dominated by money. . . .' Such was now the cost of getting married (thanks to the African custom of making a compensation payment or gift to the bride's parents) that to ask the hand of some girls in marriage was 'like asking for the daughter of a Maharajah'.[92]

Perhaps he was exaggerating. But he was not alone in his complaint. Whores and drunkards reeled across the scene. The 'old order', once it got to town, was liquidated in the literal sense of the word. Floods of booze poured in from every side. In 1951 French West Africa was importing fifteen times more alcoholic liquor than in 1938: alcohol accounted for 8 per cent of

Ivory Coast imports in 1953 and 9·6 per cent of Dahomey's . . .;[93] and this was not exceptional.

There grew up a sentiment, at least among a minority, that political independence must prove a fraud if this was all that it could offer. 'Popular morality is now a wasteland, littered with the debris of broken convictions. Concepts such as honour, or even honesty, have an old-fashioned sound; but nothing has taken their place.'[94] Those words were written of Britain in 1962; but they could as well, or rather better, have been used of Africa. Independence should offer guides through this social chaos, as well as voting rights and parliaments.

Out of revulsion from this 'European civilization in Africa' there also developed a feeling that Africa might do well to search her own past for guides. The edge of that particular feeling emerges, for example, in Senghor's bitter comparison of Manhattan with Harlem (page 75 above). Here is another tributary influence to the general theme of the African Personality. Old Africa had not been driven mad by money: maybe a new Africa could show the way to sanity?

Thoughts along these lines, one must add, made little sound in the general clamour of getting and spending. They were difficult to hear, and even when heard, they were often expressed in a style of verbal flap-doodle, not to say downright nonsense, that failed to impress. One cannot help sympathizing with the African writer who cried out, after attending yet another conference on 'African values', that he was tired of hearing about 'African this and African that', and couldn't they just discuss culture? Paintings in the central office of the Ghana Convention People's Party show how Africans invented a good many branches of modern science; while a 'historical pamphlet' reaching me the other day proclaims that practically all the great men of history, in Africa or anywhere else, were in fact Negroes.

These more or less neurotic or romantic exaggerations should not be allowed to obscure the serious reassessment of 'European values' that was taking place. On the political front this began to emerge in about 1961 with statements on 'African socialism', turned as these mainly were against the bland

Western assumption that if 'free enterprise' was good enough for Europe and America, it must necessarily be good enough for Africa as well.

That we want to banish poverty is one thing [a well-known African leader wrote to me not long ago]. The setting up, as a social aim, of the creation of unlimited wealth may be quite another. If we accept *that* as our whole aim it can quite easily lead us to a distortion of human values. For isn't it just this worship of wealth, with its concomitant distortion of values, which – in some societies – has led the masses to esteem the wealthy striptease artiste, or the adolescent 'rock' singer, above the painter or the musician? Once a society makes the creation of wealth a matter of prestige, it's difficult to persuade individuals not to adopt the same outlook.

By the end of the 1950s, a good many thoughtful folk were looking at the 'free enterprise phenomena' then developing at a tremendous speed in African towns and cities, and not liking them at all. It may be doubtful if many had read Tawney's *Acquisitive Society*: their conclusions, in a general way, were remarkably the same. President Nyerere of Tanzania, who almost certainly has read Tawney, put them in this way:

In an acquisitive society, wealth tends to corrupt those who possess it. It tends to breed in them a desire to live more comfortably than their fellows, to dress better, and in every way to outdo them. They begin to feel they must climb as far above their neighbours as they can. The visible contrast between their own comfort and the comparative discomfort of the rest of society becomes almost essential to the enjoyment of their wealth, and this sets off the spiral of personal competition – which is then anti-social.

No doubt allowing himself a little romantic licence, he went on to argue that this reckless hunt for privilege was utterly incompatible with the traditional ethos of African life.

When a society is so organized that it cares about its individuals, then, provided he is willing to work, no individual within that society should worry about what will happen to him tomorrow if he does not hoard wealth today. Society itself should look after him, or his widow or his orphans. This is exactly what traditional African society succeeded in doing. Both the 'rich' and the 'poor' individual were completely secure in African society. . . . Nobody starved, either of food or of human dignity, because he lacked personal wealth: he could depend on the wealth possessed by the community of which he was a member.

This line of thought was accompanied by another. The old ideal of African nationalists had simply been to 'join the family of independent nations'. But now it became clear that the 'family' was ferociously divided within itself. Even before the bonds of 'trusteeship' were loosened from them, Africans found their masters and governors eagerly urging them to throw in their lot, once and for all, with the 'West' against the 'East'. No doubt if there had been any strong Communist parties in Africa outside the Arab states of the north, these would have weighed in with a directly opposite appeal. As it was, the best of the leaders and parties found themselves placed before an alternative they were increasingly reluctant to take. Was their new-found independence to be submerged, even before it had really broken the surface, within another kind of alliance among the wealthy Powers? If so, what kind of independence could this mean for Africa? They increasingly rejected the alternative. Following India's lead, they declared for 'neutralism and non-alignment'.

This was at first denounced by the 'West' as undercover communism, and by the 'East' as surrender to the ex-colonial Powers. Both underestimated the drive and purpose that lay behind the independence movements, which wanted – with growing self-awareness – to find their own way forward.

Thus it came about that the central problem of transition was posed repeatedly in terms of *choice*. Whichever way they looked, leaders at all levels were faced with an imperative need to choose. They were not required, as had been promised, merely to set forth upon 'a broad clear road to freedom' made duly smooth and ready by a far-seeing and fatherly trustee. On the contrary, they were confronted with unprecedented mess and muddle – social, economic, and political. To make any sense of this they would have to select their own line of march towards the building of new and expansive systems of production.

Very few were ready for anything so difficult. Very few had any socio-political ideology that was more than a hotch-potch of colonial practice, coupled with new confusions arising from personal or group ambitions, or from the pressures of traditional habits of thought inherited from a pre-colonial independence, and now released upon the scene with disconcerting force.

Another pressure was also on the scene. This was the pressure of mass demand for a better sort of life. Driving into ideological confusion, this pressure could not be ignored. However hesitatingly, there accordingly began a search for new solutions, for new frameworks of society that should be African but modern as well.

At any rate up to 1964, the impetus of decolonization and its regenerative upsurge gave rise to an understandable 'honeymoon' of high hopes and grand designs. If these proved largely vain, that is no reason for denying the profoundly real and formative influences which lay behind them.

8 Early Approaches

The rise of popular nationalism was accordingly not just a political reaction to colonial rule. It was also a movement of social regeneration.

In this respect, of course, it was like other popular movements in other lands. Whole populations, previously quite apathetic to politics, were suddenly found to be imbued with startling new ideas. But the colonial governors, few of whom had ever known any personal political activity or thought about politics in more than the administrative sense – as a game of hide-and-seek between 'policemen and agitators' – could seldom understand or believe this new phenomenon. They therefore concluded, and with a dismal uniformity of conviction, that all demands were the work of irresponsible malcontents or sinister agents (probably Communist). To put it mildly, this led to misunderstandings.

Early in 1952 I happened to be travelling through what was then the colonial federation of French West Africa. This was at a time when the Union Française, liberal-minded legatee of the old French Empire, had lost its initially hopeful shine; and administration was retiring once more into an imperial frame of mind. Hundreds of 'agitators' were in jail. Violent clashes in the Ivory Coast a year earlier had cost the lives of fifty-three Africans even by official figures. The atmosphere was tense, not to say hostile. It became a rather delicate business, even a matter of gentle intrigue, for a foreigner to meet African leaders.

From Dakar on the far west coast I went up to Bamako – staid old market city on the Middle Niger that was then the capital of the Soudan Territory and is now the capital of the Mali Republic – with the object of meeting two prominent nationalists, Abdoulaye Diallou and the late Mamadou Konaté.

I had taken care to provide myself with a suitable note of introduction. The problem was how to present it. Bamako had no
telephone directory, or none that covered the African suburbs.
Whom should one sensibly ask for directions? I sat in a hot
little bar and found no answer. At last, prodded by a growing
sense of futility, I took the easiest course and asked the French-
speaking African barman.

The consequences of doing this were instructive.

'Look here, I've got to find Abdoulaye Diallou.'

'Ah . . .' A pause. A slight sense of pain in a comfortable face.
The withdrawal of a personality, something like a light being
switched off. I recognized the situation from experience in
occupied Europe during the war, and hastened to produce my
note of introduction.

The barman took this without pleasure and read it carefully. I
began thinking I had made a fool of myself: weren't all barmen
said to be honorary policemen? Holding my note, he stepped
into the road. I wondered where he was going. He wasn't going
anywhere. He simply stood in the road until the first cyclist
appeared. This was a ragged youth on an old bicycle. The
barman stopped this youth as though he had known him for
years, gave him my note and some vigorous instructions, and
returned to the bar, waving a signal that I should wait.

I waited. Half an hour went by. Then another. I was getting
restive, but the barman merely shook his head. Eventually the
youth came back, pushing his bicycle because he was accompanied by two fellow-countrymen on foot. One of these came up
to me. 'Well, if you don't mind walking, we can take you to
Diallou.' Which they did. Had the barman known the ragged
youth on the bicycle beforehand? No, but the youth was riding
a bicycle, and could take a message.

The passage of politics from a handful of educated men to a
mass of ordinary people was never more fully revealed to me
than during that stay in Bamako. The lessons continued. A day
or so later I was sitting with Mamadou Konaté in his big old-
fashioned house of clay in the *cité indigène*. He was surrounded by
friends and adherents; all the same, he seemed unwilling to say
very much. I was puzzled to know why. Upon returning to my

hotel, a clerk at the desk gave me a folded sheet of paper. 'I think it's from the police,' he said. It was. Would I present myself to the Chef de la Sûreté? 'I expect it's only for your passport,' said the clerk, trying to look as if he meant it.

The head of security was politeness itself. A sturdy man somewhat given to corpulence, he took after Mr Dombey's Major Bagstock, and had the same quality of sudden fervour and the same suggestion of being on the point of bursting into flame. The upshot of what he wanted to say was that he understood all about my talk with Mamadou Konaté and that what *I* should now understand – for my own good, for everyone's – was that men like Konaté were either of no importance, none at all, or else were 'absolutely on our side'.

Mamadou Konaté became one of the founders of the Republic of Mali, and Bamako today has a handsome avenue named after him. The head of security had misunderstood the political realities under his nose, though of course he was not alone in that respect. Energetic heads of security all over Africa were making the same mistake. But a further lesson of this little story emerged the following day. Two or three friends came to see me off at the airways office.

'There were spies at that meeting of mine with Konaté.' It was, I thought, useful information. They ought to know.

They only laughed. 'It's regrettable,' they agreed, after listening to my tale, 'but we knew. Two men along the wall with the others outside the big window.'

'You might have warned me.'

'Oh, we told Konaté. And if we'd told you as well those spies might have guessed we had our eye on them. Then the police might have guessed that too, and sacked them. Very bad, you see, because it takes time to discover exactly who the spies are.'

Politics in Africa during the 1950s, in short, ceased to be a minority affair and became a mass movement, passionate and popular, within boundaries shifted far beyond the narrow limits of the past.

This was the positive side to the disintegration of colonial life. And this, one may perhaps repeat, was the over-riding pressure on political leaders who might otherwise have been well enough content to let things slide, and merely feed themselves fat on the fruits of office. Not a few leaders have done just that. Some are still doing it. More than one well-known figure has arduously spent his time, these last few years, not in working for his country, but in finding ways to convert public revenue into personal income.

Yet nest-feathercrs, though not exactly rare, are none the less no longer characteristic of what really counts in the political life of the more important and dynamic independent countries. In these, even while such scandals here and there persist and flourish, the pressures of public opinion for a new society, together with the manifest incapacity of the existing order, have led to fresh upheaval and even, here and there, to useful change. Early slogans have begun to acquire new shape.

Among these were emergent policies which may be grouped under the heading of the 'one-party state', specifically defined, more often than not, as socialist in trend.

The One-Party State

Not all one party states were heading, or intending to head, in a socialist direction. The True Whig Party has ruled Liberia, with one or two brief intervals, for nearly a hundred years; but not with any socialist intentions. The political structure of another one-party state (in effect if not in theory), the Ivory Coast, has often been said to reflect little more than the interests of a ruling African plantocracy whose ideas, once again, are far removed from socialism. For even if it is true, as a sympathetic French observer has written, that although 'venerated and protected by his Negro and white entourage as though he were a Living Buddha, the object of an adulation which he has never sought but which is lavished on him both by official and unofficial people, President Houphouët-Boigny has not acted either as a dictator or a monarch',[95] the fact remains that nothing of any importance could be done in Ivory Coast without Houphouët's initiative or consent; and 'H.-B.' was certainly no socialist. There were other examples of the same kind: in August 1963 President Youlou of Congo (Brazzaville) provoked riots by his decision to form a one-party state. This decision had nothing to do with socialism, but much to do with a wish to guarantee Youlou's personal power, in which, however, it failed.

Those who have elaborated a theory or systematic defence of the one-party state in African terms, however, are all men and women who look to it as the crucial and appropriate instrument for creating a new form of *egalitarian* society. Their starting-point has been well described by Miss Margery Perham, though with a different context in mind. 'The first need for Africans [upon becoming independent],' she has said, has been 'to re-create for themselves the unity and order imposed by external authority and now suddenly removed.'[96] The first need, in short, has been to solve the central – and difficult – 'problem of power'.

In British colonies, and to some extent in French, the 'evacuating authority' left not a void but a more or less carefully articulated pattern of parliamentary rule based on European examples. There would be, ideally, a governing party and an opposition; or, with various forms of Proportional Representation on metropolitan French models, a governing coalition and a cluster of 'outs' who would form an opposition.

Now this arrangement presupposed many conditions which were in fact not present, or, if present, not significant. Above all, it presupposed a stratification of society along clearly under-stood lines of opposing interest – class interest – such as barely existed in most countries of the continent. Potentially, there might be a peasant class and a working class and a bourgeois class; but the operative word was 'potentially'. Where class divisions did seem sufficiently marked to be recognizable, as in South Africa, they proved on closer inquiry not to be class divisions so much as race divisions. Thus the white miner in South Africa belongs to the ruling group as much as the mine-owner does, at least so far as attitudes and loyalties are concerned: a situation that was crystallized long ago in that remarkable slogan of the Rand disturbances in 1913: Workers of the World, Unite for a White South Africa!

Some observers, especially Communist writers, have liked to detect a 'national bourgeoisie' in African countries, notably along the West Coast. But while it is true that the Ivory Coast, for example, has an indigenous plantocracy which is beginning to go into business, and while Nigeria and Ghana, among others, have many enterprising traders and even a few bankers, these people neither behave as an investing class nor, as yet, consider themselves to be one. They do not have 'class coherence' of the kind with which we are familiar in Europe. They are simply men and women whose position tends in that direction.

This being so, there is no basis for the parliamentary democracy along Westminster lines which has always rested, and no doubt must always rest, on clearly defined conflicts of 'class interest'. Julius Nyerere has explained this from an African standpoint. He wrote in 1963:

> The European and American parties came into being as the result of existing social and economic divisions – the second party [that is, the Opposition] being formed to challenge the monopoly of political power by some aristocratic or capitalist group. Our own parties had a very different origin.
>
> They were not formed to challenge any ruling group of our own people; they were formed to challenge the *foreigners* who ruled over us. They were not, therefore, political 'parties' – i.e. factions – but nationalist movements. And from the outset they represented the interests and aspirations of the whole nation.
>
> We in Tanganyika, for example, did not build TANU [Tanganyika African National Union, now the only party in the state] to oppose the Conservative Party of England, or to support the Labour Party. The divisions of English politics meant nothing to us. As far as we were concerned, they were all colonialists, and we built up TANU as a national movement to rid ourselves of their colonialism.[97]

When colonial power withdrew, there was accordingly no effective pattern of opposing interests which could offer the basis for a stable multi-party system. For 'now the colonialists have gone', Nyerere continued, 'there is no remaining division between "rulers" and "ruled"; no monopoly of political power by any sectional group, which could give rise to conflicting parties.' If this is the case, what interests can be served by parties severed from the nationalist movement? Nyerere's answer is characteristic of others. 'The only voices to be heard in "opposition" [today] are those of a few irresponsible individuals who exploit the very privileges of democracy – freedom of the press, freedom of association, freedom to criticize – in order to deflect the government from its responsibilities to the people by creating problems of law and order.'[98]

Why should this necessarily be so? Because, Nyerere replies, 'there can only be one reason for the formation of such parties [of opposition] in a country like ours – the desire to imitate the political structure of a totally dissimilar society. What is more, the desire to imitate where conditions are not suitable for imitation can easily lead us into trouble. To try and import the idea of a parliamentary opposition into Africa may very likely lead to violence – because the opposition parties will tend to be regarded as traitors by the majority of our people, or, at best, it will lead to the trivial manoeuvrings of "opposing" groups whose time is spent in the inflation of artificial differences into some semblance of reality "for the sake of preserving democracy". The latter alternative, I repeat, is an over-sophisticated pastime which we in Africa cannot afford to indulge in; our time is too short and there is too much serious work to be done.'[99]

Such views have been little affected, except in the way of irritation, by continuous European and American criticism that lack of an opposition must lead straight to personal or group dictatorship, with all the familiar (European) perversions of justice associated with it. African experience has so far found little indigenous ground for such criticism or its implications. South Africa, for example, has always enjoyed a multi-party system; so has Southern Rhodesia. But the situation of the vast majority of people under these multi-party regimes has been anything but 'democratic' – little different, indeed, from their situation in countries of frank dictatorship like Angola or Moçambique. If massive forced labour has disappeared in Rhodesia but not in Angola, it is because the British are a modern people who fully recognize the needs of industry, while the Portuguese are not. The question of 'local parliamentary system' appears beside the point.

Moreover, the nature of African traditional government – a theme of growing influence in these formative years – has seemed to throw convincing doubt on the relevance of European parliamentary models. Africa, it is claimed, knew democracy perfectly well in the past. The 'tribal system' had often provided for it. 'The Elders sit under a tree,' in Clutton-Brock's well-known definition, 'and talk until they agree. . . .' Those in the past who did not agree, and could not bear to continue under the rule of this or that community, either sought and secured destoolment of the elected chief, or else shouldered their spears and trekked to a new land.

Not only Africans have made this claim to pre-colonial democracy. 'It is rare,' Hailey observed in 1951, 'to find in British Colonial Africa any instance in which the indigenous form of rule previously in force could be described as autocratic, and there are not many cases' – the Zulus provide the classic exception here – 'in which it could be described in a strict sense as authoritarian.'[100] A Portuguese traveller among the Ovimbundu (Bailundu) of Angola put it rather differently in 1837, but with no less conviction. 'The government of Bailundu,' he found, 'is democratic. These heathen mix with the infamous humiliations of the orientals, the unbridled coarseness of the English people at election time in England. The kings defer to and flatter their counsellors: these are they who elevate a king to the throne and also cast him down.'[101]

Many others have reached the same conclusion. Rattray thought that the Ashanti constitution, when properly applied, was 'democratic to a degree'.[102] The notion that Britain brought democracy to West Africa, Dr Margaret Field believes, 'is quite erroneous. On the contrary, Britain did much to destroy the indigenous democracy. Neither is the idea of an opposition a new one. Alongside every chief [in Ashanti] was a *mankrado* or *krontinhene* of whom it was said, "every *mankrado* is opposed to the chief."'[103] This, of course, was 'institutional opposition': otherwise, after decisions by chiefs-in-council, popular opposition seems generally to have been regarded as treason.

The main point in this connection is that African thinkers and politicians, reassessing their past, believe that it was often as effectively democratic as the best practices of modern Europe.[104] If there were exceptions in Africa, there were surely exceptions in Europe as well; and Europeans (with so many dictators in their recent past and even in their present) may prefer not to argue. Believing this, African leaders often urge that the solutions of the past, which had so often married traditional democracy to unicephalous rule, can point the way towards marrying modern democracy to a one-party state.

But having predicated the solution of the central problem of power by means of a 'democratically representative one-party state' – with the aim of gathering all constructive energies and initiatives into cooperation for the building of a new society – there still remained the urgent problem of choosing a model.

African Socialism

An American senator lately found the Minister of Finance of the Ivory Coast 'a great believer in the private enterprise system'.[105] The Minister, if speaking his mind, is not in a majority, however – at least as far as a general belief rather than mere lip-service may be concerned. Of the leaders of Africa today it can rather be said, rephrasing Harcourt while retaining a healthy dose of Harcourt's irony, that 'they are all socialists now'. In a later chapter we shall see how widely they vary in their socialism. Here I want to look at the pattern of thought which has led to this situation.

In those few countries where the ideas of socialism are taken seriously, this pattern has had two conditioning thoughts behind it. The first of these is that *political* independence can promote no real social advance – and therefore, given the pressures of mass demand for a different and better life, no stability – unless it is followed at once by a major effort at securing *social and economic* reconstruction: at solving, that is, what I have called the real colonial crisis. The second thought, linked to the first, has concerned the *kind* of reconstruction that can and should be attempted.

Between the proffered alternatives of capitalism or socialism, and against the foregoing background, the ideologists who have made the running have all opted for socialism. They have advanced a number of reasons for doing so. At the purely practical level they have pointed to the sorry fate of Latin America. More than a century has passed since the Spanish and Portuguese colonies beyond the Atlantic broke away from metropolitan rule. Almost all have remained part of what Senator Ellender calls 'the private enterprise system'. Yet almost all of them, today, also remain poverty-stricken, chaotic in social structure, bedevilled by oligarchical corruption and ridden by dictators. None of them has really escaped from colonial bondage. Not much thought has been required to prompt the view that newly independent countries in Africa may well follow the same disastrous trail – unless they can achieve, early in their independent life, a radical reorganization of the economic system they inherited from their rulers.

A European member of the Tanganyika legislative council put the case very clearly in 1960 when he wrote that 'Tanganyika is largely condemned', through its colonial heritage, 'to a plantation economy manned by labour at subsistence level', and pleaded for a genuine effort to change this basis of inevitable poverty.[106] Having the example of many years of Liberian stagnation before its eyes, West Africa had taken the point somewhat earlier. 'With the political power vested in the people,' according to Kwame Nkrumah's basic delineation of this argument in 1959, 'we are now in a position to launch an offensive against the remnants of economic imperialism which have entrenched themselves in our country over the past hundred years'; and he went on to define Ghana's second development plan as 'an expression of the will and determination of the people to break through the barriers of economic backwardness on the broadest possible front and to make possible a great increase in national productivity'. Three years later, these general ideas were being crystallized in terms of a specifically socialist programme.

For it appeared that *radical* economic change – and nothing less was needed – could not be achieved through the efforts of private enterprise. There had been, true enough, a long history of capitalist venture by West Coast Africans. As early as 1880 Africanus Horton and others in the Gold Coast (Ghana today) had tried – and failed – to float a syndicate to mine gold.

'Inevitably, Africans found it more difficult [than Europeans] to raise capital; apart from a few prosperous traders and lawyers, the process of capital accumulation had barely begun, and the idea of investing it in business enterprise was totally new.'[107] A year earlier had also seen the floating of the West African Railroad, Tramways, and Canal Company, 'but the shareholders were not forthcoming'.

The failure continued. The years 1951–61 were something of a halcyon period for private enterprise in Ghana; but what came of them? Many individuals made money, heaps of money; few or none proved willing to put it into the kind of investment that is required to make capitalism 'work'. But how can you have capitalism without capitalists? 'You cannot mobilize capital from our traders and businessmen,' a Ghanaian leader, Kojo Botsio, commented when I raised this point with him in 1960,* 'they will not do it. We have in fact helped our Ghanaian businessmen over the past few years with loans for their capitalist development. Very large sums, too. And nearly all of it has been wasted.' Nkrumah drew the same conclusion in a key-note speech. If Ghana was really to go ahead, 'it can only be through cooperative and similar bodies, since experience has shown that private Ghanaian businessmen cannot or will not work on a sufficient scale to compete with overseas firms'.[108]

If this was so in Ghana, one of Africa's richer states, with sterling reserves of more than £200 millions on the day of independence, what could be the position in really impoverished countries like Tanganyika? When Tanganyika became independent in 1961 there were no African capitalists at all: there were a handful of European companies with oversea shareholders and a cluster of Asian traders, the first owing no final allegiance to the country and the second having no concept of developing capitalism in Tanganyika in anything but a primitive commercial sense.

To choose capitalism, then, appeared to mean one of two things: either a very long period of very slow development, the passage of enough time for a few to grow rich before 'passing on the benefits to others', or else (and perhaps in any case) an

*Mr Botsio afterwards became the Foreign Minister of Ghana.

equally long period of close economic tutelage to the wealthy countries of the Western world – the very countries, for the most part, which had combined to produce the chaos of African life. Neither possibility seemed capable of offering any genuine hope of rapid economic expansion and social reorganization. This being so, the one or the other would soon call, as indeed it has, for military forms of government capable of repressing the discontented, decapitating their leaders, and generally 'sitting on the safety-valve of social progress'. A democratic capitalism would be no more possible in Africa today than it had been in Europe a century ago. Indeed, the real danger to democracy would lie precisely in trying to stick to those very 'free enterprise' patterns so eagerly sponsored by Western Europe and America.

By 1961, with such thoughts as these in mind, all those leaders whose governments were based on broad mass movements, as distinct from minority groups of one sort or another, had opted for a non-capitalist alternative. Notable among these were the leaders of Ghana, Guinea, and Mali in West Africa, and of Tanganyika in East Africa (with those of North Africa offering some variants of their own).

In assessing their degree of conviction, and the form it took, one needs to look back a little. Many who had lived in Europe during the forties and early fifties had become strongly imbued with socialist ideas: as witness, for example, that section of the Pan-Africanist declaration of 1945 in which the delegates condemned 'the monopoly of capital and the rule of private wealth and industry for private profit alone', and welcomed 'economic democracy as the only real democracy'. And while the initial six-point programme of the Convention People's Party, formed by Nkrumah in 1949 to fight for Gold Coast independence, had contained no reference to socialism, the implications of the party constitution were a clear guide to the atmosphere of thought in which the programme was conceived. The CPP, it was laid down, should 'work with other nationalist, democratic, and socialist movements in Africa and other continents, with a view to abolishing imperialism, colonialism, racialism, tribalism, and all forms of national and racial oppression and economic inequality among nations, races, and peoples, and [should] support all action for World Peace'. The last point may seem anodyne today; in 1949, however, it was tantamount to a declaration of revolutionary opinion.[109]

Elsewhere the accent was clearer still. Small Marxist study groups came to life during 1943 in the French West African cities of Dakar, Conakry, Abidjan, Bamako, and Bobo-Dioulasso. They owed their inspiration and their lead to Communists, whether French or African, and introduced for the first time a persistently radical undertone into 'French West African' politics.[110] After 1945 the election of African deputies to the National Assembly in Paris brought close working cooperation between many of these, notably of the multi-colony Rassemblement Démocratique Africaine (RDA), and the deputies of the French Communist Party, then a member of the coalition government in France. The RDA deputies affiliated themselves to the French Communist parliamentary group: they usually declared (I was then a resident correspondent of *The Times* in Paris) that they had done this because no other French party would really bother with them; but there is no doubt that several RDA leaders, including the afterwards very anti-Communist Houphouët-Boigny, were then powerfully impressed by the Marxist case in Europe.

Translated to Africa, though, Marxist thought must quickly have withered and died unless it had found receptive soil in the circumstances of colonial and post-colonial transition. As it is, socialist declarations in Africa have taken forms and modes that often make them, from a European standpoint, notably heterodox. Of these the most interesting may be gathered under the omnibus label of 'African Socialism', itself a political complex of no mean interest. Here also we link up, among other things, with that sense of repulsion from the 'money society' of towns and cities which had begun to flourish and fester during the last phase of the colonial period.

This can be most clearly seen in the writings of Julius Nyerere, perhaps the outstanding ideologist of 'African Socialism'. 'In traditional society,' he claims, 'everybody was a worker. There was no other way of earning a living for the community. Even the Elder, who appeared to be enjoying himself without doing any work and for whom everybody else appeared to be working, had, in fact, worked hard all his younger days. The wealth he now appeared to possess was not *his*, personally; it was only "his" as the Elder of the group which had produced it. He was its guardian. . . .

'One of the most socialistic achievements of our society was the sense of security it gave to its members, and the universal hospitality on which they could rely. But it is too often forgotten, nowadays, that the basis of this great socialistic achievement was this: that it was taken for granted that every member of society – barring only the children and the infirm – contributed his fair share towards the production of its wealth. . . . Capitalistic exploitation was impossible. Loitering was an unthinkable disgrace.'[III] And he quotes a Swahili proverb which advises: 'Treat your guest as a guest for two days; on the third day give him a hoe.'*

Whether or not socialism could be regarded as 'an attitude of mind', in Nyerere's words, or rather as a structure of society based on the public ownership of the means of production, distribution, and exchange, there was no doubt that the African tradition was seen as holding within itself a main component of socialist development: *cooperative* production. Even under the colonial regime, limited forms of marketing cooperative had often proved remarkably successful (especially in Tanzania); and sociologists may be right in finding here a logical outflow from traditional attitudes to economic life. If Israeli achievement won recognition in some African countries, this was mainly because of the cooperative side of Israeli organization, although Israeli's intelligently tactful modes of capital investment in the rest of Africa had their influence.† In the thought of Nyerere

*Mgeni siku mbili; siku ya tatu mpe jembe.

†By mid-1963, 42 companies based on partnerships between Israeli and African public capital had been established. 'Instead of demanding control, or concessions for long periods, the Israelis almost invariably postulate as a condition of their participation that their shareholding *must* be minority. Contracts are limited to five years, at the end of which the local majority shareholders are given the option of buying the Israeli interest out . . . Companies jointly financed by Israeli and African public bodies have been operating in Ghana, Liberia, Nigeria, Sierra Leone, Ivory Coast, Dahomey, Niger, Upper Volta, Senegal, Tanganyika, and two or three other states. In Ghana, the Israeli shareholders in the "Black Star" Shipping Line

and those who agreed with him, furthermore, the notion of cooperation was bound up closely with family and kinship groupings. Nyerere wrote in 1962:

The foundation, and the objective, of African Socialism is the Extended Family.* The true African Socialist does not look on one class of men as his brethren and another as his natural enemies. . . . He regards *all* men as his brethren – as members of his ever extending family. That is why the first article of TANU's creed is: 'Binadamu wote ni ndugu zangu, na Afrika ni moja.' If this had been originally put in English, it could have been: 'I believe in Human Brotherhood and the Unity of Africa.'

'Ujamaa', then, or 'Familyhood', describes our Socialism. It is opposed to Capitalism, which seeks to build a happy society on the basis of the exploitation of man by man; and it is equally opposed to doctrinaire socialism which seeks to build its happy society on a philosophy of inevitable conflict between man and man . . .

Far up-country in Tanzania, towards the piling hills of the north, I asked an administrative officer of Kondoa what he thought this African Socialism, this Ujamaa, really meant? We were passing through a village. He slowed the car to a stop. 'There,' he pointed: 'look at that. Over there – *that's* Ujamaa.' Men were rebuilding a house, a clay-and-corrugated peasant house of the interior. One of them explained: 'We're neighbours. We're doing it for that man there.' The man in question hobbled on crutches, a cripple with paralysed legs. The administrative officer, not without a touch of pride, remarked: 'Neighbourliness – that's what we have in Africa. That's Ujamaa.'

From this classically utopian and moralist interpretation of socialism, we pass through many variations to attempts at a far-reaching economic reorganization in such countries as Ghana and Mali, and now Tanzania. All of them, perhaps needless to say, emphasized central planning. But this emphasis rests on a reiterated statement that 'political independence without economic freedom' – the words here being those of J. S. Kasambala,

---

and the Ghana National Construction Company have been bought out, though they have retained some of their Israeli experts . . .' – *Economist*, 24 August 1963.

*Anthropological term denoting a family which includes uncles, aunts, cousins, etc., to several degrees, as opposed to the 'nuclear family' of modern Europe.

when Tanzania's Minister of Cooperative and Community Development – 'is but an empty shell'.[112]

Accompanying this thought, there went another. If political independence could be worth little without social and economic reorganization – without the reshaping of society – then clearly this implied an entirely new kind of relationship with the former colonial powers. Even so conservative a 'socialist' as Mamadou Dia, ex-Premier of Senegal, could observe in 1960 that 'one cannot reasonably speak of a balance sheet' [of 'decolonization'] 'when one knows that political liberation does not confer economic liberation . . . [and] that aid from the West, instead of being real economic and technical assistance along the lines of mutual development, is often the result of a bargain wherein commercial preoccupations are mixed with strategic or even political calculations.'[113]

The thought behind such declarations – and there have been many such – was not that any African state could win unlimited 'economic freedom' and thereby 'go it alone', but that the necessary minimum of freedom *must* include a freedom of choice between systems. African states, it was argued, must move away from their colonial economic integration with the 'private enterprise' system of the West (without, of course, moving into the communist system of the East). Unless this happened, independent Africa could only follow Latin America into a new subjection.

Economic planning became the practical solution to this problem of 'escape'. Ideally, it was now seen as a transposition of the united nationalist movement from the political to the economic sphere: the newly-independent government, based on its own united popular movement, would move on from winning and exercising one kind of power to winning and exercising other and more potent kinds. A strong central authority would mould the scattered and chaotic fragments of the ex-colony's economy into a coherent and progressive whole, setting targets, finding resources, and realizing step by step all those objectives – schools, hospitals, higher living standards, and the rest – which mass opinion now undoubtedly demanded.

Planning became something of a panacea. Meanwhile, another

doctrine was required in order to safeguard the right to plan – the right, as it was conceived, to *choose*.

Neutralism

Many independent African states opted for neutralism. And this, in practice, has meant the refusal to enter any part of the Western defence system, notably as embodied in the North Atlantic Treaty Organization (NATO), or to make any corresponding commitment to the Communist bloc. 'Let us now look round and see what they are doing,' it was argued, 'and when we have seen all that for ourselves, and made up our own minds, then let us choose what we like – whether in one part of the world or the other – and apply it to our own problems.' The Nigerian Federal Prime Minister, the late Sir Abubakar Tafawa Balewa, was prominent among those who repeatedly insisted that 'neutralism' did not necessarily mean neutrality, but 'freedom to choose'.

The argument, really, was self-evident. Genuine political independence at this early stage – whatever might happen in the future – simply could not be made to walk in hand with anything but neutralism. Another Nigerian explained why. 'Whatever may happen in the Pan-African field,' observed the late Sardauna of Sokoto, Sir Ahmadu Bello, in 1962, 'I am convinced that our own sensible course is one of neutrality. You may ask how we can follow such a course and at the same time be the enthusiastic members of the Commonwealth that we are. The answer is that India manages to do it with considerable success, and so can we. We must not find ourselves in such a position in international affairs that we should feel morally bound to support some policy which does not win our whole-hearted or intellectual backing, or attract us by its obvious rightness.'

Did neutrality of this sort mean pacifism? Not at all. 'We must also make it clear that the word "neutrality" means avoiding commitments in the sense that we are using it. It does not have the special meaning, so often ascribed to it, of not taking part in hostilities. . . . It would be incorrect to assume that, as we are neutral in peace, we should also be neutral in war. Similarly, it would also be unwise to think that we would automatically follow the Commonwealth into a war.'[114]

The Commonwealth, in fact, has offered what many Africans have found to be a conveniently loose framework for their entry into the world of independence, though many people in Britain do not seem to have appreciated the African good-will behind such recognition. Nobody was ever more savagely criticized in British newspapers than President Nkrumah of Ghana. Yet Nkrumah, comparing the Commonwealth favourably to the French Community, expressed in 1960 a view from which he did not afterwards depart, that 'to us, the Commonwealth is a modern, flexible, and adaptable institution composed of sovereign, free, and completely independent nations'.[115] Could it be that what many British critics of Ghana really regretted was Ghana's independence? Rightly or wrongly, a good many Africans have thought so.

Neutralism was thus a diplomatic device, primarily, for gaining time. As such, it proved able to yield some useful dividends in reducing the impact of the Cold War. I think of Bamako again. In 1960 I returned there after an absence of eight crowded years. This far-inland colony of France had meanwhile become the Republic of Mali. Given its geographical enclosure, one might have expected its degree of independence to stop a long way short of neutralism. On the contrary. Staying in the same hotel, I found, were delegates of economic-aid missions from the United States and the Soviet Union, Czechoslovakia, Yugoslavia, Ghana, and France. 'East' and 'West' occupied opposite sides of the hotel lounge, but they were all under the same African roof – not far from the Boulevard Konaté. Mali's ministers were employed during those busy days in the grateful task of deciding 'what the Americans can do for us and what the Russians, what the French and what the Czechs . . .' Here was neutralism in full array; and it really seemed a remarkable achievement.

Neutralism was obviously a flexible device which could grow or dwindle in importance. French atomic explosions in the Algerian Sahara, for example, met with severe condemnation from all the important states of West Africa – and, with the Addis unity conference of 1963, from nearly all the states of Africa – while Nigeria even went so far in protest, at one point, as to sever diplomatic relations with France.

It soon became clear that there were significant differences in the degree of seriousness attached to neutralism as a state policy. Some governments have interpreted it merely as a means of squeezing money out of the East as well as the West. Others, pushing the concept a stage further, have seen it as a barrier to a new danger, which they have called Neo-Colonialism. This too has become a dominant theme, and seems likely to remain one.

Neo-Colonialism

Many definitions are to hand, the clearest coming from Kwame Nkrumah, who has called it 'the process of handing independence over to the African people with one hand, only to take it away with the other hand'. He has also defined it as 'clientèle sovereignty, or fake independence: namely, the practice of granting a sort of independence by the metropolitan power, with the concealed intention of making the liberated country a client-state and controlling it effectively by means other than political ones'.

When offering these definitions, Dr Nkrumah clearly had in mind a number of the ex-French territories, such as Niger or the equatorial lands, whose freedom of action was – and still is – very small. But the concept has a wider application. 'The greatest danger at present facing Africa is neo-colonialism and its major instrument, balkanization. The latter term is particularly appropriate to describe the breaking up of Africa into small, weak states, since it arose from the action of the great powers when they divided up the European part of the old Turkish Empire, and created a number of dependent and competing states in the Balkan peninsula. The effect was to produce a political tinderbox which any spark could set alight.'[116] Historically, the argument might be a poor one, since the colonial system had not broken up Africa into small weak states, but, on the contrary, had actually compressed hundreds of pre-colonial states within a few big colonies. But Nkrumah's listeners took his point.

The ideas of neo-colonialism have in any case added fresh

arguments against 'trying to follow the capitalist example'. Given the general absence of an investing class, according to the Guinea leader Sékou Touré, as well as the fact that foreign companies are primarily out for higher profits than they can earn at home (such being their *raison d'être*), the promotion of African independence within the capitalist system must result in surrendering the rate and course of growth to the decisive arbitration of the stronger partner.[117]

An English writer sympathetic to 'free enterprise' has recently developed the same argument. For an underdeveloped country to continue the unqualified encouragement of foreign private investment on terms the latter is willing to accept, he writes, 'would imply that, at the end of a decade, a very high proportion of the country's industry would be under the ultimate control of foreign firms . . .'[118]: would reduce it, that is, to a semi-colonial posture. So the need to change the economic system – to displace the old hotch-potch of traditional-plus-colonial economics by a modern system capable of yielding large material progress – must inevitably clash with the very requirement of those firms which are supposed to be promoting development.

The issue has appeared, basically, as one of profitable investment. What responsible foreign businessman would recommend investment of his company's funds in an African (or any other) country unless a continued high yield in earnings seemed guaranteed?* But what responsible African government could *guarantee* that the interests of his country would remain compatible with continued high earnings by foreign capital?

From the African standpoint, this could not seem an academic argument. Nationalists watched many foreign firms exporting very large profits year by year from Africa. Judged by what these men say and by what one believes they think, their main count against the colonial system has not been, as Hunter affirms, that 'colonial governments . . . failed to develop their African territories'. It has been that colonial governments developed these territories for the benefit of Europeans and North Americans,

*Very few, in fact, have: since 1945 the weight of oversea investment by British and other private investors has gone increasingly into the developed and not into the underdeveloped countries. See especially Michael Barratt Brown, *After Imperialism*, London, 1963.

not Africans. This point has been seldom understood abroad, perhaps because the large earnings of many great companies in Africa have generally been taken for granted, or else not noticed by the European or American public. Nearly £1,500 millions of British capital, for instance, are said to be invested in African countries, yielding an annual profit after local taxation of many millions of pounds, and repaying initial capital investment many times over. Another recent estimate showed that the average rate of profit on the £860 millions of British capital in South Africa amounts to about fifteen per cent, or almost £130 millions a year.[119]

The point is perhaps worth pursuing a little further, for it illuminates what sophisticated Africans have meant by the dangers of neo-colonialism. Northern Rhodesia was a colony desperately lacking in educational and other social services for Africans, the reason being, as hard-pressed administrators repeatedly explained, that there was 'not enough money' to pay for them. Yet the rate of profits-export from the mines of Northern Rhodesia has been enormous for at least twenty years: in 1956, to take a by no means exceptional year, about £50 million in company and corporation profits left Northern Rhodesia for shareholders abroad. This was certainly 'development', but of a rather special kind.

One could illustrate the same high rate of profits-export from most African territories which possess deposits of valuable minerals. An official Gold Coast report, though for restricted circulation, had this to say about the year 1949:

Of the £6.4 million earned by the exports of gold, perhaps £3 million can be considered to have been transferred out of the country. . . . Corresponding estimates for manganese place the funds remitted [abroad] at some £2 million out of a total export value of £4 million. No estimate can be given in the case of bauxite. The three estimates given [in the Report] appear to work out at *something in the region of half the export earnings* [my italics], and, bearing in mind the very tentative nature of these calculations, it seems reasonable to assume that this proportion is a fair estimate for the remittances abroad necessarily involved in the operation of the mining industry as a whole.[120]

So far as one can tell the estimate was applicable to the whole continent.

Whatever might have happened in the past, this very high rate of profits-export could no longer be regarded as acceptable; and some efforts have accordingly been made to reduce the drain of wealth. Exponents of the neo-colonialist danger have argued that there could in any case be no sense in *extending* such obligations to export wealth. The need, on the contrary, was to cut them down. But in order to cut them down, one would have to command an adequate measure of economic freedom. More than that: any later attempt to refashion the economic system along non-private enterprise lines could only be hampered by the existence of powerful foreign shareholders whose interests might then suffer; and who could therefore be expected to react in their own defence.

This line of thought has been vigorously confirmed by foreign interests, which have issued many frank warnings of the 'investment boycott' that could follow any attempt to tamper with the rights of 'free enterprise' in the former colonies. 'A break-up of the [Central African] Federation into its constituent territories . . .' thundered a semi-official pamphlet issued in 1962 by a British public relations firm in the employment of the Federal government, 'must have certain obvious economic consequences. More than fifty per cent of capital in the Federation is owned by non-residents. Even if more rigid controls than those now operating were enforced, the repatriation of investment is likely to be heavy and the re-investment of accruing funds greatly reduced. Discount houses, merchant banks, and a fairly advanced economic complex involving the Central Bank and commercial banks would need drastically to reorientate their activities in such circumstances. . . .'[121]

Such warnings have been many, and have been heeded. They have been widely taken to prove that neo-colonialism is no mere figment of a fevered political imagination, but a genuine threat to any real freedom of economic choice in ex-colonial countries. For if the constituent territories of the Central African Federation, for example, were to advance at the general rate of growth decided upon, ultimately, by foreign shareholders who owned 'more than fifty per cent of capital', then clearly independence could lead to nothing but a repetition of the past: in other words, to massive disillusionment. Either these shareholders would have to stomach a cut in their profits, or Central Africa would continue to exist without more than the sketchiest network of schools, hospitals, local industrial development, and the like.

Moreover, even if African governments were to rest content with a rate of investment controlled by the interests of foreign shareholders, what kind of investment could they expect? Here again the facts have appeared clear enough. Outside the territories of assumedly permanent white settlement, very little foreign investment has ever gone into genuine industrialization and agricultural development: an authoritative American survey of 1960, for example, showed that only about one-fiftieth of American private investment in Africa (outside South Africa) had gone into manufacturing industry, while as much as two-thirds had gone into mining.[122] Almost none at all had gone, or could ever be expected to go, into the primary modernization of social and public services. For what profits, after all, were to be made out of building schools?

Reflections such as these, more or less widely discussed, have projected on to the political scene what may be called 'the neo-colonialist stereotype' – the picture of a situation in which development by 'free enterprise' must involve a new form of indirect colonialism. This stereotype has been repeatedly stamped deeper by much that has been said and printed abroad. The enfolding within the West European Common Market of most of France's former colonies was generally greeted in West Germany as 'an opening of the doors of Africa to other nations'. There was to be 'equality of investment rights' between these African countries and Europe; but who could doubt that the equation would favour the stronger partner at the expense of the weaker? German private investors had long been busy on the scene. By the end of 1958 the Deutsche Bank had become involved in more than 100 companies in South, Central, and East Africa.[123] Yet these enterprises, it was duly noted, went hand in hand with support for regimes which had been anything but favourable to African progress. In 1959 the West German authorities made a substantial loan to the Belgian Congo government, then desperately trying to prolong its life;[124] while other reports spoke of the exports of West German armaments to the Portuguese in Angola.[125]

Controversial or not, the conclusions were uncomplimentary. Where foreign shareholders could rest on colonial or semi-colonial regimes, they would gladly do so; where they could not, they would try to slow up a rate of development which would become significantly higher than before only at the expense of foreign profits. Further, these attitudes would be transposed to the political scene in the form of pressure on African governments to preserve the *status quo*, reject 'rash experiments', and generally rest content with 'what they had got'.

Such conclusions led to a general preference for government-to-government lending and investment. More and more clearly, African countries began to develop towards a pattern dominated by state capitalism. If Western governments were initially reluctant to lend money at less than five or six per cent, they have since done something to cut down their rates under pressure of Soviet lending at 2½ per cent. African governments have lost their fear that measures unfavourable to free enterprise would bring a capital boycott in their train. In this connection, too, neutralism proved its value. By 1962, indeed, Ghana had achieved the unforeseeable success of borrowing huge sums for primary industrial development from both the United States and the Soviet Union. This process of 'looking to both sides' went so far that even so minimally independent an ex-colony as Niger has entered into cultural exchanges with Moscow. The bold were able to open the way for the timid.

A New Model

Towards 1963, accordingly, a new model of what an independent African state should be like had begun to emerge among thoughtful people. It was to be a state governed by a single party representing all or most sections of the population, politically united over and beyond the traditional boundaries of tribal or regional loyalty, equipped with rapidly expanding social services, and moving out of the colonial economic system into a national economic system based on a wide measure of cooperative effort and public ownership.

Extending the ideal, it was to be a state living in good relations with its neighbours, subscribing to efforts at African union by functional organization and coordination of foreign policy while staying clear of non-African entanglements, and willing to make its own identity subordinate to the greater claims of an all-African identity. Its peoples would look outward to the rest of Africa and the world rather than inward to their own traditional divisions and diversions.

'The time of small and jealous nationalism is past and done with,' declared Gabriel d'Arboussier in 1958 when president of the Grand Conseil of a French West Africa that was then on the eve of independence. 'African history has often been the history of large units. All the great African states of the past were large or very large, and included many peoples. This was true of Mali as of Songhay, or of others elsewhere on our continent. But what the organizers of those old feudal states did by conquest, we in our day will do by federalism and by free consent.'[126]

The new African states had not achieved this vision; far from it. Yet they had none the less been able to make cautious progress in that direction. If a good deal of politics in Africa might still sound balefully separatist and chauvinist, there was another and more hopeful side to the picture. The key slogans and signposts of emancipation continued to be couched in terms of an outward-looking humanism, not of a narrow and jealous nationalism: a fact that must surely count as one of the grand achievements of independence. And if the realization of unity across two or three crowded years, was so far much smaller than the hope of it, that still seemed no reason for disregarding the nature of the hope – nor the movement towards realizing it.

This progress could be seen at several points. Not a few outsiders had predicted, for example, that Uganda would fall apart with independence, and become the victim of its own 'tribal conflicts'. But what in fact has happened there? By mid-1963 the shrewd Milton Obote, prime minister of a government struggling hard against internal separatism, could reasonably claim a large and perhaps decisive measure of success. The Uganda People's Congress which he leads was already emerging as a dominant unifying force, and was making inroads even into Baganda separatism.

Here matters came most instructively to a head in 1966, when, evidently on the initiative of the king or *kabaka* of Buganda, there was an armed clash between the national government and the Baganda separatists. This was quickly won by the national leadership under Obote. Although use of the army now raised thorny problems for civilian rule, the year ended with no real sign of popular or 'tribal' agitation on the *kabaka's* behalf. If anything, the evidence rather suggested that most Baganda commoners were losing very little sleep over their departed king.

In the wider context of intra-African unity, progress remained far to seek. Difficulties multiplied after 1963. By 1966 they had become intense in a wide spectrum of countries, marking for many the end of the 'independence honeymoon'. Several civilian regimes broke down, displaced by soldiers and bureaucrats. Civil wars overshadowed the scene. Frontier conflicts erupted with a new violence. Organs of potential unification, notably the Organization of African Unity, fell victim to a deepening frustration.

Yet the ideal of unity, even a wide consciousness of its desirability, persisted through the disarray of the late 1960s. It survived as a dynamic element in the background of events. However hostile, the facts could not entirely be ignored. And the facts pointed with an ever more powerful emphasis to a choice, a hard choice, between forms of unity and forms of disaster.

9   Stumbling Blocks

Models are no more than models, however well designed, and human nature is not always what it should be. Anyone who leafs through the files of the first years of independence will find many occasions for stumbling over the blocks to sweet reason with which much of Africa was now bestrewn.

'Twenty-nine Europeans, including women and children, were given an hour to leave a hotel in Tanganyika today because they showed discourtesy to the President of Guinea,' then visiting that country. They had actually 'remained seated when President Sékou Touré passed through the lounge'.[127] Perhaps they had failed even to *recognize* the President of Guinea.

Prickly reactions of this kind may not be important but they have their place in the record. President Touré's Minister of Finance kept me waiting for an hour and a half, last time I arranged to be received by him in Conakry, and then without apology gave me a grudging ten minutes of his time. Travellers in Africa have learned to know that nationalism in Africa, like nationalism anywhere else, often has its underworld of thin-skinned pride and suspicion: understandable and long provoked, perhaps, but no more hopeful or agreeable for that.

Reactions of this kind would matter little if they were not the reflection of a deeper trouble. Africa won its political independence in chaotic transition from the old subsistence economies of the past to egalitarian and industrial democracy on modern lines. Withdrawing in deep water, colonial Powers left behind them far greater problems than any they had ever proposed to solve. This is not to suggest, of course, that they would have done better to withdraw later, since there was never any sign that they would allow the real problems to be tackled on a realistic basis.

Indeed, the main solutions they proposed (and to some extent promoted) have since become a large part of the trouble. For what the colonial Powers thought wise and necessary was the formation and promotion to power of 'leading élites' or 'middle classes' (those whom the French have so revealingly called *interlocuteurs valables* – 'negotiators worth talking to'): groups of men who would ensure that post-colonial government should be 'moderate and responsible' – should be, that is, a reflection of colonial government. And it is here, in growing measure, that the seat of the trouble has lain.

For it is a fact, by and large (and generalization, one may perhaps repeat, will always be unfair to someone), that such 'élites' and 'middle classes' have proved incapable of meeting the challenges of political independence. Some have retired into profitable corruption, others into old-fashioned habits of colonial authoritarianism, still others into a more or less sterile dependence on outside support. For others, again, traditionalist separatism (we may call it, with reservations, tribalism) has become a major outlet for their energy. And given their often great authority among ordinary people, the example of these educated 'élites' and 'middle classes' has echoed down the ranks of African society with curious results.

'For too many African "élites",' a notably pro-African French economist, René Dumont, has lately written, 'independence has meant taking the place of the whites and enjoying the privileges, often exorbitant, hitherto accorded to "colonials". To high salaries there are now often added fine villas splendidly furnished, or even palaces for ministers, the whole of their upkeep being paid by the budget.... To the Peugeot 403s there follow, after independence, the Chevrolets of Abidjan [capital of the Ivory Coast] and the Mercedes of Yaoundé [capital of the Kamerun Republic] – often renewed after six months, something that makes ordinary folk grind their teeth....'[128] But who in ex-British Africa could not quote similar examples?

'Independence isn't for us,' a peasant of the Kamerun countryside told Dumont in May 1961: 'it's for the people in the towns.'

All too often, pressure for 'Africanization' by 'élites and

middle classes' meant that qualified foreigners were simply displaced by Africans on the make. It seems likely that this process reached its lowest point in the ex-Belgian Congo of 1963, where Congolese were often 'occupying salaries' instead of jobs, simply because they were incapable of doing the jobs for which their salaries were supposedly paid. Here again the examples were innumerable.

They were also understandable, even natural. The same thing has been common enough in Europe. With a total of seventeen university graduates at its disposal, the Congo government was in any case obliged to choose between continuing to employ Europeans – in the event, those very Belgians who had occupied the jobs before – or promoting men without proper qualifications. Moreover, the collapse in late 1960 of the Congo's only movement of nationalist enthusiasm and self-discipline – a disaster that was mainly the work of the Belgians and their allies – also meant the collapse of nationalist morale. After that it became a question of *sauve qui peut*; and who can wonder at this?

Continued semi-colonial tutelage would have the same effect elsewhere. 'These countries,' Dumont says of some ex-French states, 'have not yet understood that they are poor, because it is still far too easy for them to sponge on us. Apart from supplying the great majority of their investments (eighty-six per cent in Upper Volta), we balance their budgets for them' with financial aid. And so a little country like Gabon, with fewer than half a million inhabitants, has a parliament with sixty-five deputies: a Gabon deputy sits for about 6,000 constituents, compared with a British Member of Parliament who has an average of about 56,000, and a French Deputy who has nearly twice that. Moreover, he gets a salary which is equivalent to about a third *more* than a British M.P.'s. 'As for the cost of the presidential and ministerial establishments, with all their more or less useless journeyings back and forth, it is probably higher, in proportion to the national income of Gabon, than the cost to France of the Court of Louis XVI in 1788. . . .'[129]

Wherever the political assumptions of the colonial period prevailed, in short, government in Africa has tended to mean government by an oligarchical élite whose members are sometimes bound together by traditional ties, but more often by a network of private interests and activities of the 'log-rolling' sort. The early years of Ghanaian independence saw some remarkable developments in this direction, a veritable efflorescence of luxury living on a scale never thought possible before. 'Come and have lunch with me,' said a leading nationalist in those years, and, when I did, showed me with pride a mansion which must have cost many thousands of pounds. Yet the nationalist in question had not been a wealthy man before. Nkrumah afterwards made some attempt to curb such spending, but with little effect.

Nowhere more deeply than in Nigeria did this 'national bourgeoisie' plunge into corruption and malversation. When the Western Region Marketing Board began amassing reserves (largely from cocoa and other farmers) for use against a rainy day, it inherited a previously collected 'pool' amounting to some £40 millions. This rose to £62 millions. But early in 1962 the Coker Commission of Inquiry into the affairs of the Board found that these resources were 'now entirely scattered and, in fact, completely dissipated'.[130] Much of the money had been properly spent on various types of national development; a significant part of it had not.

We did come across evidence of prudent and considered management and investment of public funds and we also came across evidence of reckless and indeed atrocious and criminal mismanagement and diversion of public funds. We did come across evidence regarding some bold and courageous civil servants who stuck to their guns with remarkable fortitude in the face of circumstances of a most trying order, and we also came across evidence regarding some dishonest and callous politicians who had mortgaged their consciences to dishonesty in all its manifestations and indeed demonstrated this appraisement in the way and manner in which they testified before us.[131]

But what Mr Justice Coker and his eminent colleagues of the Nigerian High Court discovered to be true in this case would also, as everyone knows though rather few care to admit, have been discovered to be true in many other cases in newly independent Africa – had they only been examined.

Early in 1963 a reporter from the Algerian weekly, *Révolution Africaine*, had lunch with President Touré of Guinea.

We were five or six at table. A member of the central political committee, some Guinean ambassadors, the Foreign Minister.... The guests get ready to leave.

'You've a car to take you?' Sékou Touré asks his comrade of the central committee [of the ruling Democratic Party of Guinea].

'No, President.'

'It's true – you sold your car and put the money in the bank.'

'One can't hide anything from you, President.'

Commenting on this little exchange, the President goes on:

There's a thousand reasons for these frauds in the civil service. Our economic difficulties are among these reasons. There are people who haven't been able to keep up with the situation, people for whom independence has become an end and not a phase.

Political independence isn't enough. What we need is to forge our economic independence. Among our party members, there are those for whom independence was first and foremost a chance to take the place of the *colon*.

But the current party congress, the sixth, would

open the phase of revolution: the strengthening of political education, the establishment of all levels of practical collective duties, the extension of criticism and self-criticism, and, above all, the reinforcement of the control to be exercised by the rank-and-file on those in power.[132]

A little earlier than that, in a dawn broadcast that was to become famous though ineffectual, Nkrumah had condemned luxury living, fulminated against the personal dissipation of national wealth, and appealed for higher standards of morality. But the get-rich-quick brigade paid little heed. Here again, there were other exceptions. One of the first actions of Tanganyika's independent government was to cut the salary of senior ministers from £3,100 a year to £1,800, and one of the first important decisions of Prime Minister (afterwards President) Nyerere was to quit his post and concentrate on organizing the rank-and-file of the nationalist movement in Tanganyika, with the purpose of setting an example for all those 'cadres' who thought, or might be tempted to think, that independence should now reward them with a lavish hand.

'Tribalism' was another stumbling block. In May 1963 Kenya had its first election on a wide democratic suffrage. Facing the major challenges of self-rule, this small country of some eight million people – deep in economic stagnation, deprived of any great mineral resources, burdened with heavy unemployment and underemployment – was none the less required to support the cost of 715 candidates for 151 seats in the two houses of the central legislature, together with another 185 seats in *seven* regional parliaments.

Kenya was thus to bear the expense not only of eight parliaments and governments, but also of eight police forces, eight sets of frontier control, eight judiciaries and other public services, not to mention an eight-fold inflation of patronage which all this administration would, in the circumstances, inevitably mean. If it is true of much of ex-French Africa, as Dumont tells us, that administration is now its principal industry – civil-service salaries apparently exhaust sixty per cent of total budget receipts in Dahomey – Kenya was surely in the fashion. A large part of its annual revenue was going to be spent in the doubling and re-doubling of jobs and responsibilities of an administrative and 'representational' order.

This retrograde 'balkanization' of Kenya – modified after independence by the wisdom of Kenya's leaders – was not without its European driving influence. But that is obviously not the whole story. It was an African party, the Kenya African Democratic Union, which was immediately responsible for this result, while tribalism – this time without inverted commas – also played a part. 'Here,' commented a conservative but shrewd English observer, 'two principles have run up against each other in a conflict fundamental to mankind from which his whole history has grown – the principle of advance, risk, change, individuality, and contest, and the principle of withdrawal, preservation, collectivity, and roots. Here is the conscious straining against the unconscious, the male against the female, the spear against the heart. Here – to put it in electoral terms –

the tribe, the ethnic family, is cast into conflict with the idea of centralized Statehood. All Africa is engaged in it.'[133]

This might be anthropologically poetic rather than incisively political. Yet even if European influences had not striven to 'divide and rule', tribalism would still have remained a factor in the present African situation. More often than some Africans care to admit, the coming of independence had meant a certain failure of nerve, a tendency to retreat within traditional enclosures, a search for new security inside an old armour of custom and belief.

Various reasons could be offered for this. One was a rekindled desire for ethnic identification after a long period of colonial anonymity. Another, undoubtedly, was the force of kinship or of 'local-ist' tradition. A third rested in the survival of chiefly authorities and systems whose sanctions have always had the compelling support of religion. When you believe that your king is also the earthly representative and spokesman of God, you may think twice before turning your back on him. In quite a few corners of the continent, the divine right of kings still had potent meaning in everyday life. The Kabaka of Buganda was head of his 'church' in a sense far more obvious and meaningful, for most of his subjects, than Queen Elizabeth II's headship of the Church of England can possibly seem to the vast majority of hers.

But the problem was more complicated than that. Popular respect for traditional hierarchies in Africa was something, or so it has appeared to me, that orthodox European opinion generally put too high. Given a chance to say so, it would seem that most people would after all prefer to govern themselves in a new way. And it remains oddly true that in nearly all those countries where tribalism has become most potent after independence, the circumstances of 'decolonization' have done a great deal to make it so.

The average educated African nationalist, if one may dare for a moment to try to summarize the views of so complex a 'person', will readily admit that a post-independence reaction towards 'balkanization' – towards the decentralization of authority – is at times unavoidable. Where strong states have survived from the pre-colonial past, even if in tutelary form, the influence of their rulers is bound to be profoundly important to a great many local folk. This we have seen in parts of Uganda and Nigeria, to mention only two examples. And the same is true, even if less emphatically so, in a number of countries where strong peoples were in more or less frequent conflict with each other during the nineteenth century: as, for example, in parts of Kenya. In cases such as these, tribalism remains a major problem, one that will not be overcome without effort and probably not without trouble.

But this heady residue of ancient loyalties has had the addition of outside influence. That is what makes its real political strength so hard to assess. Had the Belgians and their allies thrown their full weight consistently behind the concept of a strong central government in the Congo, would the tribal wars of 1960–62 have really happened? Or, if they had happened, would they have been so fierce? Had the Europeans of Kenya, with effective control of policy so long in their hands, steadily wished to have a strong African government in Nairobi, would the preindependence constitution of 1962 have taken its form of extreme 'balkanization'? Subsequent developments, whether in Congo or Kenya, certainly prompt negative answers.

Kenya has many peoples. But Tanzania has more. 'Yet here in Tanzania,' runs the argument you will hear in that country, 'we have almost none of this "tribalism" of which you speak so much. You'll find northern men administering the south, and southern men administering the centre . . .'

'But you were fortunate in being able to build a united national movement.'

'Very true, we were fortunate in that. But we were even more fortunate in not having a large European minority concentrated in the heart of our country, and given large powers by the British government for many years. That is what happened in Kenya, though. And if you look behind the scenes in Kenya, you will see that those Europeans have pushed for "tribalism" just as hard as they could. Why? But that's obvious.'

This has been, no doubt, an understandable reaction by European minorities threatened with loss of power and privilege. At another stage one may observe the same reaction in South Africa, where the Afrikaner National Party has sought to take

time by the forelock in creating 'Bantustans'; little African statelets based on regional or tribal loyalties which, it is hoped, will
reduce the pressure of explosive nationalism.

French Africa has offered other examples. There the active
survival of chiefly loyalties, tribal loyalties, was more difficult
because the French had tended to administer more *directly* –
through their own personnel or through nominated Africans –
than the British. They had thus consistently devalued and even
destroyed the old hierarchies. This, incidentally, was why the
nationalist movement in Guinea, under Touré's lead, was able
so easily to suppress the pro-French chiefs of the Fouta Djallon.
The population of those hills was in no doubt that its chiefs had
thrown in their lot with the French, and it quickly rallied to the
democratically composed village-committees of the nationalist
movement. And this was also why, a little later, the Union
Soudanaise in the Soudan Territory (Mali today) was able to
reach the same end with little more difficulty. The French had
relied on chiefs as props of colonial rule; but the white ants of
'collaboration' had eaten them through.*

Even the contrary cases prove the rule. Although commanding
a big parliamentary majority in the Niger Territory, the Sawaba
(Freedom) Party led by Djibo Bakary was overthrown after its
attempt to achieve independence in President de Gaulle's proffered referendum of 1958 (the referendum in which the nationalists of Guinea were successful); and this occurred precisely
because the chiefs in Niger were still politically strong. But the
chiefs were strong because the French had made and kept them
so; and, in turn, it was because they relied so greatly on the
French for the further protection of their privileges that these
chiefs (like some others in West Africa) were opposed to national
independence. With the chiefs' support France was able to
regain control. Niger is formally an independent state today;
but it would be absurd to suggest that it controls its own destiny

*This familiar and rather comfortable British view of French practice is not
unchallenged in France. In a brilliant and witty counter-attack, Professor Hubert
Deschamps of the Sorbonne has lately argued that French administrative practice,
up to 1945, scarcely differed from that of the British 'except for being more easy-
going and less well defined'. ('Et Maintenant, Lord Lugard?', *Africa*, October 1963,
Lugard Lecture for 1963).

in anything approaching the sense that neighbouring Nigeria does so.

Senegal has offered a more subtle case. Its long association with France makes this country somewhat eccentric to the 'French African' scene: its first deputy sat in the French Parliament as long ago as 1914, and some of its townsmen acquired French citizenship only two years later. Yet in a muted form Senegal has witnessed the same struggle between modern nationalism and traditional chiefdom – the latter taking here the special form of *grands marabouts*, local heads of powerful Islamic brotherhoods.

These often vigorous men have played, and still play, a crucial part in defending the general *status quo*; and they have invariably enjoyed important backing from the French. Even in 1961, at a time when the independent government of Senegal was preaching the virtues of African Socialism, the leader of the Muridite brotherhood could still forbid the establishment of rural primary schools and dispensaries, while conditions of work on the lands of the Muridite leaders could be likened by a careful French writer to 'near-slavery'.[134]

When Senegal and Soudan joined in the Federation of Mali, the disparity of aim and attitude between the two countries' respective leaders soon led to scission. Mali had overthrown its chiefs and was governed by a party with wide popular backing and several radical objectives: Senegal, for all the distinction and intelligence of its parliamentary leaders, was still in the grip of chiefs and religious hierarchies whose intentions were nothing if not conservative.

Morocco's recent history tells the same kind of story. There the French found it impossible to persuade Sultan Muhammad ben Youssef to denounce the rising party of Moroccan independence, the Istiqlal. Like his forbears, the Sultan looked back upon a long and sovereign past. When the French banned the Istiqlal it was the Sultan who, at least in a symbolic sense, took its place. So they exiled him to Corsica and then to Madagascar, and installed a puppet whose name was ben Arafa. That was in 1953. It proved the beginning of the end for French rule. Far from cowed into submission, the traditional followers of Sultan

Muhammad swung into line with the nationalists; armed resistance began before the end of the year.

Reacting to this along familiar lines, the French strove to bolster their power by finding other rulers who would play the tribal card. They turned to the Berber chiefs of the Atlas. Prominent among these was el Glaoui, the 'Pasha of Marrakesh'.

The Glaoui and his henchmen were painted by the French as stern traditionalists who longed to be free of the 'Arab yoke', and whose people burned with loyalty to Berber tribalism. But the facts proved rather different. At the end of 1955 the puppet ben Arafa, having spent eighteen months in his Rabat palace without daring to set foot beyond the gate, fled to Tangier. The French bowed before the rising storm and brought back Sultan Muhammad. And the Glaoui? No resistance to Muhammad or the Istiqlal came from that 'man of brothels', as one of the greatest living French Arabists once named him to me. And Berber tribalism? Its burning ardour, if it had ever had any in recent years, vanished with him.

Colonial rule was here defeated by a traditional structure which had remained loyal to its history. But just because this traditional structure was alive and meaningful, the national movement after independence could no longer remain united. Early in 1959 its radical wing, under Mehdi ben Barka, broke away from an Istiqlal government which it denounced as reactionary, and formed the Union Nationale des Forces Populaires. Moroccan politics since then have developed increasingly as a conflict between the reformers of the UNFP and the new and personally ambitious ruler, King Hassan II, son of the late Muhammad ben Youssef. In July 1963 the king's police began arresting his UNFP opponents, and by the end of the year the Moroccan regime had degenerated into a royal autocracy. As such it continued. Early in 1966 the courageous Mehdi ben Barka, still leading a democratic operation in exile, was seized on a Paris pavement and afterwards murdered in circumstances which threw a grimly sinister light on the Moroccan regime.

The other territories of the former French empire in North Africa, Algeria and Tunisia, have had different experience. In

Tunisia there was no chiefly hierarchy of any importance, but a considerable Tunisian business and farming class. It was the latter, united in the Néo-Destour Party, which led the campaign for independence. After many troubles and a brief armed struggle they triumphed in 1955, opening the way for the Istiqlal in Morocco; and their national movement has remained stable and substantially (though not entirely) united since then, while the shrewd and popular President Bourghiba has had no serious rival.

In Algeria no ruling hierarchy had survived the close attrition of colonial occupation since the 1830s, and no indigenous business class had ever had the chance to emerge. There were a few Muslim leaders of the conservative sort and a handful of wealthy Algerian landowners;* but neither of these could form a significant political grouping. There remained for nationalism, faced by an absolute French determination to treat Algeria as an integral part of France, only the route of insurrection. This was tried several times, and always with disaster until 1954. There then began an insurrection which succeeded after seven terrible years of colonial repression. In 1962 Algeria became an independent republic under the Front de Libération Nationale (FLN), with one of its outstanding leaders, Ahmed Ben Bella, as its first Premier and then President, until 1965, when an army *coup* led by Colonel Boumédienne deposed him.

Arguing from the experience of examples such as these – and others could be laid beside them – it may be seen that 'tribalism' has taken many forms, but that its effective political strength at the point of independence, or after independence, has been usually in direct relation to the policies of the withdrawing colonial power. Colonialism had divided African peoples in order to rule them. The neo-colonialist influences that remained after independence, or grew stronger after independence, have also had a divisive effect, striking along the lines of weakness within new African structures. Besides this, it is also true that ethnic separatism has continued as a factor on its own, and no

*Of native Algerian landowners, 1 per cent had 21 per cent of the land belonging to Algerians, or an average of about 620 acres each, in 1954. *Cahiers Internationaux*, 1954, No. 64, quoted by I. Potekhin in the *Journal of Modern African Studies*, 1963, Vol. 1, No. 1, Dar-es-Salaam.

doubt will so remain until local autonomies can be effectively combined with regional unities. There has been and there is, in short, both 'tribalism' and tribalism.

How far the genuine article will remain significant during the 1970s will clearly depend on the degree in which progress is made, or not made, toward social structures which are based on the peaceful integration of constituent groupings, toward societies which are capable of yielding a general advance and not a merely sectional one: in other words, toward forms of nationalism which are revolutionary in relation both to traditional structures and to colonialist structures. And this in turn, as we shall see, is likely to depend on a far-reaching shift from élitist forms of rule – of rule by privileged minorities – toward new forms of democratic participation.

10 After 1965: Independence in Travail

By 1964 the forty-odd independent governments of Africa were pledged, if with varying degrees of conviction, to construct more industry, raise standards of living, and provide many other aspects of a modern state. We have sufficiently looked at the reasons for this: the ruin and incapacity of the old way of life; the demand for a new way; the sheer weight of poverty, disease, or boredom; and a sense of profound material inferiority towards the rest of the world. All these and parallel motives had created a public opinion, eager for rapid and even startling change, which no African government could ignore and few could resist.

By 1969 it was a commonplace to say that little of this change had been achieved; that one brave hope after another had gone down in defeat; that policies of reconstruction were often reduced to garments of threadbare rhetoric; and that the whole grand surge of reassertion of the 1950s and early 1960s had vanished, or was fast vanishing, into the sands of disillusion or despair. It was a commonplace that was not always accurate, and even less often helpful. Mostly, indeed, it was not intended to be helpful. All those who had opposed the idea of African equality, or who still opposed it, felt able to beat their breasts in one degree or other of superior derision.

'We see the pandemonium which has taken place in so many countries to the north of us,' the rebel Rhodesian premier, Mr Ian Smith, felt able to explain at a moment when 'his' Africans were suitably beaten into silence or imprisonment: 'we have seen standards of western civilization completely broken down and thrown overboard' (*The Listener*, 9 October 1969). It might be replied that this displayed a peculiar concept of 'western civilization', as resting on race rule and police repression. It certainly displayed a lack of historical sense or capacity for political analysis.

Independence was in crisis: not a doubt of it. But where lay the real seat of the trouble? It would be pretentious in a short book to attempt more than a definition of the dominant lines of conflict and disintegrating pressure. Their detail runs too often through a confusion and complexity that are not surprising in a continent as large and various as this one. Yet the dominant lines of conflict, the basic reasons for frustration, the real motives for 'pandemonium', are sufficiently clear. Essentially they rest in the élitist or bureaucratic nature of the regimes installed at the time of independence, in the ideas of government promoted by retiring colonial patrons, and in the consequent failure to bridge a widening gulf between the few at the top and the many at the bottom.

This is another way of saying that 'neo-colonialism' during the second half of the 1960s acquired a native dress and form, so that political independence, more often than not, remained little more than a façade for ideological and economic subservience. To this extent, of course, the crisis was and is not only African. Far more than that, it was and is part of a wider crisis in which the modern world, apparently incapable of resolving its problems allows a few rich peoples to become continually richer while ensuring that many poor peoples, no matter how hard they run, should fall ever more deeply into poverty.

This being the case, it is a question whether one may not even welcome – aside from its tragic aspects – the breakdown of regimes installed at the time of independence. For this breakdown was also the witness to a widespread refusal by Africans to accept rule by privileged minorities, unconscionable élites, or individuals incapable of putting the interest of their countries above the advancement of their careers. Distressing though the condition of much of Africa might be in 1969, it was at least one in which the determination to find better leaders, more hopeful forms of society, a kindlier future, stayed vibrantly alive.

It is also a question whether things could have been any different. People who think like Mr Smith may find repressive laws and ample jails a sufficient guarantee of 'civilization'. But those who look for something rather less ungenerous will scarcely expect the jagged upheavals of decolonization to give way, as by the waving of a wand, to the pleasant order of a tolerant and peaceful life. Large and difficult transitions, reaching over from one mode of society to another, simply do not happen that way.

The true position is contradictory. There may be much frustration. Yet this is in some measure a product of the very advances made since the 1950s. Africa today may face a major crisis of growth. But at least there is no independent African people today that is not far better placed to understand the problems of this crisis, if not to solve them, than in previous years.

The contradiction between progress and stagnation, even regression, has been present everywhere, even in those countries which have seemed most stable. Thus President Tubman of Liberia and Emperor Haile Selassie of Ethiopia, both of them conservative by formation as well as confronted with strongly traditional conservatism in their regimes, have each been engaged in pushing their countries, if by very different routes, into the middle of the twentieth century. Ethiopia is no longer the merely feudalistic structure of its long history, though it remains partly that. By this fact alone Ethiopia is latently, perhaps actually, in critical instability: new pressures thrust forward, new aspirations demand freedom. But to see only the local crisis – the need for a new framework to displace imperial authority – is to ignore the constructive reasons for it.

Modern Liberia is likewise different from the mere coastal oligarchy of American settlers, floated off the rocks of insolvency by the cash of an American rubber corporation, that President Tubman took in hand nearly thirty years ago. Liberia's regime may still look like 'a virtual oligarchy', with 'corruption ... possibly more deeply engrained in the Liberian polity than anywhere else in West Africa'. Tubman's policy has none the less been 'an effort to redress the balance of power in favour of the tribal elements of the interior at the expense of the settler minority around the capital'.[135]

Yet the legacy of the past is also still there. A group of American experts found in 1961-2 that 'the lives of all Liberians could be markedly improved within a generation', provided that the government were to operate 'an intelligent and honest development policy'. Liberia, in other words, suffered and suffers with other countries from élitist forms of rule, no matter what President Tubman may intend. The same experts discovered to their indignation that 'the relinquished developmental opportunities because of prestige outlays are very great. Government expenditures on diplomacy amounted to 8 per cent of the 1960 budget, while those on education amounted to only 10 per cent. Some $50 million have been spent during the past five years on expensive public buildings ... The primary obstacles to economic progress in Liberia are not technical but social – political and institutional residues of an earlier era.' And, to spell out the real nature of the trouble, these experts went on to assert that 'Liberia is being run – and run inefficiently, in terms of development – by a handful of people. Close family ties developed in response to earlier pioneer conditions inhibit efficient conduct of government by encouraging nepotism and large-scale outlays for unproductive purposes.'[136]

This was no longer quite the situation of 1969, when new and healthier trends were making themselves felt. But one may note in passing, as one of the problems with which reforming Africans have had to contend, that these opinions were produced by experts sent to Liberia by the U.S. Agency for International Development, an arm of the U.S. Government. Like other such agencies, AID has frowned most disapprovingly on those very countries which, by moving toward non-capitalist forms of development, have tried to break away from the sort of élitist structures responsible for 'close family ties', for 'nepotism', and for 'large-scale outlays for unproductive purposes'. The experts of the West may have seen the need for radical change in Africa; their governments have had quite another idea of what is desirable.

The Ivory Coast, a potentially rich ex-colony of France in West Africa, has offered and offers the same contradictions in still more startling form. Since independence in 1960, the Ivory Coast under President Felix Houphouët-Boigny's thrusting leadership has shown, according to the U.N., an economic growth rate of well over six per cent, and an annual national income considerably higher than the African average. Investment has risen steadily; recurrent budget surpluses have allowed spending on development; expenditures for administration have been comparatively a good deal lower than in many other countries.

But does this 'economic miracle' mean that Houphouët's regime has found its new society, its liberating structure, its pathway to a better future for its people? A closer glance can suggest otherwise. For the 'miracle' has evidently rested on no basic structural change from colonial times, on no subsequent narrowing of the gap between the few at the top and the many at the bottom, on no sure advance to self-determination. If there is a boom in agriculture, it is a boom in export crops, very much according to the colonial pattern. In 1969 the Ivory Coast was a net *importer* of food – and this in a relatively rich country where farming plays a dominant role in the economy. Increased food exports have been obtained much too easily, according to one observer, 'with little direct investment in agriculture itself (only in transport infrastructure)'.[137]

Another side to the Ivory Coast picture returns the same conclusion. Partnership with French and other European Common Market investors exacts its price, whether in sovereignty or in direction of development. The same observer could find that 'the employment – at very high rates – of foreign capital, whose domination over the whole of the country's economy is exercised in the most absolute way, means that the country's growth has been purely dependent on outside factors'.

All the same a useful development of capitalism, a new system of enterprise? There may be some reason to doubt it. For if it is true that there are more Ivory Coast capitalists than before, it is also true that rather few of them are Africans. Here, as elsewhere, the ruling élite is essentially bureaucratic and entrepreneurial: 'If one can speak of the development of capitalism in the Ivory Coast, one cannot speak of the development of an Ivoirian capitalism.'[138]

Mr Smith and his friends may rejoice in the friendly stability of this booming oligarchy, always willing to set 'practical questions' above 'ideological sentimentalism', and to remember that business is business. Others may wonder about the true condition of the mass of food producers in a country which has concentrated on the export of plantation crops at the expense of local food consumption, or about the likely feelings of all those thousands of migrant workers who, year after year, tramp down from the Volta Republic to man plantations for wages which, to put it mildly, are far from 'miraculous'.

There have been, there are now, other regimes which have preferred the easy road of minority enrichment to the tough work of solving basic problems. This, as will be seen, is precisely what took place in the first Nigerian federation after 1960.

The degree and direction of change are obviously governed to a large extent by the 'inherited situation'. One sees this very clearly in North Africa. If it was possible for independent Tunisia to avoid major upheavals, at any rate so far as the basic economic structure of society was concerned – even to the point, indeed, where the national economic plan could be officially described as 'a sort of councilling agency to assist private companies in defining their projects'[139] – this was certainly not the case with Egypt.*

Egypt was a country, characteristic of its semi-colonial type, where the rich were getting richer and the poor more numerous at a visible annual rate, and where the poor vastly outnumbered the rich. Nothing short of great structural reform could have prevented this society from deepening internal crisis. Much of this reform, duly undertaken by Gamal Nasser's regime in the past fifteen years, was necessarily in a radical direction: the expropriation of royal and some other large estates, massive public investment in land reclamation and hydraulic works, widespread promotion of forms of peasant cooperation – these and other such steps were scarcely open to question if the regime were to show any real progress, although this did not mean that they were therefore easy to take.

*An initial land reform in Tunisia has limited holdings to a maximum size of 50 hectares (110 acres), and in 1963 there were moves toward further structural re-organization.

The question for Nasser then became: what next? Beyond such reforms there was a choice to be made. Nasser's choice of 'Arab socialism' or 'democratic cooperative socialism', as it was variously described in the official press, bore the imprint of many traditions: Muslim conservatism, the mental formation of Egyptian officers, socialist agitation as well as capitalist pressure, but above all, perhaps, the country's ancient habit of highly centralized direction.

By 1962 this particular choice had begun to make itself felt. In some ways it seemed a contradictory sort of choice. The government was claiming to have helped the mass of people by redistributing about ten per cent of the total area under cultivation; but most of the 226,000 families who benefited from this were small rather than landless peasants, and the needs of the latter were barely touched.[140] 'Arab socialism' was claiming to have set the people free; but the prisons were crammed with socialists, and of course, communists. The further question for Nasser then became: could his choice now find ways of stabilizing – and this, in the circumstances, meant democratizing – a new structure imposed from the top, since its capacity for social growth was otherwise all too likely to remain minimal? The year of 1963 brought some interesting answers to this question: among them, indeed, a steady release of political prisoners and a further instalment of social reform, especially on the land.

Egypt after 1963 thus presented the encouraging spectacle of a country where necessary structural change was already taking place, or was at least intended. Yet the will to effect such large and difficult transformations in social structure supposed a means, in popular understanding and support, that were scarcely present. To switch from the narrow and restrictive concepts of military rule to a democratic system of 'people's rule' proved a transition altogether too hard for the available bureaucracy and its emanations in party politics. Orders might be given at the top; it was far from certain that they were followed lower down, or, if followed, understood. Egypt's rulers came up against the harsh fact that you cannot build a revolution from the top: you have to start at the bottom, you have to hand over power to the people down below. President Nasser himself remained a powerful and popular figure, even in spite of the destructive blows struck by Israel; the structure of the regime, for the most part, barely changed. Yet it could still be said that the way ahead had at any rate been opened.

Nothing like this could be said of Morocco. There a 'leftist' foreign policy has been utilized, not without skill, to cover a general domestic stagnation. No structural reforms of any magnitude have yet occurred in the antiquated landowning and *métayage* systems; French investment capital has dried up and little has yet been found among businessmen at home; while the population is said to have increased by more than a fifth in the past ten years. Here the 'inherited situation' has continued to obstruct new policies of growth. Morocco is a country which has yet to find its way ahead.

In Algeria, next door, the FLN early declared that its war for independence must aim at a complete renewal of society: the sufferings and sacrifices could be justified by nothing less. Radical reorganization of land ownership and land use was high on the programme. Not surprisingly. 'At the beginning of the Algerian Revolution' – November 1954 – 'six million Algerians were living or rather subsisting on an average annual income per head of 16,000 old francs (about £12) ...'[141] This being so, the 'Algerian Revolution ... is not and cannot be a simple fight for the conquest of political power. For us ... it is a political, economic, and social Revolution.'[142] *El Moudjahid*, official journal of the FLN explained in 1960 that 'the land reform of tomorrow will be necessarily and ineluctably an *agrarian revolution* [italics in original] or it will be nothing'. In December 1961 the journal went further. The reconstruction of Algeria could take place only on the basis of 'a genuine land reform which will allow a progressive structure of landownership', and 'will banish capitalist forms of production by decisively limiting the size of individual property ... Whether within the framework of family holdings, or within that of much larger properties taken in hand by the community, or by the state, we must prepare for the collective organization of farming – alone capable of improving the productivity of the land by the use of modern methods and means of cultivation.'[143]

Taking over a ravaged country from which most of the European landowners had fled, and where thousands of peasants had lost home and livelihood, the newly independent government headed by Ben Bella had gone some way by the autumn of 1963 to make good these wartime promises. They were helped in this by the voluntary abandonment of French estates in the fertile regions. During the winter of 1962 peasant workers had begun cultivating land left idle by their former employers. In March the government legalized these 'take-overs', covering in all about 3,300,000 acres of the country's best farming country. In the following October Ben Bella declared that 'every hectare' of land belonging to French settlers was now nationalized, thus adding about another 3,000,000 acres to the expropriated total. At the same time it was announced that large Muslim landowners would also lose some of their property, though it had still to be decided exactly how much. The eventual aim was to bring under public ownership about half of Algeria's cultivable land.

An essential feature of this structural change was that the nationalized estates were not divided among individual peasants but handed to the community of all those who worked on them. These communities formed *assemblés d'autogestion* which in turn elected *comités d'autogestion*, self-management committees; and these, flanked by government-appointed managers, numbered by October as many as 1,800, with others being continually formed.[144] Though suffering from a desperate shortage of cash, mechanics, and book-keepers, and still lacking an efficient administration to take the place of the French, the new machinery of state and of workers' self-management had begun to appear as much more than a promising experiment.

Later events threw doubt upon these hopes of radical enlargement. The military who came to power in 1965 (see p. 145) might broadly accept the need for the kind of advances promised by the FLN during and immediately after the war of 1954–62: land reform, self-management by peasant and workers' collectivities, the building of an industrial base for Algeria's economy, a large expansion of social and educational services going hand-in-hand with new democratic structures. And on the technical side the soldiers proved far from incapable. The Boumédienne regime proved able to strengthen the Algerian state, to repair much of the material damage of the war, and to take a strong line with foreign owners and investors. They successfully encouraged the growth of new industries, particularly in textiles and fertilizers: a steel works built by collaboration with France, the U.S.S.R., West Germany and Italy – itself no mean proof of the regime's capacity for 'constructive neutralism' – is expected to produce a million tons of steel in 1976.

Early in 1970 President Boumédienne was insisting once again on the need for new democratic structures, and on his government's determination to set about building them. But here the weakness in basic political thought seemed very evident. The 'internal revolution' had failed to arrive; and not surprisingly. Shortly before being ousted by the military in June, 1965, Ben Bella had offered the key to understanding this failure. Robert Merle hands it on in his book about Ben Bella, published later in the same year. 'The Algerian revolution,' Ben Bella had said then, 'was a revolution made without an ideology. This lacuna permitted a broad union against the colonial power during the time of our war. Once peace came, it proved a dangerous void.' Technicians greatly concerned with efficiency and action, the soldiers were able to fill this void only with hopeful words. The lands placed under peasant self-management might cover most of the property formerly owned by European settlers, and total about a third of cultivable land; but in 1969 the promised land-reform for the rest of the country had still failed to materialize. Workers' self-management in industry included only 15,000 workers out of a total of about 130,000. Temporarily thrown off in the euphoria of liberation, the veil was once again the rule for the vast majority of Algerian women. Education had made considerable progress, yet more in form than in content.

The regime, true enough, still liked to call itself socialist. But 'when you take a close look,' according to a generally sympathetic review of 1969 by Claude Collin in the Paris political quarterly, *Les Temps Modernes*, for November 1969, 'you see that the system is socialist in no more than name, and that the term 'state capitalism' would suit it far better, a state capitalism resting on technocracy and highly centralized national corporations.' Real power lay with a 'new class' of businessmen, young technicians, and civil and military bureaucrats. 'Against a dying private sector, and a bloodless self-management sector, this "new class" is profoundly influential in the present regime, and generally controls the apparatus of State and Party.' The same writer went on to recall that the Algiers Charter of 1964, aimed at laying the ideological foundations of a new Algeria, had warned against the danger of 'a bureaucratic bourgeoisie formed within the apparatus of government, state and party'. Today, he concluded, this bureaucratic bourgeoisie 'appears firmly established and in place for a long time . . .' To build new democratic structures capable of engaging the active participation and enthusiasm of the masses of the people would clearly be a painful task in this situation. At the same time it was also clear that expansive aspects of the regime installed in 1965 were none the less able to give reality to the idea of Algerian independence, as well as to promote a certain economic progress.

These North African contrasts in policy and posture have been reflected in the countries south of the Sahara, though in a different context of daily life and traditional attitude. Here, too, there has been a common point of reference in emphasis on public investment – on state capitalism – whether for public utilities and services, for raising the productivity of farmers, or for laying the foundations of industry.

Yet here again the contradiction between post-colonial advance and post-colonial frustration remained obvious in every region. Everywhere, by 1969, the root problem was the same: how to move forward from a merely political independence, often little more than a verbal independence, with its correspondingly shallow base in popular involvement, to a much deeper independence such as could inspire and liberate the energies and determination, as well as the self-sacrifice, of millions of ordinary folk. The 'myths and slogans' of the run-up to political independence had well served their purpose. Now, in the more testing circumstances of the late 1960s, something more solidly helpful was required. The root problem, in other words, was how to produce democratic systems capable of meeting the challenge of far-reaching social and economic change. No kind of 'rule-by-decree' could hope to do this job, no kind of 'police socialism', no kind of militarized 'law and order'.

Nobody who has thought deeply about Africa will ever have doubted the magnitude of this problem, or looked for any quick and painless solution. Outside the rhetoric of propaganda, the case for decolonization had never rested on any belief that Africans would at once accede to an untroubled peace and progress. The case for decolonization lay in the simple fact that no movement towards peace and progress could be possible without decolonization. Before anything else could be attempted, it was necessary to get rid of colonial rule. Getting rid of colonial rule was the indispensable condition for advance. It was in no sense a guarantee of advance. Its blessing was an opportunity.

African peoples have grasped this opportunity according to their circumstances and their chances. Some were very small or very poor, and found the task extremely difficult. Even in 1969, for example, the ex-colonies of French Equatoria were still at an early stage of transition from traditional and colonial ways of life. They had been the Cinderellas of the French Empire. Milked by concession companies from 1900 till 1930, they were never able to achieve the comparatively favoured posture of some of the French West African territories, not to speak of some of the British ones, whose position was better again.

Other peoples, such as those of Southern Rhodesia, South Africa, and the Portuguese colonies – constitutionally called 'oversea territories of Portugal', a distinction without a difference – had not been able even to begin their work of reconstruction. Albeit with growing resistance, they continued to live within the structures imposed by colonial or apartheid rule.

Others again, including those of Ghana, Guinea, Mali, Tanzania, had embarked with varying results on the hard road to structural change, to forms of political life such as could embrace village people as well as urban masses. We shall take a look at these in a moment. Before doing that, however, it will be useful to consider some large examples of frustration.

Nigeria is perhaps the crucial example. The most populous and in some ways the most exciting country in all Africa, this great territory is remarkable for its rich history, range of traditional wisdom, variety of energetic populations, and actual or potential wealth in soil and oil and minerals. By 1967 the country was falling apart, and yet it was fairly remarkable that it should even have begun independence as a federation, since it contains three major regions of which each has a population as large as many other African states. Had these three regions fallen to the 'tutelage' of different European powers, or within different colonial frontiers, they could scarcely have come together. Each has strong characteristics of its own. Each has a long and in many respects sovereign history of its own – the history of Yorubaland in the West, of the Hausa, Bornu, and Fulani states in the North, of those of the Niger Delta and the Ibo in the East. Within all these regions there are many lesser contrasts, so many indeed that political programmes often spoke of the need to 'regionalize' Nigeria into twenty or even more autonomous states. If the same ideas had governed British policy in Nigeria during the pre-independence years as governed British policy in Kenya during the same period, Nigeria might indeed have embarked on independence as a cluster of states. Paradoxically, the chances of future Nigerian unity might then have been much greater.

But Nigerian nationalism during the 1950s – aided by a clear British preference for the territorial *status quo* – desired unity; and this proved decisive. That in itself was much, and it may be unrealistic to have expected any more. The major effort at winning independence within a Nigerian framework, coupled with the often ticklish problems of combining this with a reasonable measure of regional autonomy, occupied all energies.

The late Sardauna of Sokoto put this point with a graceful irony when writing, in his autobiography of 1962, of the problems of political growth.

So far, none of the 'political' parties have produced programmes markedly different from each other. ... The reason is simple. In the old days, when the British were the 'government', all parties concentrated on demanding self-government to the exclusion of all else. . . . Attacking the existing government was the main occupation, and it was not particularly difficult and did not demand any real thought. Naturally, when the British withdrew gradually, and the power passed, there was no one to attack and, as we had got self-government, there was nothing more to be said about it. So far no burning question has arisen on which we are likely to take sides strongly.

The upshot, as an American investigator, Professor Bretton of Michigan University, observed in 1963, was that Nigeria had come to independence 'without any real ideology, even a negative one, in its ruling circles'.[145] This seemed also true of Sierra Leone, a country which deserves far closer attention than space will here allow.

These Nigerian 'ruling circles' in any case found it difficult to see the present in terms of dynamic transition to a different future. They were heavily weighted on the traditional and conservative side of African life, especially in the North, where power had passed largely into the hands of the traditional Fulani emirs – much less open to democratic pressure, as the Sardauna of Sokoto himself pointed out,[146] than in pre-British times – and in the West, where that subtle nexus of political and commercial interest represented by the enterprising chiefs of Yorubaland had remained the real seat of authority. This conservative pattern of political life, anointed in 1960 with the unction of Westminster parliamentarianism, misled many non-Africans into imagining that Nigeria was, in fact, really no different from a rather poor though promising member of the West European community of nations. Hence it came as a bitter disappointment when this 'most promising' of all the 'Western bulwarks', welcomed as showing so many signs of having embraced 'Western civilization' in its most parliamentary sense, broke down in 1966, passed through two military *coups*, became the scene of massacre by one people of another, and in 1967 was most bitterly at war with itself.

Some critics seized this opportunity to speak glumly of a 'reversion to tribalism'. This was another misunderstanding. The concept of 'tribalism' was perfectly inadequate to explain the manifestations and rivalries of ethnic and cultural separatism which had long existed here. Aside from this, the trouble clearly lay much deeper than disruptions caused by local loyalties in conflict with central government. The crisis, essentially, was not of 'tribe against tribe', but of traditional modes of political life and attitude at grips with modern problems and demands.

Individuals were partly to blame. It was manifestly true, as the Coker Commission showed, that a number of people in Nigeria's 'ruling circles' saw their country not as a society to be passionately believed in, but – the words are Bretton's – 'one which was more of a vehicle for personal advancement'. Others saw it as a vehicle for conserving customary forms of hierarchical power. Yet these individual attitudes were also the personal reflection of a national problem. Could traditional modes of political life, even though modified by parliamentary processes, possibly avail to shift Nigeria out of her poverty and ignorance into the leading position she could undoubtedly aspire to claim? Falling standards of living for many people in the towns, far too slow an advance in the countryside, haphazard or superficial planning: all these seemed to answer in the negative. This vast and many-sided country certainly enjoyed a high measure of stability; but the stability appeared to have come perilously near stagnation. And nobody seemed to have any clear or consistent policy for getting on the move again.

Towards 1963, accordingly, bitter troubles began to gather force. 'Today,' wrote a distinguished Nigerian schoolmaster and journalist, 'one thing is clear in the minds of the young elements in our country – Nigeria is not being effectively governed. Our government is a hydra-headed octopus that veers and backs, depending on the prevailing planetary and political winds, and that oscillates and flounders and hopes, whatever happens, for the best. It is not purposive; it is not logical; it is not disciplined.'[147] Another well-known Nigerian journalist, Gabriel Fagbure (Lagos *Sunday Times*, 15 December 1963), condemned 'the appalling mismanagement of our public affairs, the lack of sense of direction on the national level, the moral depravity of our society . . .'

London's most consistently intelligent commentary on Nigerian affairs put it more gently: 'The real crisis in Nigeria is its unique experiment of meeting the challenges of a new, vast, multi-tribal state in Africa with all the borrowed apparatus of Western democracy. Nigerians are now deciding whether this structure should be modified or whether they can, after all, make it work as it is.'[148] In other words, the central 'problem of power' was resolved for the time being, but resolved in a conservative sense. Though often locally effective, this solution was soon to be revealed as totally incapable of facing the severe challenge of modernizing a united Nigeria.

One saw all this most clearly in Nigerian ideas about planning for development. Some forms of planning had been undertaken by the British, and with positive results. By the end of 1952–3 a total of £28·5 millions had been spent under Nigerian programmes of the Colonial Development and Welfare Scheme, just over half of which had come from Nigerian sources.[149] But this was planning of a primitive sort, limited to little more than raising funds and spending them on desirable objectives, stopping far short of the principles of a planned economy which were to emerge later. There was to be state enterprise and private enterprise, but which was to control the other? The question was crucial in deciding the shape and direction of Nigeria's economic growth; but it was not asked.

'We intend,' declared an Eastern Region planning report of 1955, 'that statutory corporations should be created with the idea of administering certain new and complex functions for which civil-service organization is inadequate whilst, on the other hand, private enterprise is too mercenary and profit-seeking.' But this report could none the less recommend the creation of a Finance Corporation which should make 'liberal advances to hard-pressed business organizations'.[150] And the same ambivalent attitude to the vital question of economic control, to the choice of direction – *either* towards state capitalism leading into socialism *or* towards state capitalism leading into 'free enterprise' – governed the later and much larger all-Nigeria economic plan of 1962.

It might be a good aspect of this ambitious plan that the lion's share of responsibility and spending should lie with the federal government, whose authority and influence would be correspondingly reinforced to the advantage of Nigerian unity. But the plan itself was on the old 'shopping list' lines. Its root idea seems to have been that state investment should pave the way for private investment. Great hopes were placed in stimulating the growth of private business among Nigerians: a sum of £4 millions, for example, was allocated to the establishment of a Development Bank 'in which private Nigerian investors, foreign private investors, and the International Bank and its affiliates will, it is hoped, participate'. Meanwhile, large industrial and utility projects were planned for which the state (whether by federal or regional government) and foreign capital would join in common effort. Of the total projected sum of £676 millions to be spent in development over six years, foreign aid was to provide £339 millions, or just over half.[151]

This was an almost classical application of a colonial policy dominant during the 1950s. A responsible 'middle class' should take over power, operating through parliamentary institutions as nearly like those of Westminster as possible, and should promote its country's interests by advancing its own. By such means, Nigeria was supposed to emerge in a few years as a democracy founded not only on the patterns of Westminster but, much more important, on the reality of a flourishing middle class. This 'middle class solution' would remould Nigerian institutions – pushing ahead with education, developing industries and communications, laying 'tribalism' finally on the shelf – and would turn Nigeria, in so doing, into a bastion of the Western way of life.

No such thing came to pass. This was indeed precisely an extension of what Bretton shrewdly called the 'new myth of wishful thinking' about Nigeria which had grown up in Europe and North America – the myth which 'mistakes the community of interests between the leading Western countries and a group of Nigerian leaders oriented towards the *status quo* for a valid formula to cope with Nigeria's problems'. In order to be a 'valid formula' of this kind, Nigeria's middle class would have had to be large, coherent, inured to political responsibility, and widely spread throughout the regions.

Now the middle class of Nigeria might be in a healthier

condition than most 'middle classes' in Africa, but it was scarcely any of these things in adequate measure, while events after 1963 in the Western Region proved that its readiness for political responsibility would often fall short of the most minimal requirement. And while parallels with Europe or South America may quickly mislead, the world has often seen that representative government cannot in any case be reconciled with rule by a financial and commercial oligarchy – even if Nigeria's middle class could claim to have reached that status. Long before the *coup* of January 1966 it was evident that the system of power in Nigeria, insistently aiming at the promotion of a middle class which was to dominate the country, must either run aground on its own incapacity or else, provoked by growing popular pressure for a better life which it could not provide, open the road to autocratic forms of rule. Here again it was demonstrated that a *democratic* installation and early growth of capitalism could be no more possible in Nigeria than it had been in Europe.

It remains true that Nigeria moved significantly in the years after 1960. Primary as well as secondary education achieved much progress in the two southern regions, and began to do the same in the very conservative north; while the Plan, whatever its basic failings, took care to provide plenty of money (potentially at least) for medical and other services. Universities expanded with help from the United States and elsewhere, and with much drive and enthusiasm at home. Yet the very success of Nigeria's widely spreading educational facilities again acutely raised the problem of development. A record number of children left primary school in the Eastern Region in 1963; but how many could be sure of finding a quick road to skilled employment, or even any gainful employment? The answer is suggested by experience in the Western Region. Of about 100,000 children leaving primary school every year in the Western Region, a White Paper of 1963 pointed out, only half 'gain admission into other schools for further education, *or find useful employment*' (my italics).

This was one cause for worry that began to lead Nigerians to question the 'middle-class' theory of growth. It was not difficult to understand their doubts. By the methods of 'free enterprise' – of promoting a large and responsible middle class through state capitalism and foreign private investment – the building of a 'welfare economy' must clearly take a long time, even (on precedents abroad) a very long time. Yet it was time, precisely, that remained in short supply. Aside from the question of post-primary employment, there was the even more pressing problem of what happened to the large numbers of young men and women whom the country's multiplying secondary schools were now turning out every year. These young folk might be excused for wanting well-paid 'nine-to-five' jobs in city commerce and the professions; yet what the country really needed of them was low-paid service in humble schools and remote villages. But the familiar pressures of middle-class formation in an economy of 'booming individualism' continually presented them with the glittering ideal of the *personal career*, and, by so doing, continually devalued the ideal of service to the community in favour of service to self.

Aside from this question of service, however vital to continued social and economic growth, there was another pressing problem. What were these young folk going to do and think when they could not find the *personal careers* to which they had been led to believe themselves entitled? Would they really be content to put their certificates into a drawer along with their white collars and ties and neat blouses, and labour quietly at low-paid work until the slow processes of capital-formation and investment had provided what the economists call 'take off' – had fired that swift and sudden rise to higher standards which are possible, or should be possible, once the infra-structure of industrial development is laid? Putting it another way, how could you achieve an atmosphere of social service in a system geared to personal advancement?

In a somewhat different direction, it was relevant to such questions that a great deal of planned development was to be provided by the investment of state-accumulated reserves from various forms of taxation and marketing-board activity. A sound and necessary policy: but were those farmers whose work had created these reserves, or a large part of them, really going to be content to see them concentrated on the building of a commercial and industrial middle class? And if not, what influence might such pressures bring to bear on Nigeria's already precarious structure of parliamentary government? The private interests of a small minority – and this is what a middle class must here remain for a long time to come – were increasingly revealed as incompatible with the interests of the majority of people.

This deepening unpopularity, not to say growing hatred, of the new 'middle class' of Federal beneficiaries was quickened by another emotion still more explosive – the connected southern fear of permanent northern domination, 'constitutionally' or not, through an alliance between a sufficient number of these beneficiaries and the conservative rulers of the north. People watched events in the Western (Yoruba) Region and saw in them a dreadful warning of the probable shape of things to come.

When the Federal bubble burst in January 1966, the West had been in uproar for months. Dozens of people, perhaps hundreds, had been killed in political riots. I know of no more succinct account of the reasons for this than a report in *Time* magazine for 19 November, 1965. Three years earlier a frankly minority government under Akintola had been imposed on the West by Federal – indirectly, that is, by Northern – command. In October there were new regional elections. *Time* recalled (what everyone knew) that 'Chief Samuel Akintola's pro-North government faced apparently overwhelming opposition. Akintola himself had little popular support; he had been appointed Premier three years ago after a blatant power play that sent anti-North Chief Obafemi Awolowo to jail. But when regional elections rolled around last month [October 1965], Akintola showed that there was more than one way to win the West. To the surprise of hardly anyone, he rigged the elections.

'Key election officials were kidnapped, key opposition candidates kept off the ballots entirely. In heavy Awolowo precincts, polling places mysteriously ran out of ballots, and Akintola's stalwarts stuffed the ballot boxes in others...' The Akintola faction 'won' by 78 seats to 18. This meant that the Northern leader, Sir Ahmadu Bello, could now continue to dominate the Federal parliament through an alliance between this faction and the Northern People's Congress which Bello controlled. But his triumph was a brief one.

Early on 15 January, and with initial success, a small group of army captains and majors declared themselves in revolt. They appear to have had three principal aims. One was to break the Bello-Akintola alliance beyond hope of repair. Another was to end the division of Nigeria into water-tight regions. And a third, closely linked to these, was to eliminate from power the most hated of the 'middle class' beneficiaries, headed by that master in the techniques of getting rich quickly at the expense of the public purse, the Finance Minister Okotie Eboh. Nigeria could then make a fresh start with clean hands. But these military rebels were nearly all Ibos of the East, and their enemies at once declared them the tools of an 'Ibo plot' to dominate Nigeria.

The men of 15 January went a long way towards securing their aims by the simple if odious method of assassination. Bello, Akintola, Okotie Eboh were all killed at once, and also, more puzzlingly, the (Northern) Federal Prime Minister Sir Abubakar Tafawa Balewa. In widespread southern rejoicing, the Federal regime vanished overnight, and the 'revolutionary majors', at least in the south, became popular heroes. Almost immediately, however, their *coup* was taken over by the army commander, General Aguiyi-Ironsi, who put them in jail and tried to govern himself. He made some effort. He abolished the federal system, appointed military governors for each of the Regions, and proceeded towards the establishment of a new and unified structure in which all real power was to be at the centre in a country which was to be divided into thirty-five provinces with purely local authority. Civilian rule was to be restored 'as soon as possible', although how this was to be done without calling back the politicians, now entirely out of office and, in some cases, up before courts of inquiry into corruption, was a different question.

It was never answered. On the night of 28 July, 1966, Northern sections of the army mutinied in the Western Region. Aguiyi-Ironsi, who happened to be in the Western city of Ibadan at the time, was taken and shot, though his death was concealed for many months. The rulers of the North had bided their time; now they moved in. A new military leader, Lieutenant-Colonel

Gowon, took over power on behalf of an army whose effective fighting units and command were nearly all men from the North. Unfortunately for Gowon, a reasonable man of good intentions, there were those who now wanted more than power. It became evident that they also wanted revenge. This might have mattered less if Gowon had then possessed any strong power inside the Northern Region: at any rate at first, he could act as little more than the man in the 'central office' in Lagos.

Fearful events shook the country. Their pattern had been set in the previous May. Hundreds of Ibos living in the North, where they had an active part in local trade, were killed by Northern mobs; countless others had lost their property or jobs, or both. Now, in September and October 1966, the Northern Ibos suffered again, this time far worse. Many thousands of Ibo men, women and even children were massacred. It was said afterwards that scarcely a single family had escaped some grievous loss and tragedy. Inevitably, those who managed to survive fled to their homeland. There came a mass withdrawal of Ibos into the Eastern Region; and talk of secession now acquired a new realism. By early 1967 the Eastern Region had become to all intents and purposes a separate state, although efforts continued to be made to patch up some minimal compromise whereby at least a notional all-Nigerian government might continue to exist. Little came of these efforts: by now, the gap was fatefully wide. Federal pressure grew stronger. Then on 30 May the Eastern leader, Colonel Ojukwu, declared Eastern Nigeria a secessionist state as the Republic of Biafra, and outright warfare followed.

It was a sad *dénouement*. Fifteen years of the 'middle class solution', eight before independence in 1960 and seven after, appeared to have gone for nothing; and all the early hopes of unity and progress seemed now to have been swept away on a torrent of unresolved problems, whether national or local.

Greater sadness followed. Launched in June 1967, the war bitterly continued. If by the end of 1969 the territory still held by Ojukwu's army and administration was little more than half the Ibo homeland and only about five per cent of the whole territory of Nigeria, it was still the scene of costly resistance. Countless thousands had lost their lives in the previous three years, chiefly by starvation; much had been wrecked; hatred and resentment had grown with fear and desperation. Foreign intervention made matters worse, together with an ardent pro-Biafran propaganda in the outside world which, not seldom, served purposes that had nothing to do with African advancement.

The federal government in Lagos under General Gowon's leadership countered on two fronts. Militarily, his army continued to recover control of the old Eastern Region, rapidly enclosing Enugu, the capital, and installing a new administration under an Ibo official, Ukpabi Asika. Growing in stature and experience, Gowon also pressed on with a political solution. The reshaping of the Nigerian Federation from four into twelve autonomous states, proclaimed on 31 May 1967, was not forgotten; some progress was made towards realizing it. This progress was especially important in the centre and south-east. In the centre the Tiv people won their long-desired autonomy within a new Benue Plateau State. In the south-east, two new states were carved from the old Eastern Region (the area claimed as Biafra). These were the Rivers and the South-East States, giving the Kalabari, Efik and other non-Ibo peoples of the Delta a real say in running their own affairs. Meanwhile there was similar progress towards carving up the rest of the old Northern Region, with the emergence there of five new states as well as the Benue Plateau State

Though strangely ignored in the outside world, this reshaping opened the prospect of a very different kind of federation from the one that had acceded to independence in 1960. At the end of 1969 the emergent picture looked like this:

States of the Reorganized Federation

(populations in millions)

West	9·5	Benue Plateau	3·8
North East	7·9	South East	3·6
East Central	7·2	Mid West	2·5
Kano	5·8	Kwara	2·4
North West	5·7	Rivers	1·5
North Central	4·1	Lagos	1·4

Critics argued that this reorganization was far from complete – rather as though it should somehow have been fashioned overnight – and that 'common services' institutions still tied the states of the old Northern Region into the same structure. The federalists replied that devolution was going steadily ahead, and would be carried to the end. In their own defence they could also point to another argument for believing that the old Federation of four states or regions was well and truly dead. This was the undoubted emergence of three autonomous states for the Tiv and Delta peoples. These lost no time in making it clear, at least to anyone who cared to ask them, that they had no intention of giving up their gains.

Even assuming that peace were established within a twelve-state federation, the end of 1969 showed that many great difficulties must still remain. These were most acute in the old Western Region, where the intra-Yoruba conflicts of 1965 had yet to be resolved. It would be optimistic to think that the old lords of the North might not try, even at this late hour, for a come-back. The problems of building a new political life, infused with new political ideas and led by new political thinkers, were similarly obvious. None of this was denied. What was claimed in Lagos was that a new and workable federation could now take shape, politically better balanced than before, and capable of yielding economic progress for the many as well as for the few. It was a claim that nobody who looked at the facts, with whatever degree of scepticism, could easily set aside.

Unhappily, outside Nigeria, there were a great many people who refused to look at the facts. As the embattled Ibo multiplied their appeals for aid, they became generally presented as the victims of a Muslim (old Northern Region) conspiracy against Christians, or, alternatively, of the machinations of British imperialism. The one picture might be as unreal as the other. Yet a large number of folk without the least experience of Nigeria, or indeed of any other part of Africa, suddenly became sure that they were 'experts' for whom the Biafran cause was practically a holy crusade.

This took place in spite of alliances which seemed extraordinary at the time, as well as for long afterwards. While multiplying their military effort against the nationalists in their own colonies, the Portuguese Government and army came forward with supplies to Biafra of warlike stores, as well as with critically useful logistic support, so that the Portuguese airbase of Bissau (in Guiné) and another Portuguese airbase on São Thomé island (likewise a Portuguese colony), became of continuously crucial value to the Biafran leaders and their armed forces. The South African regime hastened in with cries of approval, and, according to *The Times* (12 March 1968), with military help by way of Portuguese airfields. The French Government, a major arms supplier to South Africa, obeyed its own logic by becoming, at least in 1968, a major arms supplier to Biafra as well.

None of this, it was noted with astonishment, dissuaded otherwise radical Frenchmen and others from denouncing the federal Nigerian cause as though it represented the long arm of the Devil himself. I recall arguing in Paris, one evening of 1968, with a well-known French writer who was and is generally regarded as a pillar of radical thought. He clearly thought me just another 'sell-out to British imperialism'; but his own knowledge of the case appeared perilously small. When I spoke about the new autonomy of the Tiv, as pointing to a clear termination of the old solidity of the North, he asked me who the Tiv might be and how their name was spelt.

Like many others, he confused the Ibo case with the case for Biafra, merely ignoring the difficult fact that some two-fifths of the area claimed as Biafra was inhabited by non-Ibo peoples who opposed the Biafran cause. Aside from this, it was and is obvious that the Ibo had a great deal of right on their side. They suffered appallingly in the tumults after 1965, and they rightly wanted to be sure they would not suffer again. Yet it seems likely that they did not always suffer in the subsequent war as much as the propaganda made on their behalf would have us believe. After federal forces had taken Umuahia, a temporary headquarters town of Ojukwu early in 1969, a team of international observers found none of the scenes of carnage and destruction which foreign 'pro-Biafrans' had predicted. 'The observers were able to visit all parts of the deserted town and, although distant sounds of fighting could be heard, they saw little war damage. Both the market place and railway station are intact.'[152]

When the war at last ended, and Colonel Ojukwu had fled to the Ivory Coast, the irresponsible nature of 'pro-Biafran' propaganda in Europe and North America became painfully clear. Having moved in with federal troops to the last secessionist enclave of East-Central State (northern half of the old Eastern Region), British, Canadian and Swedish military observers 'reaffirmed findings in earlier reports that [their team] had neither seen nor heard any evidence of genocide in the newly captured areas it visited' (*The Times*, 17 January 1970). The 'pro-Biafran' publicity machine had claimed a death roll of two millions: it now remained to ascertain the exact dimensions of a far smaller figure. While a major effort of reconstruction would be required in Ibo areas, it was likewise obvious that material damage was less severe than this well-fed publicity machine had claimed.

The healing task called for a spirit of forbearance and reconciliation such as now appeared in the immediate wake of the fighting. Over and beyond that, however, it called for a new political system as well as for a new federal structure. This, to succeed, would have to be emphatically non-élitist, 'non-middle-class' in the old federal sense. The energy and genius of Nigeria's peoples were again to be challenged by the need to develop both federal and regional loyalties through the evolution of intra-regional democratic parties and effective forms of popular representation.

Other countries faced problems of the same nature, though much differing in degrees of acuteness.

Milton Obote's government in Uganda met and overcame the separatism of Baganda chiefs, seeming to achieve by 1969 a balance that gave fair promise of new opportunities for forward movement later on. Less could be said of the vast provinces of the ex-Belgian Congo. Born in tumult, the Congo Republic continued in tumult for several years, facing secession on one hand and radical upheaval on the other, and emerging only in

1967 with a stability which looked dangerously like stagnation. Even when one sets apart all foreign intrigues and interventions – and it is difficult to do that, for they were many and persistent – it remains easy to see where the shoe pinched. Once the rigid colonial framework of the Belgians was removed, this enormous country of a hundred languages could be held together only by a copy of that framework, imposed by military rule, *or* by the unifying force of a national movement based on the supra-ethnic loyalties of people in countless little towns and villages. Patrice Lumumba had understood this, but was murdered by his rivals, in 1961, before he could have any real chance of promoting any such unity. Taking his place, there came a foreign-backed élite and its almost inevitable culmination in military rule.

Kenya struggled with other problems of unification, and made a good beginning. Under the prestigious leadership of Jomo Kenyatta, the Kenya African National Union proved able to bring peace and the promise of good government to the confusion, violence and bitterness that had reigned over the last few years of British colonial rule. Yet two disturbing factors soon appeared. One was the consolidation in government of a Kikuyu élite; the other was the rapid crystallization of this élite into a power structure of its own. In 1967 an opposition critic could write, in words that many government supporters would not have quarrelled with, that:

If Kenya started *uhuru* [freedom] without an African élite class, she is rapidly acquiring one. Ministers and top civil servants compete with one another to buy more farms, acquire more directorships and own bigger cars and grander houses. False standards are set with salary scales for M.P.s, Ministers, and top civil servants that the country cannot possibly afford . . .

In 1963 M.P.s earned £620 a year. This was increased to £840, then to £1200 a year, making three increases and a doubling of salary in less than three years . . . Civil servants are still paid according to the old colonial salary structure. In six months an M.P. receives more money than the average peasant earns in half a life-time . . . The spirit of national reconstruction is killed. An inner core of party leaders accumulate office inside the party and in government, a vast edifice of self-interest is erected while the people wait for land, jobs, schools, and hospitals. The man in the street or in the field is called upon to work hard, to sacrifice for freedom; yet he sees the ostentatious display of wealth by government leaders and administrators who earn salaries of astronomical sums compared with his earnings ...

'High salaries,' continued this critic, himself a former Vice-President of Kenya, 'are not the whole of the story. Gradually, political control and business interests have begun to intertwine. Many have begun to use their positions in politics to entrench themselves as a propertied economic group. A self-entrenched class of politician-businessmen is growing up in the cities, and in the countryside a large land-owning class' that was no longer merely white.[153]

As in Nigeria, this trend was inseparable from certain types of outside pressure. The men who ruled Kenya after 1963 were, with few exceptions, energetic and intelligent politicians whose enterprise was admired even by British Conservatives. But they inherited a country with enormous problems. Not the least of these was represented by the great city of Nairobi, the wealthiest business centre in East Africa. If KANU leaders were to carry out their promises of 'African socialism' – meaning, at the least, the erection of a non-élitist structure of government and administration – they would have to transform a great deal of the powerful network of capitalist enterprise concentrated in Nairobi. This, to put it mildly, would be difficult. Meanwhile, problems multiplied: an annual population growth rate of three per cent; a consequent flooding of rural poor into Nairobi, which now began to grow by about seven per cent a year (1969); and a tide of primary school-leavers expected to rise to about 500,000 a year in 1972. With all this, nothing was easy.

Up to 1965 the options remained fairly open. Justifiably proud of their success in mastering the immediate problems of independence, Kenya's leadership still felt that it could manoeuvre between opposed policies. Perhaps a crucial change occurred with the assassination in February 1965 of Pio Gama Pinto, a radical KANU leader, in circumstances which have yet to be made clear. With that, tensions inside KANU rapidly tightened; manoeuvre between opposed policies became increasingly difficult. Most of the leadership now went rapidly to the right; 'free enterprise' became the ruling if unconfessed doctrine. Early in 1966 the radical minority in the leadership, headed by Oginga Odinga, split away and formed an opposition party called the Kenya People's Union. The KPU had little success in subsequent elections, being also harried and hampered by administrative obstruction, but acquired some footing in Luo territory, most of its leaders being of Luo origin. So the government was now seen as Kikuyu, and the opposition as Luo. Thus 'tribalism' once again emerged from policies of élitist rule.

Late in 1968 it was evident that fresh trouble was on the way. The first blows fell in the middle of 1969. One of the most effective of all the KANU leaders, a prominent Luo named Tom Mboya in whom, it appeared, President Kenyatta had particular confidence, was shot down in a Nairobi street. A Kikuyu named Njoroge, of no known importance, was arrested and found guilty at a trial in which the assessors differed on the value of the evidence, and hanged soon afterwards. It might or might not be material that Njoroge had stoutly denied his guilt; there were in any case few who felt that his trial had plumbed the depths of this dark affair.

Their doubts were rapidly reinforced by events of quite another kind. Hard on the heels of Mboya's murder came disturbing reports of new 'oathing ceremonies' among the Kikuyu, designed this time, it was alleged, to keep the Kikuyu ruling group in power against any attempt to unseat them. A Kamba minister of the government called a press conference in which he said that Kikuyu-solidarity oaths were being taken even by Kikuyu living in London. Three resident British journalists, cautious and experienced men, gave some newspaper space to this minister's statement. They were forthwith expelled from Kenya at one hour's notice.

That was on 26 September. Yet only one week earlier the Vice-President of Kenya, Mr Daniel Arap-Moi of Kalendjin origin, had declared that 'the Government condemns those who are going round the country molesting people and forcibly administering oaths and collecting money illegally...'[154] And only four days before the journalists' expulsion the official radio station, *Voice of Kenya*, stated in a commentary on current events that 'it would be futile to pretend that something terrible is not going on in some parts of the country . . .'[155] At the same moment *The Times* printed a story from Nairobi which helped to explain what this 'something terrible' might be. The Nairobi police, it reported, said that they were investigating the death of a Kikuyu Christian minister, the Rev. Samuel Mwai, who was alleged by Church authorities to have died of severe wounds after refusing to participate in an illegal oath-taking ceremony.

One blow now followed on another. On 25 October President Kenyatta paid a visit to Kisumu, the capital of Luoland in north-western Kenya. Incidents occurred which included police volleys into a crowd. This shooting was officially explained as a necessary response to the crowd's hostility and throwing of stones. It was noted that others offered a different explanation. Late in November the London *Observer* printed a letter signed 'Eye-Witness', the writer supplying his name and address but insisting these not be published. This letter denied that the crowd at Kisumu had got out of hand, and claimed that the police had gratuitously opened fire:

I was close enough to the shooting to collect one dead schoolboy about 14 years old and one badly injured man shot in the back. I have also spoken to a number of eye-witnesses and have met only one person who saw *one* stone being thrown. Tear gas grenades were thrown into the crowd, the crowd ran for cover and were shot at as they ran without any shots being fired over their heads . . .

There are only three possible explanations of the gratuitous shooting on the crowd:

1. It was a deliberately created incident to justify the banning of KPU [the mainly Luo-backed opposition party].

2. It was the result of irrational anger on the part of the President caused by some members of the crowd shouting the KPU slogan.

3. The President's escort panicked needlessly.[156]

But the government insisted that the incidents were fomented by the KPU for subversive ends. On 30 October, accordingly, they banned the KPU; and its leaders, including ex-Vice-President Odinga, were taken into custody and kept there.

With this, as many thought, the scene was set for events still more dramatic. As it happened, general elections followed quietly in December, and were distinguished by allowing many candidates within KANU, now the only legal party, to contest seats against each other. It turned out that 108 out of the 170 seats were to be occupied by politicians entirely new to Parliament; once again the resilience and originality of African political systems were displayed to advantage. Many of the new M.P.s, moreover, belonged to that expanding educated minority whose rivalry with the established élite had already appeared upon the scene. 'Cautious optimism about the new phase of Kenya's national history,' Mr Patrick Keatley felt able to conclude in the *Guardian*, 'is the mood in that part of East Africa today... The political atmosphere seems reasonably encouraging...' Others felt less optimistic. The long-range question was evidently whether a new version of the 'middle class' solution, however skilfully applied, could do better than the old.

Given the international pressures now in play, it could in any case be asked whether there was any real alternative, in most independent African countries, to the 'middle class' solution and its consequent 'pandemonium'.

The records show that there were always Africans who thought that such an alternative would have to be found, and that they had thought this even in the 'early days' at a time when independence was little advanced beyond an anthem and a flag. Some of these Africans advocated socialism of one type or another, and were rapidly labelled by their rivals as the stooges or agents of the communist powers. Such accusations were the less effective, however, because it was noticed – and often said – that they came most energetically from men who appeared to have no objection to lining themselves up as the representatives of the capitalist powers. Other Africans who favoured socialism were ignored as foolish visionaries; others again were swept aside by intrigue or foreign intervention. A few survived on the political scene. By 1963 or so they had moved from an initial utopianism to a firmer grip on the realities they faced. Here and there they began to acquire an audience. They began to wield influence. They began to grope their way toward new solutions, new directions.

They had varying degrees of success or failure. The experience of Ghana has been much in point. Always controversial, the leadership of Kwame Nkrumah was as variously judged.

How one regards these various efforts will partly depend on what they do, but also on who one is. 'Ghanaians comprehend representative government,' *Time* remarked with effortless condescension some years ago, 'but Moscow-leaning Kwame Nkrumah misrules [his] country as [an] autocracy.'[157] Yet a few months later another prominent American magazine, the *Atlantic Monthly*, had concluded that 'on paper, the Ghana program seems no more socialistic than Nigeria's $1·8 billion six-year plan of development. But there is a huge difference in atmosphere. Nigeria in some ways resembles nineteenth-century America, with foreign capitalists rushing in, hoping for quick profits, and with land bloating in value. Although the state plans a good deal of supervision and interference, the Nigerian economy basically is capitalist in atmosphere.

'Ghana is different,' continued the *Atlantic Monthly*. 'While Nkrumah has kept nationalization (with liberal compensation) to a minimum, Ghana is committed to a socialist future. It has a calm, ordered atmosphere and moves in a disciplined way ...' No mention of 'autocracy' here: on the contrary, Nigeria and Ghana 'may be proceeding in the only economic way possible. And Ghana's way, because of its size, may be the easiest.'[158]

The notions of 'capitalism' and 'socialism' were of course relative. Africans often emphasized this. Thus the late Dunduza Chisiza of Nyasaland (Malawi) told an American audience that 'the chances of either of these systems being adopted in an un-adulterated form are very slim'.[159] But the need for *choice*, as we have seen earlier in this book, was not relative: it was an ab-solute element in the situation. By making a clear choice in favour of a radical reconstruction of society – one that could draw the vast majority of people into active and conscious participation – the 'committed countries' could show a stability and solidity which their neighbours seldom shared; and this was also true, one may note, of Ghana under Nkrumah until the bottom fell out of the world price for cocoa.

Failure to understand this commitment led to a number of disappointments in Europe and North America. In Julius Nyerere, for example, the governments of the West have generally seen a man who, they believed, would take a predictable road towards modelling Tanganyika on examples proffered by themselves. There, if anywhere, parliamentary democracy and free-enterprise would surely flourish? Yet within a year of independence Nyerere had declared Tanganyika a one-party state vowed to socialism. *

With no money in the till, though with less acute problems than those of Kenya, an impoverished Tanganyikan government had one card to play. This was political unity. By a tremendous effort in the middle and late fifties, the Tanganyika African National Union had won the adherence of nearly all Africans and not a few among the European and Asian minorities. By 1963 TANU was not only the party of central government – with a virtual monopoly of parliamentary representatives – but had become, in a literal sense, the whole of government in Tanganyika, even down to occupying junior posts in the administration.

The logic of this was clear enough. If the hundred-odd peoples of Tanganyika could unite for large political objectives, what agency except TANU could keep them united? And how could TANU do this unless it were not only the central government and parliament – far-away abstractions in Dar-es-Salaam for most of the country's two million peasant and fisherman families – but also the day-to-day village and regional government as well? There were great and simple difficulties to be faced. There was acute shortage of cash, partly because of natural disasters and partly because of failure to pay taxes (itself a consequence of peasant expectation that 'everything must be different' after independence). In the train of all this, hard decisions had to be taken and realized. That was the work of the administration. Yet the administration, in 1960, was much

*After Zanzibar became independent in 1964, it carried through a social revolution and joined Tanganyika in a federal structure, the Union of Tanzania.

the same in personnel – or so it would have appeared to the average peasant – as the colonial administration before it.

Unless TANU were to be associated with this administration – were even to *become* this administration – unpopular but necessary decisions could scarcely be carried through. Little by little, Nyerere and his colleagues were driven to the conclusion, fully embraced at the end of 1961, that TANU must not only govern but must also administer. A year later this process was almost complete. The political party and the civil service had, in large degree, become one and the same organization.

This radical solution of Tanganyika's 'problem of power' carried obvious dangers. Who was to control the controllers, once parliament and administration were so closely identified? Occasional abuse of power and some patently wrong appointments soon raised this question to a national issue. Early in 1963 the TANU national committee – by then the country's effective parliament – began casting round for 'checks and balances'. Nyerere, for example, proposed that TANU members might stand in opposition to TANU official candidates at parliamentary elections. He argued that this was advisable since no non-TANU candidates had any chance of being elected, such was the party's popularity at village level. A more serious danger seemed to lie in the general lack of political ideology: it was hard to see how TANU could keep safely moving forward if it lacked a set of rules for navigation. In 1963 Nyerere began to propound some rather vague and romantic rules for the achievement of 'African socialism'.

But the system also bore some powerful advantages, at least for the time being. It dispensed with the waste and frivolity of political conflicts whose reality was nothing more than personal ambition or clannish conservatism. While Kenya next-door was busy dividing itself into ever smaller units of 'tribal nationalism' – to borrow again Miss Arendt's phrase about Europe – Tanganyika's many peoples became less disunited. Moreover, the system evolved by TANU put politicians in the best possible posture for behaving as good men: it made them publicly responsible, in short, for the day-to-day application at village level of the decisions they had taken in Dar-es-Salaam. They could blame their failures only on themselves. This encouraged social responsibility in contrast with the nest-feathering so common in some other countries.

Even so, how to solve the basic problem? How to involve Tanganyika's population of about two million peasant families (and a few townsmen, Europeans, and Indians) in an active, voluntary, and united effort at total reconstruction and modernization? Nyerere and his leading colleagues had always been clear that the 'middle class solution' – the solving of the problem by the slow growth of a capitalist class at the expense of the majority of the people – could never be made to work, and should not even be attempted. Other pressures now hardened this conviction, not least the revolutionary atmosphere and activities of Zanzibar, now joined with Tanganyika in the Union of Tanzania. They began to face problems with a new realism.

The answer to the problem seemed to be two-fold. One part of it was to avoid the Algerian and Ghanaian failure to transform the *national movement* into a *democratic party* of the masses. The other was to apply the ideas of socialism to the realities of Africa. The first part was tackled by continuing efforts at democratization. The second was approached through a long debate which culminated in the Arusha Declaration of TANU in January 1967. This Declaration could be seen as a milestone, for it was the first coherent attempt to reduce the concept of 'African socialism' from demagogic verbiage to practical policy. It analysed the country's social structure with a generally hard-headed realism, and spoke in words not heard before. Attached to it, hitting at the 'middle class solution' (with thoughts of Nigeria perhaps in mind) was a resolution which stated, among other things, that:

1. Every TANU and Government leader must be either a farmer or a worker, and should in no way be associated with the practices of capitalism or feudalism.

2. No TANU or Government leader should hold shares in any company.

3. No TANU or Government leader should hold directorships in any privately-owned enterprise.

4. No TANU or Government leader should receive two or more salaries.

5. No TANU or Government leader should own houses which he rents to others.

A week later, applying this Declaration, the Tanzania government took over all banks and insurance firms, eight large import-export companies which were, it was announced, to form the nucleus of a State trading corporation, and several other foreign-owned enterprises. At the same time Nyerere made a major policy statement in which he lashed out at everyone who thought that Africa could be saved by anything but African work, devotion, and intelligence. Begging from others could never do the job. 'We have now decided to blot out this policy of begging. We enter on the policy of self-reliance. Our country's development depends on our own hard work and willingness to fulfil our own activities.'

Other élites might fatten on the honeypot of office and 'connections'. Nyerere set his face against that. Arusha declared that all who held office must be free of business interests, property deals, the accumulation of salary-paying posts. Not surprisingly, there were cries of pain from the *beati possidentes*, and several foreign newspapers lost no time in interpreting these wails of dismay as the prelude to Nyerere's downfall. The 'gentle moderate' had turned on them and bitten hard: understandably, they were upset with him. But Nyerere did not fall.

It was not an easy moment. 'We are,' a TANU official commented to me in December 1967, nine months after Arusha, 'at war with ourselves' – a war, he explained, between personal interests and community interests. Yet only two out of thirty-two top leaders preferred to pull out of politics, and keep their business and property activities. All the rest, if with misgivings, stayed put and carried on.

This led to some refreshingly frank talk. What many leaders hoped from independence was now revealed in one of the most unexpected documents ever to be issued by a government in Africa, or perhaps anywhere else. This was a pamphlet, freely on sale in Dar-es-Salaam bookshops, from the office of the government printer, called '*Answers to Questions*'. Obviously though not explicitly written by the President himself, these answers were in promised response to questions raised by the Arusha

Declaration. Such questions, Nyerere had hoped, would relate to basic problems of aim and policy. He was disappointed.

'Unfortunately,' said the pamphlet, 'almost all the questions received related to just one section of the Arusha Declaration – that on qualifications for leadership. There was not one question on Socialism and Self-Reliance', the declared principles set forth at Arusha.

In fact, the problems of political leadership during the 1960s were seldom more clearly defined than in some of these questions and answers. Consider, for example, Question 10 and its reply.

Question: A politician has no security. Today he is a Minister, tomorrow not; today he is an M.P., after five years he is not; today he is a Regional Commissioner or Area Commissioner, tomorrow he is unemployed. . . . Why does the Arusha Declaration prevent such leaders from providing by other means for their future?

Answer: What other means? Leaders ask this question more than any other question, and it is the most serious and dangerous question of all. The Arusha Declaration says that a TANU leader will be a peasant or a worker. Before he is chosen as a leader he will be working as a peasant, working for wages, or working on his own account as a carpenter, blacksmith, goldsmith, etc. This is the work by which he meets his needs now, and through which he prepares for his future security. . . .

[But] which is the politician who went to the people at election time and asked them to elect him so that he could provide for his future? Which Area or Regional Commissioner or other TANU worker got his job by saying that he wanted to improve his personal position, and get security for his future? Whenever a person seeks political work, whether it is through election or by appointment, he says he wants the opportunity to serve the people, to guard their interests and to further their aspirations. What right has such a person, once he has the appointment he sought on this basis, to use his responsibility for his own betterment?[160]

There was much else to the same effect. It was not liked; but it was accepted. TANU leaders stopped providing for their future 'by other means'. Within a year it was clear that the early objectives of Arusha were assured. The new national trading bank was on the way to a profit. None of the upheavals forecast abroad had come about. Progressive taxation was cutting into the prospects of a crop of 'beneficiaries': in October 1967 Nyerere could say that 'there are only ten people in our whole country who have an income of Shs. 300,000 or more a year (£15,000 or more), and these people each pay more than two-thirds of that amount to the Government in direct taxation.'[161]

Modesty of aim and language were the order of the day. Tractors for farmers? One day, perhaps: meanwhile, something simpler would do better.

In many parts of the country we are beginning to follow the advice of our agricultural experts. But our major tool, the *jembe* (hoe), is too primitive for our present-day needs. We must now abandon it and replace it with the oxen-plough. We cannot make progress by waiting until every peasant is able to possess his own tractor which he can drive and maintain. Indeed, if we wait for that we shall never leave the hoe behind us, for our present methods are too inefficient ever to produce the wealth which would enable us to buy tractors for all parts of the country, or to train people to drive and maintain them. We are not ready for the tractor, either financially or technically; but we are ready for the oxen-plough . . .[162]

For whose benefit?

We still have in this country a predominantly peasant society in which farmers work for themselves and their families, and are helped and protected from exploitation by co-operative marketing arrangements. Yet the present trend is away from the extended-family production and social unity, and towards the development of a class system in the rural areas. It is this kind of development which would be inconsistent with the growth of a socialist Tanzania in which all citizens could be assured of human dignity and equality, and in which all were able to have a decent and constantly improving life for themselves and their children.[163]

Hence the need, Nyerere went on to argue, for the growth of

economic and social communities where people live together and work together for the good of all, and which are interlocked so that all the different communities also work together in co-operation for the common good. . . . The basis of rural life in Tanzania must be the practice of co-operation in its widest sense – in living, in working, and in distribution. . . . This is very different from our present organization of society, and requires a reversal of the present trend.[164]

To achieve this reversal it would not be enough to create new institutions. It would be still more necessary to create new attitudes, new understandings, new types of education. Tanzanians, said Nyerere in another of his 1967 pamphlets, suffered from the wrong type of education. They had inherited from the British a system of education, as of educational values, which was

based on the assumptions of a colonialist and capitalist society. It emphasized and encouraged the individualistic instincts of mankind, instead of his co-operative instincts. It led to the possession of individual material wealth being the major criterion of social merit and worth. This meant that colonial education induced attitudes of human inequality, and in practice underpinned the domination of the weak by the strong, especially in the economic field.[165]

All this must be changed, however difficult that might be; and Nyerere proceeded to offer some practical proposals.

These trends of thought and action were at an early stage in 1970. Yet by then they were three years old. It could be said that the outline of a new society was at least taking shape.

Three countries in West Africa – Ghana, Guinea, and Mali – had earlier made some effort in the same general direction. But Ghana must have most of our attention, for it was the most important of the three. With just over seven million people, Ghana was one of Africa's smaller countries. In terms of wealth, social and political cohesion, and dynamic leadership, however, it was well out ahead of almost all the field. In more ways than one it was a pace-maker, a position which seldom made for popularity, but could none the less command attention and respect, even from opponents and critics.

Ghana had also been independent Africa's biggest surprise. If any country should have been content to settle down under a 'new middle class', this was surely the one. With more than £200 millions of sterling assets on the day of independence, an average standard of living that was probably somewhat higher than in Portugal, and a numerous trading community whose contacts with Europe had more than four centuries of varied experience behind them, the new government might surely have sat back in 1957 and happily let things slide.

Yet Ghana by 1962 was launched on a far-reaching programme of social reconstruction, industrialization, and modernization on a radical plan; her overall productivity was vastly higher than it was a decade earlier; large new investments were in hand; while 'domestic fixed-capital-formation' is said to have as much as doubled since 1956. Estimated at £532 millions in 1962, Ghana's gross national product had risen to an outstandingly high point for ex-colonial Africa. The slipshod days of early independence, when personal fortunes mushroomed in a boom of corruption and careerism, had at least begun to give way to a better atmosphere. Why and how had this come about?

At the usual risk of over-simplification, one can reply that the story begins with the efforts of Kwame Nkrumah and a handful of like-minded young nationalists to transform the United Gold Coast Convention from a staidly respectable pressure-group of elderly lawyers and chiefs into a 'party of the masses'. That was in 1949. Denounced and rejected with dismay by the leaders of the UGCC, Nkrumah and his friends broke away altogether, formed the Convention People's Party, won mass support up and down the country and turned in 1950 to 'positive action'.[166] They were put in prison for this but released a year later when elections gave decisive victory to the CPP. Nkrumah became the leader of a Gold Coast government with limited domestic powers. Following on their experience with India, Britain's Labour government were ready for a gradual but decisive transfer of power. Nkrumah's main achievement lay not only in forcing the pace but, even more, in drawing very large numbers of ordinary people into political action. Despite much opposition from those who had wanted only minimal forms of change, there thus emerged a widely democratic basis for independence.

Full sovereignty was conceded in 1957. What was the position then? Politically, the new regime had one great asset and one great liability. Its asset was its widespread popularity with the common man and his wife, the latter no mean factor in any

part of West Africa. Its liability was a corresponding unpopularity with all the important chiefs of the inland country,
who rightly saw the CPP as a potent threat to their traditional
influence and privilege. Few leading chiefs wanted independence;
some opposed it vigorously. I remember being received by one
of these in the 'throne room' of his large old country house a
few days before independence. His mood was one of sadness. He
saw no good in what was happening. 'Ah, my boy,' he said,
shaking his handsome old head, 'it all began with that man
Creech-Jones.' He shrugged. 'Now we have a gentleman in
charge, Mr Lennox-Boyd. He will try to do the right thing. But
it is too late, too late.'*

The first independent government, therefore, began life
with a tough challenge to its authority, and this challenge was
made even tougher with the encouragement given to traditional
chiefs, especially in Ashanti, by an independence constitution
which allowed for the formation of strong regional governments.
The object of the chiefly opposition was now to secure a transfer
of power to the regions at the expense of the central government in Accra. Whether he wanted it or not, Nkrumah was thus
faced with an unavoidable choice: either he must break the
power of the principal chiefs, or else resign himself to being
little more than a figurehead. It was very much the situation
that Kenyatta and his colleagues would be required to face in
Kenya seven years later.

Had Nkrumah been a weaker man, or one who believed less
fervently in his mission to take Africans altogether out of their
'second-class citizenship' in the world, he might have accepted
the comfortable role assigned to him by a regionalist constitution. In that case there can be little doubt that Ghana would
have split away on the Nigerian pattern into several conflicting
regions, most of whose leaders would have done their best to
conserve the *status quo*. But the *status quo* was precisely what
could *not* be made compatible with a general reconstruction of
the country on modern lines.

*Mr Arthur Creech-Jones had been Secretary of State for the Colonies in Britain's
post-war Labour government; in 1957 Britain had a Conservative government and
Mr Alan Lennox-Boyd was Colonial Secretary.

This being so, it was possible for Nkrumah and the CPP to quell the opposition of the principal chiefs. They went far to unite the country. Deprived of any considerable local power, the regions found themselves under a single government. This was to be the foundation for every major advance the country has since achieved. It was not done easily or peacefully. There were months and even years of sporadic violence or near-violence in Ashanti. But when it was over, surprisingly few had died. And while Ghana had political prisoners, some of whom were grossly abused, it may at least be remarked that she had no political executions, although a new wave of terror-bombing, aimed especially at Nkrumah, began in 1962.

Only those who prefer that Ghana should have remained a congeries of traditional little statelets with no effective central power can fairly criticize Nkrumah's policy of unification. Yet the curious fact remains that many otherwise thoughtful people in Europe and North America none the less interpreted this policy as one of dictatorship, while some Western newspapers quite recklessly plastered the government's reputation with accusations of 'autocracy' and the like. This badgering of Ghana sometimes reached an astonishing point. In May, 1963, for example, the head of the department of East European studies at London University felt able to compare Nkrumah's government with the racialist dictatorship of the Afrikaner National Party in South Africa. 'The Labour Party [if it accedes to power] has promised action against South Africa, whose government subjects Africans to political persecution,' wrote Professor H. Seton-Watson to *The Times*, which gave his letter prominence. 'It has yet to announce its intentions towards Ghana, whose government also subjects Africans to political persecution.'[167] To place the breaking of an often violent and reactionary separatist minority in a new state on the same level as the behaviour of Verwoerd's regime in South Africa – under which one fifth of the population is intended to remain complete and permanent master of the other four-fifths – might seem a comical misunderstanding of the truth if it came from a less portentous source. The effect of such criticism in Ghana, of course, was to lead no small number of Ghanaians to believe that influential persons in Britain simply did not want them to make a success of independence.

Having united the country, what next? By about 1959 it once again appeared that the CPP leadership would be content to settle into peaceful comfort, of which, by now, they had plenty. Yet the same mass pressures which had made unity possible now thrust the country forward into a new direction. No doubt Nkrumah's socialist convictions played their part: they could have availed for little, however, if standing still had seemed possible or easy. But it did not. Certainly there was progress. Cocoa-farmers' incomes rose from about £27 millions in 1957, according to official figures, to £48 millions in 1960, while the (official) cost-of-living index rose only from 106 (1954 = 100) to 112. Yet wages stagnated at a low level; and popular demand for higher living standards now began to take the form of open discontent. Besides that, the writing on the wall was anything but hopeful even for the maintenance of existing standards within the *status quo*: cocoa prices might still be high, but the terms-of-trade had been moving decisively against Ghana (as against every primary producer) since the middle fifties. Very large sums were being spent on the import of food, let alone of manufactured goods. And there were here, of course, the same acute problems of post-school employment as in Nigeria. 'Despite the stupendous increase in output,' an official circular commented with an admirable frankness, 'the country is only running in order to stand still.' Once more the CPP leadership was faced with an ultimate choice between abdication or movement forward to a large expansion of the economy. It began to try to move forward.

It moved notably in 1962 with the promulgation of a seven-year development plan which aimed at being more than a list of desirable targets and possible donors. This provided for a large expansion of the state-capitalist sector, abandoned previous and vain attempts to 'make local capitalists do the job', and placed primary emphasis on raising agricultural productivity together with a major effort in many sectors at transforming a one-crop economy (based on cocoa) into a diversified and industrial complex. In contrast with other countries which had also opted for a measure of state capitalism, here the 'state capitalist content' was presented as a prelude to a socialist system.

'Socialism,' Nkrumah told a meeting of CPP organizers in April 1961, 'is the only pattern that can within the shortest possible time bring the good life to the people . . . [but] all talk of socialism, of economic and social reconstruction, is just empty words if we do not seriously address ourselves to the question of basic industrialization and agricultural revolution in our country . . .'[168]

From about this time the government made successful if expensive efforts at buying up important foreign concerns, notably in gold-mining, and laid down careful conditions under which future private investment could be made. Founded half a century earlier, the gold-mining companies had realized their original investment many times over. Until 1944 they had remained 'with no levy on their exports other than insignificant rents to the chief and a slight tax to the government. All income tax was paid within England itself.'[169] About half the gross income of the mines went year by year, as we have seen, almost untaxed abroad. After 1944 small domestic taxes were imposed, and these were later somewhat increased.

But with 1960 the government moved into the mining field itself. It purchased five mining companies in the Tarkwa region at a cost of £5½ millions, a fairly generous but sensible transaction which cost about the value of one year's annual output of gold; and in 1964 Ghana's state mining corporation produced just over half of the country's gold. Although rather more than half of total diamond production remains in foreign hands, diamond dealing was also transferred to Accra with a consequent effect on revenue. Among other purchases was a large retail-marketing concern; and a beginning was then made in state retail-trading through 'people's shops', under the direction, interestingly enough, of a former senior British executive of the United Africa Company. In farming, meanwhile, the 'agricultural stations' of former days were transformed into more than a hundred state farms; unemployed men were absorbed into many other farms run by the Ghana Workers' Brigade; and there was a wide and not altogether unsuccessful promotion of cooperative marketing and production.

At the same time a large proportion of sterling reserves, accumulated under the colonial regime and held for a long time as 'blocked balances' in London, were used in primary development, notably in completing a new deep-water harbour and township at Tema, east of Accra, at the cost of nearly £30 millions, and in work on the huge Volta dam at Akosombo, towards which Ghana contributed £35 millions,[170] and which was completed, ahead of schedule and below cost, in 1965.* Much other money was going into the improvement of farming methods, fertilizers, and types of seed.

Ghana also took its 'neutralism' seriously and to active purpose. After some hesitations, the United States and other Western official lenders agreed to devote no less than £93 millions to the Volta dam and its connected enterprises, whether in hydro-electric power or the mining and processing of bauxite, while the Soviet Union was committed to another dam on the Volta and granted credits worth about £29 millions for repayment in ten years at 2½ per cent, the repayment to be largely by the proceeds of Ghanaian exports, or, in other words, cocoa. Other communist countries agreed to comparable credits on a smaller scale. The objective of all these Eastern agreements was agricultural and industrial diversification, with payment in cocoa. 'The Eastern bloc are paying for this cocoa at the rate of 55 per cent in hard currency and 45 per cent in goods and services ... [They have] guaranteed Ghana a total of £100 millions in credits for new industries to be planned and eventually built by their own technicians.'[171]

A consistent policy towards private investment was also projected. The government would henceforth recognize 'five sectors, all operating side by side in the nation's economy. These sectors are:

1. State enterprises.

*The huge lake formed by the dam at Akosombo soon became a valuable source of food. 'After intensive stocking operations, fishing in the man-made 3,300 square-mile Lake Volta is now,' reported *West Africa* on 20 December 1969, 'reaching some 10,000 tons a year under a U.N. Development Programme assisted project, and is expected to expand at an annual rate of 2,000 tons ... The lake has a shoreline of 4,500 miles and possesses high fishery potential ...'

2. Enterprises owned by foreign private interests.
3. Enterprises jointly owned by the state and foreign private interests.
4. Cooperatives.
5. Small-scale Ghanaian enterprises.'[172]

State-controlled enterprise, in other words, was intended to dominate the economy. But while pointing the economy away from 'free enterprise', the government took some care to welcome foreign private investors who might be prepared to cooperate on acceptable terms. 'All enterprises', that is to say, would be 'expected to accept the economic policy of the government as the basis of their activity.'[173] In mid-1963 the Ghanaian ambassador to the United States assured a business audience in Washington that 'foreign investors had nothing to fear in Ghana'.[174]

Part of this new attitude to private investment consisted in an attempt to persuade foreign companies to invest some of their profits in the processing of locally produced raw material. Some large firms quickly agreed. In 1963, for example, the United Africa Company (Unilever) built a soap-and-toothpaste factory in Ghana at the cost of £2 million. This plant, Nkrumah claimed when opening it, was proof of a new relationship with foreign investors. In the past Unilever had bought palm-oil in Africa and brought it back again as soap made in Europe. 'Now the wheel has turned full circle, and Lever Brothers, who originally came to Ghana for the raw material, are today manufacturing here the finished product.' In this way, as well as by public investment, Ghana's narrow 'industrial base' was being steadily broadened.

By 1964, accordingly, the pressures for a better life could begin to be met, if cautiously, with solid claims to have opened out the future. Though events in the political field were now – perhaps inevitably – to take an increasingly abrupt and controversial turn, it could at least be argued for the regime that it had squarely faced the challenge of large-scale economic reconstruction as well as of social change; that it had scored a number of outstanding initial successes; and that with hard work and a measure of good fortune Ghanaians could now hope

within a fairly short time to see their country vastly more re-
silient, wealthy, and agreeable to live in than before. In this
connection, the British High Commissioner, Sir Geoffrey de
Freitas, was more than merely courteous when he opined in
1963 that 'of all tropical African countries, Ghana has the best
prospects economically'.[175]

The gains secured under Nkrumah's leadership were undoubtedly considerable in many fields. Between 1951 and 1961,
for example, the numbers of children in primary schools rose
from 211,000 to 484,000, with comparable expansion at the
secondary and university levels. Yet these gains were by no
means well reflected in the voting strength of the ruling party,
Nkrumah's Convention People's Party. The CPP never managed
to win more than 60 per cent of the votes in general elections
which seldom brought out more than 60 per cent of the electors.
This political weakness, partly inherent in the country's traditional divisions, was greatly increased, after 1961, by a persistent
failure to enlarge or even maintain the democratic structure
of the CPP. More and more, the CPP degenerated into a
self-perpetuating oligarchy of competing interest-groups with
Nkrumah, willy nilly, driven into the posture of a supreme
arbiter obliged to play off one group against another. History
may reach a judgement on how far this degeneration could have
been averted. As things were, it became increasingly fatal to all
Nkrumah's plans.

He himself was clear that the 'middle class solution' – development by the building of a full-scale local capitalism in
alliance with that of the West – could not succeed, and that only a
boldly radical alternative would realize the promises and hopes of
independence. But he was forced to work with men who seldom
shared his convictions, and whose personal ambitions often
turned them, here as in Federal Nigeria, into speculation and
careerism. On top of this there were other strains. A Preventive
Detention Act was introduced and widely used. Hundreds of
critics went to jail, and many suffered badly there. To bomb
outrages by unknown opponents, the regime answered with more
arrests. Tensions grew.

They became acute in 1965, but for another reason. Cocoa

prices collapsed. The world price of cocoa had been £247 a ton in 1957 at the time of independence. In 1961 it was down to £177. In the summer of 1965 it dropped well below £100. Inflation and bad management, including corrupt management, now added their woes.* Food prices doubled in the towns, especially in Accra, where the CPP had never won a firm electoral hold. Foreign debts soared as cocoa revenue dwindled. Foreign creditors began threatening to foreclose.

The end came in February 1966, at a moment when Nkrumah was in Peking on the way to Hanoi for a peace mission at the invitation of the government of North Vietnam; but not as the result of a popular rising. A *coup* was staged by the Ghana army, which took over the country. The CPP regime was overthrown without a hand being raised to save it – some indication, perhaps, of its loss of popularity with the public – and many of its leaders were jailed. A new attempt at the 'middle class solution' was launched by a National Liberation Council under the leadership of General J. A. Ankrah, backed by leading opponents of the CPP such as Dr K. A. Busia.

This military regime showed itself as tough and hard-working. While passing draconian laws against anyone who might support or be likely to support the return of Nkrumah – something apparently thought quite possible – it proclaimed the intention of returning to civilian rule. Meanwhile it dismantled much of Nkrumah's structure by returning state-controlled enterprises to private hands, and generally gave signs of returning Ghana itself to the ranks of Western approval.

In April 1967 a small section of the army attempted another

*After their *coup* the soldiers showed a laudable energy, as General Aguiyi-Ironsi had done in Nigeria, in exposing scandals of corruption. With one of their principal aims, however, the blackening of Nkrumah's reputation, the truth was far from simple. There was much other evidence to show that the Nkrumah regime had accumulated funds for purposes quite other than personal comfort. Not a few struggling independence parties in countries still under colonial rule had reason to be grateful for substantial though secret gifts from non-budgetary sources in Ghana. In one such case, known to me personally, a Central African independence party, in desperate need of money for political purposes, received a (to them) critically useful cheque for £10,000 from President Nkrumah's London representative. To the Sandhurst-trained soldiers who made the *coup*, of course, all this was deplorable subversion: they, after all, were the strictly non-participant and 'respectable' beneficiaries of the struggles for African independence, a cause for which they themselves, as good exponents for the 'middle-class solution', had precious little sympathy.

coup, murdered General Kotoka, General Ankrah's righthand man, but was at once put down. This outbreak of military gangsterism appeared to prelude new currents of dissent. According to London *Amnesty* (August 1967), detentions increased rapidly; by July of 1967 there were said to be more than a thousand political detainees. But the trouble blew over, and most were afterwards released.

Another attempt to overthrow General Ankrah and his National Liberation Council was alleged by the authorities in February 1969, this time implicating Air Marshal Otu. According to the public prosecutor, the plot was to have been carried out in the previous December, when the NLC leaders were to have been killed and Nkrumah brought back to power.[176]

In spite of these alarms, civilian rule was duly restored. Parties were legalised in May 1969; elections followed in September. Though generally well conducted, they revealed a clear trend toward parties based on ethnic groups. Drawing strength from the Akan-speaking peoples of Ghana, Dr Kofi Busia's Progress Party emerged as easy victors. With this, all question of 'socialist experimentation' was at an end, at least for the time being. Dr Busia set about reinstalling the 'middle class' solution. It remained to be seen how far it could be made to work under this new management, even with the advantage of cocoa prices now much recovered from their low of 1966.

Two other countries need some mention under the general if clearly very far from definitive label of 'committed'. They are Guinea and Mali, whose policies have also been based on the belief that the ex-colonial countries can and should rebuild their economies on a non-capitalist basis, and that failure to achieve this must result in new if indirect forms of quasi-colonial subjection.

With a population less than half of Ghana's (and a little smaller than Mali's) Guinea achieved independence in late 1958 with the handicap of acute rural poverty and in face of a complete rupture with France. The French departed suddenly, cutting off all aid, facilities, and good will. In this absolute break with the colonial power there lay an immediate gain to which Sékou Touré and the Parti Démocrate de la Guinée were by no means blind. They could attempt without further hindrance a radical reform of the whole spirit as well as personnel of the administration. Their Ghanaian contemporaries, by contrast, had often complained of Britain's slowness to move. Yet the disadvantages soon became apparent. Guinea sorely lacked capital and trained men. Knowing this, the newly independent government tried from the first to restore friendship with Paris (to which many of their members and intellectuals were in any case emotionally committed), though this was to prove possible only in 1963. In their helpless isolation, meanwhile, they turned for help to those who would give it. They forged new and valuable links with Ghana, but also with the Soviet Union and some other communist countries.

By the end of 1960 they were running into fresh difficulties, largely caused by trying to go too far too fast. They overstrained their resources in experienced manpower, available capital, and popular political understanding; and they planned on a level that proved over-ambitious. Far-reaching economic reconstruction ran into crucial problems of revenue and credit. State monopolies in foreign and domestic trade attempted to solve some of these problems, but merely got into a mess. A three-year plan proposed to give the country a firm industrial base with a proportion of domestic capital-formation of only about a fifth of the total thought to be required (relying on foreign aid for the rest), whereas India had allocated about 88 per cent for capital-formation from her own resources, and China as much as 96 per cent, in their respective 'first national plans'.[177]

There were painful consequences, perhaps inseparable from any attempted transition of this kind; but there were also helpful consequences. People learned. Incompetents were exposed. The whole experience of braving the difficulties of the non-capitalist solution proved a good school of practical enlightenment. Life in Guinea might change slowly, often not at all. Yet there were growing numbers of men and women who came to grips with problems as they really were, and not as romantic delusions might present them to be. Remaining skilful in manoeuvre,

Sékou Touré held to his political line. There was here some-thing of the same modesty of style and language that one noticed in Tanzania.

In 1970 Touré was heading for his thirteenth year in power, and the prospects suggested continuation. The Guinea over which he now presided was not a socialist country in any formal sense. Would 'socialism-in-one country' be in any case think-able for a land with fewer than five million inhabitants, much poverty, little or no industry? But neither was Guinea a country where the rich were getting richer and the poor were getting poorer, nor a country where foreign agents or advisers sat behind the chairs of ministers and top officials. In a sense that was not true of most of the ex-colonies of the French Empire, Guinea was an independent and sovereign country with policies and executives of its own, a country where the gap between 'rich and poor' scarcely existed. All this betokened stability.

It also betokened forward movement. There were gains in the educational field; gains in the field of an improved status for women; gains of a subtler sort such as could give ordinary people a new measure of their collective problems. Poverty made any rapid progress impossible. Peasants without material incentives are likely to be peasants who produce little or badly; Guinea found it hard to provide any such incentives. Mean-while, plans were afoot to make this less difficult in the future. Realization of the country's riches in bauxite had gone ahead, during the 1960s, under agreements with foreign enterprises which at least gave Guinea a substantial share in the profits. One American group (Olin Mathieson and others) were active in exploiting deposits at Fria. Another took shape in September 1968, when agreements were signed for the exploitation of neighbouring deposits at Boké. These agreements had an interesting history.

In May 1958, a few months before independence, a French consortium, Bauxites du Midi, had obtained the right to pro-duce at Boké. It was a valuable right: Boké bauxite has an alumina content of about 55 per cent, compared with Fria's 33 per cent average. But Bauxites du Midi appear to have dragged their feet, or else been incapable of meeting their deadline, which was to get Boké into production by 1964. In 1961, accordingly, the Guinea government nationalized Boké, and tried to run the mines with technicians from Eastern Europe. This failed; production fell heavily; Fria remained the principal producer. Then came a new American interest.

The agreements of September 1968 provided for an investment in Boké of $185 million by the World Bank, the U.S. Agency for International Development, and seven American companies banded together in a corporation called Halco. Besides mining, this capital was also to build an 85-mile railway from the Boké region to the sea, as well as a port and harbour works. The Boké deposits were to be mined by a company called Bauxite de Guinée, jointly owned by the government (with 49 per cent) and Halco (with 51 per cent). By 1972 the Halco companies were to have found £100 million; they were to purchase from Bauxite de Guinée an initial 4.7 million tons a year, and somewhat more than that after the sixth year of production. Bauxite de Guinée hoped to sell another one and a half million tons to other consumers.

Neo-colonialism? There were those who thought so. Yet neo-colonialism, it was replied, consists not in small and impoverished ex-colonial countries having to remain in a posture of economic dependence on powerful outside buyers: nothing else is remotely possible in the world of the 1970s. Neo-colonialism consists in allowing these buyers to secure control over domestic policy: even more, it consists in handing power to domestic cliques or élites who become, willingly or not, the local representatives of foreign interests. Neo-colonialism, in short, is the situation which reproduces in an ex-colony a necessarily weak and corrupt copy of a 'middle class' society.

In Guinea, it was further argued, the profits and pickings of bauxite development were not going into the pockets of a privileged few. They were not rebuilding Conakry, the country's capital, as a lavish little copy of London, Paris, or New York. Conakry remained little more than an overgrown village. Critical journalists could regularly report the grass growing in its streets. Others could find a 'profound crisis' in the absence of luxury goods in its shops. All this might be true: to most of the population it mattered not in the least. The country was living within its means; and the means were gradually growing a little less slender for people to whom luxury goods could have little or no importance

The point is worth enlarging. Any immediate comparison between Guinea and the Ivory Coast, by 1967 or later, revealed a far more brilliant picture in the second. Abidjan, capital of the Ivory Coast, was no longer the little town of colonial times. It had become a fine city of tall buildings and fashionable stores. But how much of this luxury had seeped down into the villages, into the crowded urban peripheries? Touré's Guinea, by contrast, had taken a far more difficult line of advance. Here, at least, there was no aping of Paris, no copying of an imported system of values, no widening of the gap between rulers and ruled, no proliferation of foreign advisers and entrepreneurs. It would be interesting, during the 1970s, to see which of these two countries could show the wider social progress, the deeper degree of social and community integration, the larger welding of constituent peoples into new structures of co-operation and production.

Where does the wide grassland republic of Mali stand in this configuration? Here too the nationalist movement had gathered all effective opinion behind it during the run-up to independence in 1960, and was able to conserve this for most of the decade in a broadly-based party. Led by radicals such as Modibo Kéita, the new government sought to advance in a generally non-capitalist direction by relying upon the promotion of co-operative enterprise, by cutting free from the constrictive limits of the French franc system, and by extending state control into manufacture and distribution.

In spite of difficulties caused by the breakdown of Mali's federation with Senegal in 1961 – difficulties enhanced by Mali's landlocked position and poor rail-road communications with the outside world – there were some marked successes. Writing of the period 1964–5, one thoughtful observer could, in 1969, summarize them in this way:

There have been many changes in the Mali countryside as a result of socialist policies. Some of these changes represent a successful transfer from socialist blueprint to social reality; others represent the adaptation of those new institutions to local ends . . .

The Mali achievement is to have brought all the disparate elements of the country together in a single social system. Though the peasants might resist intrusion into local affairs, and did not have to defend the internal organization of their villages, they did not hesitate to participate in national political, social, and economic activities. Herein lies perhaps the most profound change wrought by Mali's socialism: the creation of a new set of social and economic institutions for the rural areas, which, having become naturalized, are the basic framework for a new nation.[178]

It was no small achievement, but it was not enough. The sheer difficulty of modernizing a country such as this, and in ways which offended powerful interests abroad, revealed their harsh obtuseness as early as 1966. Inflation, import scarcities, faults in administration, personal failings: all these piled into a major devaluation of the Mali franc, in May 1967, which formed the price of resumed French aid. Chastened and uneasy, Mali reverted to the franc system, with all that this entailed. Natural disasters added their toll. 1967 brought a plague of locusts, and bad Niger floods. 1968 added a damaging drought.

A not unsympathetic researcher commented in 1968:

Looking back on the past two years, one can see that Modibo's position was becoming increasingly impossible, ever since the agreement of February 1967 to change course and return to the French orbit. To appease his own disillusioned militants he dissolved the party's political bureau and launched Year 1 of the Mali revolution, with its progressive purges of right-wing and moderate elements, culminating in the dissolution of the National Assembly.[179]

There followed a period of demagogic turbulence and increasing threats of a *coup* by those who, for whatever reason, thought that 'things were getting out of hand'.

The *coup* duly came in November 1968. Army officers under Lieut. Moussa Traoré took power and installed a government which, in the words of its foreign minister, intended to put an end to 'the radicalization of the Marxist regime' of Modibo Kéita. In more senses than one, it was Ghana all over again. Once again it would be for the 1970s to prove whether a 'middle class' type of solution in Mali could do more than deepen the problems of socio-economic transition to urbanism and industrialism.

It scarcely needed the growing frustration of the Organization of African Unity, during the second half of the 1960s, to show that the whole future of African liberation was now in question.

Launched as a political slogan, 'neo-colonialism' had acquired a perilous reality.

There was abundant evidence, on every hand, of the frailty of the independence gains of the early 1960s.

As matters stood in 1970, few of these many countries stood firmly on their own ground. Few national leaders showed any realization of the need to combine together in structures that were supra-national, and so avoid the growing dangers presented by élite-promoted separatism, whether within their own frontiers or between their respective countries. Most leaderships continued to go from month to month, somehow hoping for the best. There continued to be, as Fanon had remarked long before, a great deficiency of long-range thought.

There were and are exceptions. By 1969, President Nyerere in Tanzania was outstanding among these. Others, notably President Kaunda of Zambia, were moving in the same direction, grappling with the basic truth that African national parties must either democratize or perish. In 1967 Zambia's ruling party began trying to put down deeper roots in the villages and towns, to draw rank-and-file supporters into the framing and enforcement of policy, as well as to stretch a firm line of working communication between village councils, urban councils, and ministerial departments.[180]

These few men, and those who supported them, were working against time. By 1970 the prospects for an enlarged liberation – for progress towards economic as well as political enlargement – were no longer anything like so favourable as ten years earlier. It was not simply that a dozen countries had fallen under military rule, nor that the outside world is failing, ever more tragically, to make good its promises of aid, nor that population growth is now at a rate which threatens a general impoverishment of all African populations, nor even that budding 'middle class' élites have repeatedly shown their irresponsibility or incapacity to rule well. All these factors have been in play: each has had its weight. But they, in a sense, were or are naturally there: no easy road to wider liberation could in any case be possible.

Beyond these factors, there now lay another and more menacing threat to African advancement, as well as to the gains already made. By the late 1960s a new imperialism was taking shape in the south, but with ambitions pointing far across Middle Africa. For long on the defensive, white South Africa and its partners were turning to the attack. The consequences could not be small.

11 A Neo-Imperialism? Menace and Resistance

The expansive capacity of white-supremacy rule in southern Africa could well seem small in 1960, the 'year of Africa's independence'. Barricaded within its laager, the Purified National police-state was deep in troubles of its own. These were dramatized for the rest of the world in events that followed a non-violent African campaign against the apartheid pass laws. 'The campaign was met with deliberate violence by the police' in shootings at Sharpeville and Langa: between 21 March and 9 April 1960, 'a total of eighty-three non-White civilians were killed and 365 injured by police bullets ... Some 2,000 leading figures in the Congress movement, Pan-Africanists, Liberal Party members, and others were detained without trial for up to five months. Almost 20,000 Africans were arrested under another section of the emergency regulations and thousands of them were sent to prisons or work camps after conviction at secret trials held in the jails. . . .'[101] Could any system as sorely rent within itself prove dangerous to its neighbours? There seemed some grounds for thinking not.

Those who drew any such conclusion were proved wrong. Just as an earlier hope – that the general economic development of South Africa, drawing in non-whites as well as whites, would have a moderating effect on the rigidities of Afrikaner National policy and action – was falsified by the parallel development of police repression, so now did the new prophecies of change prove empty. 'The radical vision failed to materialize. South Africa uniquely demonstrates that a dominant racial minority can perpetuate social rigidities and feudalistic traits on an advanced and expanding industrial basis.'[182] By 1970 the rulers of South Africa had fully recovered from their loss of prestige and confidence after Sharpeville and Langa in 1960. More than that, they had achieved an unprecedented strength and influence. More than that again, they could even claim to stand upon the threshold of a still wider deployment of their power, of the forging in Africa of a new system of empire. Such was the unfolding situation, in 1970, that words like these could not appear inflated.

South Africa was now a country stacked high with capital accumulated from its own domestic enterprises or invested from abroad. While at the beginning of the 1960s there had been 'a net outflow of capital' from South Africa, by 1965 it had become apparent that 'investors' confidence had recovered from the setback of the earlier years, and a substantial inflow of capital was recorded during the period 1965 through the first quarter of 1968': an inflow which continued after that.[183]

Already in 1966 the total value of foreign investments in South Africa was calculated in the same report at $5,313 million, an increase of about ten per cent over the total for 1965. Nearly all this – some 84 per cent – was in private industrial or commercial enterprise. About 60 per cent of the total had come from the United Kingdom, with the United States as the second biggest but now most active source of private investment in South Africa.

Exploiting cheap African labour in mines and other enterprises, South African corporations paid out millions of dollars every year. 'Earnings on United Kingdom and United States private direct investment in South Africa have amounted to $159 million and $124 million respectively in 1966, the most recent year for which data are available. The rates of return on these two countries' direct investment in South Africa also registered substantially higher rates than those on investments held oversea elsewhere.'[184] Partners in the police state, powerful investors in Western Europe and America saw good reason to protect their profits. International action against South Africa's racist policies was correspondingly weak.

From this flowed another contradiction of the 1960s. While world opinion was increasingly mobilized against apartheid, even to the point where there could be serious international discussion of the possibilities of applying economic sanctions,[185] the South

African regime benefited at the same time from growing foreign support. This could be clearly seen in Britain, where a Labour Government's partial ban on arms exports to South Africa met with sharpening denunciation from the Conservative opposition.*

It was not a new Conservative theme. Defending the slave trade two centuries earlier, a British Colonial Secretary had argued that Britain could not afford 'to check or to discourage in any degree a traffic so beneficial to the nation' – by which, of course, he meant the owning and merchanting section of the nation. His successors now said the same about the arms trade. It was not an elevating spectacle, this scene of comfortable investors worried by a threat to the value of their shares. But it was not a surprising or a new one. Long before, Henry Nevinson had described it with an asperity provoked by scenes of slavery in Angola. 'Civilized people may whine and blubber over their imaginary sufferings in plays and novels, but touch their comfort, touch their property – they are rattlesnakes then!'[186]

A second consequence of South Africa's accumulation of capital was to have still deeper meaning for the continent. Production boomed: 1967 alone showed an increase of 50 per cent over 1966 in the share of manufactured goods and machinery in South Africa's exports.[187] As production boomed, so did the search for markets and raw materials grow more extensive. Where better to look than in Africa? By 1965 the notion of a new imperialism in southern Africa, an 'internal' neo-imperialism exercised by South Africa over countries to the north of it, perhaps far to the north of it, had become common talk in Pretoria and Johannesburg. It took the form of advocating a Southern African Common Market. This would extend, it was argued, not only over the small republics of Lesotho, Botswana, and Swaziland, but also, little by little, over other and larger republics further north.

*Not, however, unanimous. 'If our businessmen want to invest up to £1,000 million in South Africa, they should be free to do so. But it does not follow that they should then expect the Government to give moral encouragement to their investments, or even that these investments should force a Government into an erroneous belief that South Africa has become a strategically vital area. It is, by almost common agreement, a poisonous regime in Pretoria. Before we take the poison, it should be made absolutely clear we are doing it only for the money' – Charles Douglas-Home, Defence Correspondent of *The Times*, 24 January 1969.

Malawi was a first target, and easily achieved. Its President, Dr Hastings Kamuzu Banda, found it well to greet the new guest with open arms, though there was also something to suggest, at least in private, that he was not without misgivings. Borrowing £11 million from South Africa for 'development projects', including the building of a new administrative capital, the actual need for which was far from obvious to his critics, Dr Banda declared that South Africa was 'in every sense a friend in need – which is a friend indeed'.[188]

Other targets were also on the list, most obviously Zambia and Congo (Kinshasa), while South African investment in Angola and Moçambique, Portugal's colonies in southern Africa, now became important for the first time. At the same time the South African government embraced the secessionist cause of Biafra, while making efforts towards joint action with any African state, such as Ivory Coast and Ghana, whose government would allow it.

These moves provoked outbursts of indignation from a section of the Purified National Party. Men like Dr Albert Hertzog, following what was now called a *verkrampte* or 're-stricted' line against the *verligte* or 'enlightened' policy of northward penetration adopted by Prime Minister Balthazar Vorster, found it sinister that black diplomats should be allowed to live in whites-only suburbs, and eat in whites-only hotels. But the *verkrampte* politicos were in a small minority. Though numerous enough to break away from the main block of their party and form a new party (just as the Purified Nationalists had broken away in 1933 from the old National party), they found the whole swing and thrust of South African neo-imperialism against them. Another Great Trek was now in motion. For the first time in several decades, white South African influence was moving actively again towards the north.

The decade of the 1960s, in short, brought a turn-about in South African policy. Pretoria's aims were now increasingly aggressive. And this aggressiveness was by no means only in the economic and commercial fields. It was military as well. The mounting armament of white South Africa might be excused, in official propaganda, by some supposed need to meet African armed resistance within South Africa or African attack from the north: its actual scale and content revealed that the basic motivations went far beyond any such 'defensive' role.

In April 1969 it was announced that the government would spend nearly £1,000 million on its military forces and their equipment up to 1974. About £140 millions would be spent in 1969–70, or nearly 17 per cent of the national budget, compared with 6·6 per cent in 1960–61.[189] These armaments were to include conventional small arms and automatics, French helicopters and other equipment, which could serve in anti-guerrilla as well as 'regular' campaigns. Over and beyond all that, they were also to include naval vessels, fast bombing aircraft, rockets and guided missiles, radar and other navigational gear – and, as appeared from what became known of secret agreements signed with France, some advance toward nuclear-armed warheads with their necessary propellants. None of this could be required by any kind of anti-guerrilla operations.* A South African White Paper said as much: 'Although an unconventional threat already exists in the form of terrorism, the possibility of a conventional attack is not excluded.'[190] It called for little reading between the lines, given the military weakness of all the independent African states, to see that the real implication was not an attack on South Africa, but an attack *by* South Africa.

The truth was that the 1960s had drawn white South Africa step by step, though not always willingly, outside its traditional 'redoubt'. There were several sides to this expansive movement.

In November 1965 the White settler government of Ian Smith in Rhodesia rebelled against the British Crown and declared Rhodesia independent. Backed by South Africa and Portugal, which together broke a punitive oil blockade imposed by Britain, the Smith regime set about transforming Rhodesia

---

*After 1963 the French government and French private companies became the principal suppliers of advanced arms and military equipment to South Africa. In return, South Africa became France's principal supplier of uranium for the purposes of building the French government's nuclear weapons armoury. In May 1969 Mr P. W. Botha, speaking for the South African regime, announced with pride that French financial and technical aid had enabled South Africa to manufacture a new air-ground guided missile, 'Cactus'. Italy and Western Germany were also active in supplying arms to South Africa. See an important analysis by René-Georges Claude, 'Le Gaullisme et l'Apartheid', in *Temps Modernes*, Paris, June–July 1969.

into a full-blooded apartheid copy of South Africa. Unwilling to use force, the British government came very near to surrender in 1966. But the extremism of the Whites in Rhodesia prevented this; and, early in 1967, the voluntary sanctions imposed by Britain and such of her friends as were willing to follow suit were enlarged into selective mandatory sanctions applied by the United Nations. The advocates of economic sanctions now argued that these must prevail in the end. They pointed out that Rhodesian exports had been reduced from £145 millions in 1965 to about £80 millions in 1966, and that UN sanctions were expected to reduce them by another £20 millions. Meanwhile, Rhodesian imports were down by a third, and the country's economy was beginning to feel the strain. But the sceptics replied that White South Africa would always be rich enough to succour its little brother across the Limpopo, and that economic sanctions could never do the job.

Events have shown that the sceptics were right. Advancing to full-blooded apartheid on South African lines, the Smith regime proved able to keep going thanks to South African and Portuguese aid. Yet from South Africa's official standpoint, Smith's success was by no means altogether welcome. It carried serious disadvantages for the new policy of 'reconciliation and absorption'. This policy would have much preferred a tame black-and-white regime in Salisbury – one which could prevent any real development of African majority rule, but at the same time provide safety-valves for African protest, as well as disarming the hostility of the outside world. As it was, Smith's open stand for an apartheid-type regime, and a continuation of sanctions under the aegis of the United Nations, meant that the greater part of the outside world had now declared itself, however partially and hesitantly, to be at limited economic war with race rule in what was now a satellite of South Africa. This interposed a barrier to South Africa's continued expansion northward, and it was bitterly regretted in Pretoria. Vorster accordingly tried for a settlement.

'There are,' reported the Salisbury correspondent of *The Times* on 4 October 1968, 'four reasons for the South Africans' desire to make a settlement':

They do not want to end up carrying the Rhodesian economy on the back of the Reserve Bank in Pretoria. They do not want to have to increase the extent to which they are committed to giving para-military assistance to the Rhodesians to help them in combating terrorist activity.

The sophisticated outward-looking policy of Dr Muller, the South African Foreign Minister, hopes to include Zambia one day in the concord which he has established with Malawi and the former High Commission protectorates inside South Africa. Fourthly, South Africa is anxious to achieve a rapport with the West, and particularly Britain and America, on the arms embargo [applied with some success by the United Nations in 1964 and after].

These arguments were pressed on Smith, but Smith would not settle because he could not settle: his electors would not let him. By 1969 the South African regime had absorbed this situation. The 'new' Rhodesia was effectively within the South African system. Like it or not, South Africa's military frontier had advanced north to the Zambezi.

The point was rammed home by the building of a major military air base in the so-called Caprivi Strip of South West Africa (now renamed Namibia by its African nationalists, as Rhodesia was renamed Zimbabwe). This base was only a few miles from the Zambian frontier. Meanwhile South African armed police – no doubt, in fact, units of the South African army specially formed for the purpose – continued on patrol in Rhodesia against any recrudescence of the guerrilla attacks launched there in 1967 and after.

By this time, moreover, South Africa's regime had begun to feel the northward pull of another scene of African resistance, this time against the Portuguese colonial systems in Angola and Moçambique. With some 80,000 troops from Portugal actively committed against perhaps a tenth as many African guerrillas in these two colonies,* the Portuguese had become white South Africa's cannon-fodder along the front lines of the whole white-supremacy system in the southern continent. During the 1960s

*With 30,000–35,000 troops of all arms in Guiné (Portuguese West Africa), the Salazar-Caetano regime had at least 110,000 men fighting in Africa at the end of 1969; the actual total of metropolitan troops was almost certainly higher than this, and perhaps as high as 130,000, not counting some thousands of African mercenaries.

these colonies had provided the scene of the largest, longest, and in some ways most ferocious colonial wars that any part of Africa had ever known, except Algeria in 1954–62. Could the Portuguese make good their desperate effort to remain an imperial power? If not, what must then become of white South Africa's hopes for expansion to the north?

Although Portugal's wars in Africa lit the decade of the 1960s with the flames of napalm and the smoke of burning villages, they were remarkably little noticed in the outside world. They were, of course, inconvenient to the orthodox: as a member of the North Atlantic Treaty Organization, 'little Portugal' was supposed to behave itself, not least in refraining from the use in Africa of arms provided by NATO. When Portugal's masters trampled such promises underfoot, and proceeded to smash up African populations with bombs and bombers made in various NATO countries, scorch them with napalm of similar provenance, and pour out on 'their Africans' the shot and shell of NATO factories, the orthodox preferred to look elsewhere. A tremendous shout emerged from many lips in protest against limited British arms supplies for the Federal Nigerian Government's limited war against Biafran secession: no such support during the 1960s was ever accorded to the Africans caught in the holocausts of Portuguese imperial repression.*

This was all the more strange because of the duration and the size of these colonial wars. At the end of 1970 African nationalists were nearing the end of their tenth year of armed resistance in Angola, their eighth year in Guiné, and their sixth year in Moçambique. For most of these years the Salazar regime had committed to *each* of these colonies an army that was consider-

*Fighting movements in the Portuguese colonies received military aid from the U.S.S.R., China, Czechoslovakia, and other Communist countries; some of these also helped with the training of doctors, soldiers and other technicians. In its early days FRELIMO received money from the U.S. Ford Foundation for a secondary school established in Dar-es-Salaam; U.S. Church sources also donated money to FRELIMO. The Swedish Government, through a para-state body, the Swedish International Development Authority (SIDA), gave FRELIMO, a total of 1,750,000 Swedish crowns for educational purposes between 1964 and 1969 (about £140,000 or $330,000); while in 1969 the same Swedish Government agency devoted one million Swedish crowns (about £81,000 or $190,000) to the purchase and shipment of food, textiles, and medical stores for the PAIGC's needs in their liberated areas of Guiné.

ably larger, in comparative population terms, than the United States army in South Vietnam.

The indifference of the outside world became stranger still when one considered the nature of this African resistance. For the leading movements in these colonies had achieved a success that was unique in the history of guerrilla warfare. They had cracked the towering problem of how to gain a hearing among pre-literate and pre-industrial peoples, of how to mobilize these peoples, of how to persuade these peoples to embrace the cause of armed resistance. Aside from that achievement, their rise and growth were of a general historical importance in the study of African nationalism, for they were governed by circumstances markedly different from those obtaining in the British and French empires. They took shape, that is, in circumstances where no 'reformist option' was present, and where, accordingly, forward movement was possible only in terms that were revolutionary.[191]

While much of black Africa could and did take advantage of the possibility of constitutional reform, and was able to achieve political independence by methods of largely peaceful pressure in the wake of the second world war, the budding nationalist movements of the Portuguese colonies had no such prospect. They were faced with a blank refusal of reform, even minimal reform, of any kind that could lead to African enfranchisement and sovereignty. For them, there was only a choice between two forbidding courses of action. They could disband their clandestine groupings, and accept defeat. Or they could embark on a resistance capable of making Lisbon listen – and this, in the circumstances, could only be an armed resistance. The late Eduardo Mondlane wrote in 1968:

By 1961, two conclusions were obvious. First, Portugal would not admit the principle of self-determination and independence, or allow for any extension of democracy under her own rule.... Secondly, moderate political action such as strikes, demonstrations and petitions, would result only in the destruction of those who took part in them. We were, therefore, left with these alternatives: to continue indefinitely living under a repressive imperial rule, or to find a means of using force against Portugal which would be effective enough to hurt Portugal without resulting in our own ruin.[192]

It stands squarely on the record that they found this a means of effective action against Portuguese imperial rule. Not easily, not quickly, nor without failures and false starts. Yet by 1969 the Movimento Popular de Libertaçao de Angola (MPLA) – launched in clandestinity in 1956, all but wiped out in 1961, reformed in exile in 1963 and embarked on new operations in 1966 – had rooted itself deeply in the wide grasslands regions of eastern and east-central Angola, despite intensive Portuguese efforts to destroy it by ground and air operations. Though traversing a leadership crisis after the unexplained assassination of Eduardo Mondlane in January 1969, the Frente de Libertaçao de Moçambique (FRELIMO) had shown itself capable of securing the military initiative throughout the northern provinces of Moçambique, and of establishing its control over broad rural areas there, once again in face of determined Portuguese warfare. Far away in Guiné, on the tip of western Africa, the most successful of all these movements, the Partido Africano por la Independência de Guiné e Cabo Verde (PAIGC), had swept the Portuguese out of some two-thirds of that colony, and gained a clear military initiative at all points on the mainland.

Still more interestingly, these movements had shown themselves persistently capable of effective political action. Though impressive, their military success was the lesser part of their achievement. To be convinced of that, one needed only to walk through areas under their control and note the schools, hospitals, clinics, productive and economic organisms they had brought into being in combination with village committees which pointed to new structures of self-government.* Here, in the midst of bitter warfare, a new type of political system appeared to be taking shape, such as might be capable of bridging the gulf between these technologically deprived populations of Portuguese Africa and the modern world outside. It was moreover a type of political system which might even have an exemplary importance for the Africa of the 1970s. *Ex Africa semper aliquid novi*: the old saying could still ring with an insistent truth.

Facing this determined armed resistance not only to the Por-

*By 1970 quite a few visitors had done this. I myself was briefly in guerrilla areas of the PAIGC in 1967, of FRELIMO in 1968, and of MPLA in 1970.

tuguese, but also to the development of their own hegemony in central-southern Africa, the men in Pretoria increased their effort to present it as 'the long arm of Communism'. In this they were avidly seconded by the Rhodesian rebels and the Portuguese themselves. It seemed likely to be a theme of which much would be heard – and from which, as many feared, much evil might now flow.

The consistently non-alarmist Nyerere summed up this fear when addressing the University of Toronto in October 1969. Like Portugal, he said,

South Africa claims to be a bastion against communism in Africa. The regime in Rhodesia claims that it is defending its part of Africa against communist-inspired chaos. These states are all anxious that their struggle against the freedom movements should be interpreted in the West as part of a world-wide anti-communist struggle. The real danger which worries me is that the West will accept this interpretation, and that it will, in consequence, betray its own principles by supporting these Southern African regimes.

He went on to point out that

the freedom fighters use communist arms and are trained in communist countries because they have no choice. This is happening now and it will continue. And then South Africa and Portugal will proclaim to their allies this 'proof' that they are fighting communism. They will show captured communist weapons and display some hapless prisoner-of-war (whom they will describe as a criminal) in order to persuade those opposed to communism to support their war against the freedom fighters. ... In the face of this kind of psychological pressure, I am afraid that Western states would strengthen their support for the Southern African regimes. They would argue that for their own protection it was necessary to prevent Africa from falling into the hands of communists. ... And gradually this conflict will become the ideological conflict which at present it is not.

At that point, because Africa does not look at things through cold war spectacles, the nature of the conflict may change again: it may become a confrontation between the poor, coloured world and the rich, white world. ...

It was a sombre warning. Yet it was hard, as the decade of the 1960s came to an end, to say that it overstated the conflict that could now unfold.

12 Which Way Africa?
The Challenge of the 1970s

The long-range answer to the question of Africa's future will depend on pressures that are probably beyond the reach of anyone's present understanding, and are certainly beyond mine. But it appears already obvious that the crucial pressures will be those of a public opinion increasingly impatient of 'things as they are'. Such pressures have been growing rapidly since 1963. 'Our leaders must realize', ran one fairly typical statement of this mounting impatience, 'that we have put them where they are not to satisfy their ambitions nor so that they can strut about in fine clothes and huge Cadillacs as ambassadors and ministers. . . . Selfish power-seekers will have to go.'[193] Thoughts like these could be heard all over the continent, though not until lately in such forthright words.

Furthermore, these growing pressures of public opinion seemed likely to operate within the framework of four dominant trends. These trends were partly negated by subsequent events, but are still worth summarizing here.

To solve the central 'problem of power' – of 'who governs whom and how' – there was first of all the trend towards the one-party state, towards concentration of all effective and even legitimate action within a single organization, within a 'liberation movement' transformed and deepened into a 'reconstruction movement'. More and more leaders had been recognizing the strength of this trend. 'As things are,' the late Sardauna of Sokoto was noting of Nigeria at the end of 1962, 'there is no real reason to think that the Opposition in the Regions are ever likely to be in a position, in the foreseeable future, to form a Government. . . .'[194]

On the same point, a little earlier, the Minister of the Interior of Mali, Modibo Kéita, had argued that full recognition of the reality of this situation – acceptance, that is, of a single unified party of 'government and opposition' – made for 'greater honesty, greater disinterestedness, greater devotion' among politicians, and all the more because in Africa today 'you cannot remain a leader for very long unless you are really effective'.[195] Public opinion, in other words, could not be ignored; and public opinion wanted progress.

To solve the problem of development – of economic and social progress – there was the trend towards state capitalism, and, among the committed countries, its deliberate extension in the direction of socialism. Thirdly, to the problem of the cold war and its conflict of loyalties, the general answer was a more or less emphatic neutralism. And, last but not least, in response to the problem of inter-African relations there was the effort to secure continental unity of policy, action, and institutions.

It was early in the day to be sure of what the atmosphere, the mood and style of independent African civilization, would be like. On the whole, though, it appeared that this atmosphere would not be narrowly nationalist, intolerant, or bellicose. There were, true enough, signs to the contrary. White racism has sometimes tended, most obviously in South Africa, to produce its African counterpart. But even here the signs are far from clear. Quite often they seem to owe less to reality than to European imagination. The Malawi Congress party in Nyasaland, it may be remembered, was accused of conspiring to massacre Europeans; but the charge was then shown by a British judicial inquiry to be groundless.[196] The following extract from a British newspaper suggests that accusations of chauvinism and violence should be received with caution.

During the recent election campaign in Nyasaland [that of 1961] a fierce campaign was waged by a section of the Press of this country and by a group of Tory M.P.s against Dr Banda's Malawi Party, alleging that it was victimizing its opponents by burning down their homes. At one stage the campaign reached the point where Sir Roy Welensky (then Federal Prime Minister in Central Africa) canvassed the idea of putting off the elections because of this alleged victimization.
The worst incident was said to have occurred at Mbobo, where three

houses were destroyed, including that of Mr Chijalo, the local chairman of Sir Roy Welensky's United Federal Party. At the time two of Dr Banda's supporters were convicted; one youth was given twelve strokes with a cane. Last week Mr Chijalo was himself convicted for conspiring to defeat justice and sentenced to eighteen months' imprisonment. He has also been charged with two other members of the United Federal Party with burning down their own houses. It is a pity that these events have not been given equal prominence in those papers which gave so much prominence to the allegations against Malawi at the time. The boy who was whipped after being wrongfully convicted has been paid £10 as compensation.[197]

Europeans, of course, found many occasions for irritation – some petty and spiteful – in independent Africa. I have already quoted the case of the twenty-nine Europeans who were turned out of a Tanganyika hotel for failing to recognize President Touré of Guinea. But all in all it is hard to understand how a newspaper like the *Guardian* could bring itself to write that 'Africa has not yet had time to throw up the new generation of leaders who will see Africa as something more edifying than a racial battleground'.[198] For the weight of evidence had been remarkably at odds with any such conclusion. Victorious Algerians had not massacred Frenchmen; independent West Africans had not ceased to employ large numbers of whites; emancipated East Africans had not turned their backs on European friendship. Even a 'hard-core detainee' of the 'Mau Mau' emergency in Kenya, J. M. Kariuki, could write after seven years of detention in fourteen camps and much beating and harsh treatment that 'there will be no spirit of revenge to destroy our new Kenya'; while Dr Margery Perham noted in her foreword to his book that she found Kariuki possessed of 'a healing desire for reconciliation with those Europeans or Africans who had ill-treated him'.[199] The general temper of Africa appeared to be resiliently tolerant and healthy.

These neat and somewhat oratorical perspectives for continental progress through the techniques of mass democracy, socialist organization, neutralist policy, and African unity, were the hopes of 1963. Not surprisingly, they have run into many storms and upsets. Events in Nigeria and Ghana in 1966 were paralleled by military *coups* in eight other countries, including Sierra Leone in March 1967. Seen from the midway point of 1967, most of independent Africa was now locked in struggle with acute problems inherent to its situation, and there is no good reason for thinking that the process can soon be over.

This brief survey has had to omit a great deal of supporting evidence. Yet it may be adequate to indicate at least the general framework and dimensions of this continental search for progress in stability. Since 1963, true enough, the prevailing atmosphere has been darkened here and there by violence and civil war; all the same, the general temper has remained surprisingly tolerant and pacific. The themes of 1963 have taken a battering at several points, and yet they likewise remain at the centre of debate.

Essentially, the problem remains one of unification at two levels: intra–territorial unification of states whose frontiers were fashioned by Europe and include within themselves a far larger number of pre-colonial states; and, secondly, inter-territorial unification of these states within the boundaries of Africa itself. What has really changed since 1963 is that things are clearer than before. Myths have been vanishing – myths of charismatic leadership, myths about the miracles to be performed by foreign aid, myths around the true nature of the modern world. Otherwise the heart of the matter remains where it was. It is to know how to activate and enthuse millions of rural Africans for efforts at the forging of new attitudes to work, new ways of cooperation, new methods of production, new forms of organization.

More and more, African national leaders and parties have come to understand that they must democratize or perish. The failures of élitist forms of rule, seeking to impose their hegemony within structures taken over largely from the colonial past, have repeatedly made this clear. Many had learned this lesson by 1969; others who had not, or who preferred to ignore it, seemed due for disagreeable surprises. Only new structures of mass participation seemed now capable of mastering the future.

Independence created an opportunity, but little more than that. There is here an analogy with Russia. Professor Carr has remarked that Tsar Alexander's emancipation of the serfs in

1861 did not, in any absolute sense, free the peasant from his bondage. 'Where no alternative employment or avenue of escape was available, it could not materially raise the level of the peasantry as a whole. It ushered in a period of growing population and chronic hunger in the Russian countryside, culminating in the drastic famine of 1891.'[200] What was needed was an entirely new social and economic framework. In the event, only revolution provided that.

Much the same is true of Africa. Political emancipation offers the key to a different and better future only if it can unlock the gate to major structural changes in every field of everyday life. And by 1967 the lesson was being hammered home by population experts who estimate that Africa's population may well have grown to 700 millions by the early years of the twenty-first century. Only great and systematic increases in production can now prevent the disasters of widespread famine. But these in turn must depend on far-reaching advances in methods and relations of work.

And so we come back to the question of *choice*. By what system can these advances be assured? In practice, of course, the choice is concerned with African realities, and to that extent must be original and unique. Theoretically, though, as documents like the Arusha Declaration show, it is a choice that is ultimately between a form of colonialism and a form of socialism. By 1967, too, the choice was clearer because the chances for an indigenous capitalism in Africa no longer seemed as bright and easy as before. Federal Nigeria had been the great exemplar of the capitalist choice; and Federal Nigeria had failed. The lessons were many, and they were pondered.

There were other lessons of the last few years, notably on the practical limitations of foreign aid. It had fallen steadily in quantity, and seemed bound to fall further. 'The present status of aid today,' commented the late Tom Mboya, speaking for the Kenya government at a session of the UN Economic Commission for Africa, 'holds no promise for the future. Optimistically, it means gently rising *per capita* incomes to achieve for the very poor countries perhaps $200 per annum by the end of the century; it means rising debts and perennial balance of payments problems; it means continuously falling terms of trade and continued barriers to the sale of industrial products; it means no escape from the abyss of primary production.'[201]

Various conclusions were drawn. At one extreme there were Mr Mboya and others who thought with him. They continued to call for a vast increase in aid: for a 'Marshall Plan for Africa', 'a massive inflow of capital over perhaps 30 years and an equally massive inflow of technical assistance personnel over 10 to 15 years'.[202] At the other extreme there were Nyerere and the socialists who replied that in the first place there was no real hope of any such aid, and, secondly, even if there were, it would be highly undesirable, because it would lead, in one way or another, to a new if indirect bondage:

We have made a mistake [said the Arusha Declaration] to choose money, something which we do not have, to be our major instrument of development. We are mistaken when we imagine that we shall get money from foreign countries – firstly, because to say the truth we cannot get enough money for our development, and, secondly, because even if we could get it such complete dependence on outside help would have endangered our independence and the other policies of our country.

Those who still held firm by the capitalist or 'middle class' solution did so, like the new military rulers, with their eyes shut or as if discussion of any other solution must be treason at worst and foolishness at best; or, like Mboya, they whistled to keep their courage up and vainly exhorted the rich countries, then eagerly retrenching on their aid programmes, to dip more deeply into increasingly reluctant pockets.

Meanwhile it seems clear that the emergent middle classes on whom the capitalist solution must depend are in for a rough time. Deprived of expanding inflows of foreign capital, whether private or public, these 'beneficiaries' are now likely to appear, still more obviously and intolerably than before, as power cliques concerned mainly with accumulating personal wealth at the painful and growing cost of the mass of ordinary folk. What looks probable now is an extension of military or other authoritarian rule as the only way of protecting the class-formation that must now be necessary, whatever the cost in social justice, if an African capitalism is to have a chance to flourish. And onward from there, faintly in the future but steadily drawing nearer, there can also be descried the grim possibility that Africa may after all follow Latin America, and reduce its political life to a mere battle between contending oligarchies while the masses hunger, or are at any rate deprived of all real participation in public affairs.[203]

Not that the alternative, the only alternative – the move towards non-capitalist solutions, eventually socialist solutions – can be easy or painless. As those few leaderships who have embarked on this alternative have good reason to know, their success will depend on strong courage and firm faith in human nature, on a moral commitment willing to throw everything into the balance, on a hard-headed realism that must shift mountains of misunderstanding or disbelief. Much of independent Africa in 1970 faced a new peril of impoverishment, whether through population growth or worsening terms of international trade. Much of it faced a new danger of subjection, whether through the weakness of its governments in face of outside pressure and ambition, the irresponsibility of its 'beneficiaries', or the intentions of South Africa and the backers of South Africa.

All the same, one may emphasize, the overall situation is in many important ways much better than before. The choice is clearer. Not only is the debate still open: it is advanced by several stages. If the past few years have brought setbacks to those who believe that nothing short of profound and therefore radical structural change can save Africa from a new subjection, they have also brought a new clarity, an end to many illusions and delusions. Africa remains deep in conflict on the means and possibilities of continental transformation. But today there are many Africans who measure the problems of the present and the future far more realistically than in the past. Ten years of independence have brought great and creative changes to many fields of life and thought.

The mists of nationalist euphoria, the smokescreens of charismatic demagogy, the fogs of Cold War propaganda – all these have felt the useful blow and blast of many gales of argument and action. The 1950s presided over the struggle for political emancipation. But the 1960s, whatever trials they have brought, have not been wasted. They have successfully opened the way for another necessary struggle, a struggle for the fruits of political emancipation, for that new and unified society without which the peoples of Africa cannot even keep the freedom which they have, let alone enlarge it.

Summer 1970

On the Record
The Charter of Unity

Addis Ababa, 25 May 1963

We, the Heads of African States and Governments assembled in the city of Addis Ababa, Ethiopia;

CONVINCED that it is the inalienable right of all people to control their own destiny;

CONSCIOUS of the fact that freedom, equality, justice, and dignity are essential objectives for the achievement of the legitimate aspirations of the African peoples;

CONSCIOUS of our responsibility to harness the natural and human resources of our continent for the total advancement of our peoples in spheres of human endeavour;

INSPIRED by a common determination to strengthen understanding and cooperation among our states in response to the aspirations of our peoples for brotherhood and solidarity, in a large unity transcending ethnic and national differences;

CONVINCED that, in order to translate this determination into a dynamic force in the cause of human progress, conditions for peace and security must be established and maintained;

DETERMINED to safeguard and consolidate the hard-won independence as well as the sovereignty and territorial integrity of our states, and to fight against neo-colonialism in all its forms;

DEDICATED to the general progress of Africa;

PERSUADED that the Charter of the United Nations and the Universal Declaration of Human Rights, to the principles of which we reaffirm our adherence, provide a solid foundation for peaceful and positive cooperation among states;

DESIROUS that all African states should henceforth unite so that the welfare and well-being of their peoples can be assured;

RESOLVED to reinforce the links between our states by establishing and strengthening common institutions;

HAVE agreed to the present Charter.

Establishment

Article I. (1) The High Contracting Parties do by the present Charter establish an organization to be known as the 'Organization of African Unity'.

(2) The organization shall include the continental African states, Madagascar, and all the islands surrounding Africa.

Purposes

Article II. (1) The organization shall have the following purposes: (a) to promote the unity and solidarity of the African states; (b) to coordinate and intensify their cooperation and efforts to achieve a better life for the peoples of Africa; (c) to defend their sovereignty, their territorial integrity, and independence; (d) to eradicate all forms of colonialism from Africa; and (e) to promote international cooperation, having due regard to the Charter of the United Nations and the Universal Declaration of Human Rights.

(2) To these ends, the member states shall coordinate and harmonize their general policies, especially in the following fields: (a) political and diplomatic cooperation; (b) economic cooperation, including transport and communications; (c) educational and cultural cooperation; (d) health, sanitation, and nutritional cooperation; (e) scientific and technical cooperation; and (f) cooperation for defence and security.

Principles

Article III. The member states, in pursuit of the purposes stated in Article II, solemnly affirm and declare their adherence to the following principles:

(1) the sovereign equality of all member states;

(2) non-interference in the internal affairs of states;

(3) respect for the sovereignty and territorial integrity of each member state and for its inalienable right to independent existence;

(4) peaceful settlement of disputes, by negotiation, mediation, conciliation, or arbitration;

(5) unreserved condemnation, in all its forms, of political assassination as well as of subversive activities on the part of neighbouring states or any other states;

(6) absolute dedication to the total emancipation of the African territories which are still dependent;

(7) affirmation of a policy of non-alignment with regard to all blocs.

Membership

Article IV. Each independent sovereign African state shall be entitled to become a member of the organization.

Rights and Duties of Member States

Article V. All member states shall enjoy equal rights and have equal duties.

Article VI. The member states pledge themselves to observe scrupulously the principles enumerated in Article III of the present Charter.

Institutions

Article VII. The organization shall accomplish its purposes through the following principal institutions:

(1) the Assembly of Heads of State and Government;

(2) the Council of Ministers;

(3) the General Secretariat;

(4) the Commission of Mediation, Conciliation, and Arbitration.

The Assembly of Heads of State and Government

Article VIII. The Assembly of Heads of State and Government shall be the supreme organ of the organization. It shall, subject to the provisions of this Charter, discuss matters of common concern to Africa with a view to coordinating and harmonizing the general policy of the organization. It may in addition review the structure, functions, and acts of all the organs and any specialized agencies which may be created in accordance with the present Charter.

Article IX. The Assembly shall be composed of the Heads of

State, Government, or their duly accredited representatives, and it shall meet at least *once a year*. At the request of any member state, and approval by the majority of the member states, the Assembly shall meet in extraordinary session.

Article X. (1) Each member state shall have one vote.

(2) All resolutions shall be determined by a two-thirds majority of the members of the organization.

(3) Questions of procedure shall require a simple majority. Whether or not a question is one of procedure shall be determined by a simple majority of all member states of the organization.

(4) Two-thirds of the total membership of the organization shall form a quorum at any meeting of the Assembly.

Article XI. The Assembly shall have the power to determine its own rules of procedure.

The Council of Ministers

Article XII. The Council of Ministers shall consist of Foreign Ministers or such other Ministers as are designated by the Governments of member states.

The Council of Ministers shall meet at least twice a year. When requested by any member state and approved by two-thirds of all member states, it shall meet in extraordinary session.

Article XIII. The Council of Ministers shall be responsible to the Assembly of Heads of State and Government. It shall be entrusted with the responsibility of preparing conferences of the Assembly.

It shall take cognizance of any matter referred to it by the Assembly. It shall be entrusted with the implementation of the decisions of the Assembly of Heads of State and Government. It shall coordinate inter-African cooperation in accordance with the instructions of the Assembly and in conformity with Article II (2) of the present Charter.

Article XIV. (1) Each member state shall have one vote.

(2) All resolutions shall be determined by a simple majority of the Council of Ministers.

(3) Two-thirds of the total membership of the Council shall form a quorum for any meeting of the Council.

Article XV. The Council shall have the power to determine its own rules of procedure.

General Secretariat

Article XVI. There shall be an Administrative Secretary-General of the organization, who shall be appointed by the Assembly of Heads of State and Government, on the recommendation of the Council of Ministers. The Administrative Secretary-General shall direct the affairs of the Secretariat.

Article XVII. There shall be one or more Assistant Secretaries-General of the organization, who shall be appointed by the Assembly of Heads of State and Government.

Article XVIII. The functions and conditions of service of the Secretary-General, of the Assistant Secretaries-General, and of other employees of the Secretariat shall be governed by the provisions of this Charter and the regulations approved by the Assembly of Heads of State and Government.

(1) In the performance of their duties the Administrative Secretary-General and the staff shall not seek or receive instructions from any government or from any other authority external to the organization. They shall refrain from any action which might reflect on their position as international officials responsible only to the organization.

(2) Each member of the organization undertakes to respect the exclusive character of the responsibilities of the Administrative Secretary-General and the staff and not to seek to influence them in the discharge of their responsibilities.

Commission of Mediation, Conciliation, and Arbitration

Article XIX. Member states pledge to settle all disputes among themselves by peaceful means and, to this end, decide to establish a Commission of Mediation, Conciliation, and Arbitration, the composition of which and the condition of service shall be defined by a separate protocol to be approved by the Assembly of Heads of State and Government.

Specialized Commissions

Article XX. The Assembly shall establish such Specialized Commissions as it may deem necessary, including the following:

(1) Economic and Social Commission;
(2) Educational and Cultural Commission;
(3) Health, Sanitation, and Nutrition Commission;
(4) Defence Commission;
(5) Scientific, Technical, and Research Commission.

Article XXI. Each Specialized Commission referred to in Article XX shall be composed of the Ministers concerned or other Ministers or Plenipotentiaries designated by the Governments of the member states.

Article XXII. The functions of the Specialized Commissions shall be carried out in accordance with the provisions of the present Charter and of the regulations approved by the Council of Ministers.

The Budget

Article XXIII. The budget of the organization prepared by the Administrative Secretary-General shall be approved by the Council of Ministers. The budget shall be provided by contributions from member states in accordance with the scale of assessment of the United Nations; provided, however, that no member state shall be assessed an amount exceeding twenty per cent of the yearly regular budget of the organization. The member states agree to pay their respective contributions regularly.

Signature and Ratification of Charter

Article XXIV. This Charter shall be open for signature to all independent sovereign African states and shall be ratified by the signatory states in accordance with their respective constitutional processes.

The original instrument, done, if possible, in African languages, in English and French, all texts being equally authentic, shall be deposited with the Government of Ethiopia, which shall transmit certified copies thereof to all independent sovereign African states.

Instruments of ratification shall be deposited with the Government of Ethiopia, which shall notify all signatories of each such deposit.

Entry into Force

Article XXV. This Charter shall enter into force immediately upon receipt by the Government of Ethiopia of the instruments of ratification from two-thirds of the signatory states.

Registration of the Charter

Article XXVI. This Charter shall, after due ratification, be registered with the Secretariat of the United Nations through the Government of Ethiopia in conformity with Article 102 of the Charter of the United Nations.

Interpretation of the Charter

Article XXVII. (1) Any question which may arise concerning the interpretation of this Charter shall be decided by a vote of two-thirds of the Assembly of Heads of State and Government of the organizations.

Adhesion and Accession

Article XXVIII. (1) Any independent sovereign African State may at any time notify the Administrative Secretary-General of its intention to adhere or accede to this Charter.

(2) The Administrative Secretary-General shall, on receipt of such notification, communicate a copy of it to all the member states. Admission shall be decided by a simple majority of member states. The decision of each member state shall be transmitted to the Administrative Secretary-General, who shall, upon receipt of the required number of votes, communicate the decision to the state concerned.

Miscellaneous

Article XXIX. The working languages of the organization and all its institutions shall be, if possible, African languages, English, and French.

Article XXX. The Administrative Secretary-General may

accept on behalf of the organization gifts, bequests, and other donations made to the organization, provided that this is approved by the Council of Ministers.

Article XXXI. The Council of Ministers shall decide on the privileges and immunities to be accorded to the personnel of the Secretariat in the respective territories of the member states.

Cessation of Membership

Article XXXII. Any state which desires to renounce its membership shall forward a written notification to the Administrative Secretary-General. At the end of one year from the date of such notification, if not withdrawn, the Charter shall cease to apply with respect to the renouncing state, which shall thereby cease to belong to the organization.

Amendment to the Charter

Article XXXIII. This Charter may be amended or revised if any member state makes a written request to the Administrative Secretary-General to that effect, provided, however, that the proposed amendment is not submitted to the Assembly for consideration until all the member states have been duly notified of it and a period of one year has elapsed. Such an amendment shall not be effective unless approved by at least two-thirds of all the member states.

In faith, whereof, We, the Heads of African States and Governments, have signed this Charter.

Done in the City of Addis Ababa, Ethiopia, this 25th day of May, 1963.

1. Algeria: Premier Ahmed Ben Bella
2. Burundi: King Mwambutsa
3. Cameroon: President Ahmadou Ahidjo
4. Central African Republic: President David Dacko
5. Chad: President François Tombalbaye
6. Congo-Brazzaville: President Fulbert Youlou
7. Congo-Leopoldville: President Joseph Kasavubu
8. Dahomey: President Hubert Maga
9. Ethiopia: Emperor Haile Selassie I
10. Gabon: President Leon M'Ba

11. Ghana: President Kwame Nkrumah
12. Guinea: President Sékou Touré
13. Ivory Coast: President Félix Houphouët-Boigny
14. Liberia: President William V. S. Tubman
15. Libya: King Idris I
16. Malagasy Republic: President Philibert Tsiranana
17. Mali: President Modibo Kéita
18. Mauritania: President Makhtar Ould Daddah
19. Niger: President Hamani Diori
20. Nigeria: Prime Minister Alhaji Sir Abubakar Tafawa Balewa
21. Ruanda: Foreign Minister Callixte Habamenshi for President Grégoire Kayibanda
22. Senegal: President Leopold Sédar Senghor
23. Sierra Leone: Prime Minister Sir Milton Margai
24. Somali Republic: President Abdullah Osman
25. Sudan: President Ibrahim Abboud
26. Tanganyika: President Julius Nyerere
27. Tunisia: President Habib Bourguiba
28. Uganda: Prime Minister Milton Obote
29. United Arab Republic: President Gamal Abdul Nasser
30. Upper Volta: President Maurice Yaméogo

Not Present:

1. Morocco: King Hassan II
2. Togo: President Nicolas Grunitzky

THE RESOLUTIONS

I. *Decolonization*

The Summit Conference of Independent African States meeting in Addis Ababa, Ethiopia, from 22 May to 25 May 1963; *having considered* all aspects of the questions of decolonization; *unanimously convinced* of the imperious and urgent necessity of coordinating and intensifying their efforts to accelerate the unconditional attainment of national independence by all African territories still under foreign domination; *reaffirming* that it is the duty of all African independent states to support dependent people in Africa in their struggle for freedom and independence; *noting* with deep concern that most of the remaining dependent territories in Africa are dominated by foreign settlers; *convinced* that the colonial powers by their forcible imposition of the settlers to control the governments and administration of those territories are thus establishing colonial bases in the heart of Africa; *have agreed* unanimously to concert and coordinate their efforts and action in this field, and to this end have decided on the following measures:

(1) *Declares* that the forcible imposition by the colonial powers of the settlers to control the governments and administration of the dependent territories is a flagrant violation of the inalienable rights of the legitimate inhabitants of the territories concerned;

(2) *Invites* the colonial powers to take the necessary measures for the immediate application of the declaration on the granting of independence to colonial countries and peoples by insisting on the fact that their determination to maintain colonies or semi-colonies in Africa constitutes a menace to the peace of the continent;

(3) *Invites* further the colonial powers, particularly the United Kingdom with regard to Southern Rhodesia, not to transfer the powers and attributes of sovereignty to foreign minority governments imposed on African peoples by the use of force and under cover of racial legislation. A transfer of this kind would amount to a violation of the provisions of United Nations resolution 1514 on independence;

(4) *Reaffirms* its support of African nationalists of Southern Rhodesia and solemnly declares that if power in Southern Rhodesia were to be usurped by a racial white minority government, the states members of the Conference would lend their effective moral and practical support to any legitimate measures which the African nationalist leaders may devise for the purpose of recovering such power and restoring it to the African majority. The Conference undertakes henceforth to concert the efforts of its members to take such measures as the situation demands against any state according to such recognition;

(5) *Reaffirms* that the territory of South-West Africa is an African territory under international mandate and that any attempt by the Republic of South Africa to annex it would be regarded as an act of aggression; *Reaffirms* also its determination

to render all necessary support to the second phase of the South-West Africa case before the International Court of Justice; *Reaffirms*, further, the inalienable right of the people of South-West Africa to self-determination and independence;

(6) *Intervenes* expressly with the great powers so that they cease without exception to lend directly or indirectly any support or assistance to all those colonialist governments which might use such assistance to suppress African national liberation movements, particularly the Portuguese Government, which is conducting a real war of genocide in Africa. *Informs* the allies of colonial powers that they must choose between their friendship for the African peoples and their support of powers that oppress African peoples;

(7) *Sends* a delegation of Ministers of Foreign Affairs to speak on behalf of all African states at the meeting of the Security Council which will be called to examine the report of the United Nations Committee of 26 on the situation in African territories under Portuguese domination;

(8) *Demands* the breaking off of diplomatic and consular relations between all African states and the Governments of Portugal and South Africa so long as they persist in their present attitude towards decolonization;

(9) *Asks for an effective boycott* of the foreign trade of Portugal and South Africa by (a) prohibiting the import of goods from those two countries; (b) closing African ports and airports to their ships and planes; (c) forbidding the planes of those two countries to overfly the territories of all African states;

(10) *Earnestly invites* all national liberation movements to coordinate their efforts by establishing common action fronts wherever necessary so as to strengthen the effectiveness of their struggle and the rational use of the concerted assistance given them;

(11) *Establishes* a coordinating committee consisting of Ethiopia, Algeria, Uganda, U.A.R., Tanganyika, Congo-Leopoldville, Guinea, Senegal, and Nigeria, with headquarters in Dar-es-Salaam, responsible for harmonizing the assistance from African states and for managing the special fund to be set up for that purpose;

(12) *Establishes* a special fund to be contributed by member states with the deadline (15 July) to supply the necessary practical and financial aid to the various African national liberation movements;

(13) *Appoints* the day of 25 May 1963, as African Liberation Day and will organize popular demonstrations on that day to disseminate the recommendations of the Heads of State Conference and to collect sums, over and above the national contributions, for the special fund;

(14) *Receives*, on the territories of independent African states, nationalists from liberation movements in order to give them training in all sectors, and afford young people all the assistance they need for their education and vocational training;

(15) *Promotes*, in each state, the establishment of a body of volunteers in various fields, with a view to providing the various African national liberation movements with the assistance they need in the various sectors;

(16) *Fixes* a deadline for the accession of all African territories to independence.

II. *Apartheid and Racial Discrimination*

The Summit Conference of Independent African States, *having considered* all aspects of the questions of apartheid and racial discrimination; *unanimously convinced* of the imperious and urgent necessity of coordinating and intensifying their efforts to put an end to the South African Government's criminal policy of apartheid and wipe out racial discrimination in all its forms; *have agreed* unanimously to concert and coordinate their efforts and action in this field; and to this end have decided on the following measures:

(1) Creation of a fund for concerted financial assistance to the anti-apartheid movement in South Africa.

(2) Effective assistance of every kind to anti-apartheid movements in South Africa to help them carry out their struggle for freedom efficiently.

(3) The immediate release of Mr Mandela, Mr Sobukwe, and all other political prisoners in South Africa.

(4) Granting of scholarships, educational facilities, and

possibilities of employment in African government service to refugees from South Africa.

(5) Supporting the recommendations presented to the Security Council and the General Assembly by the Special Committee of the United Nations on the apartheid policies of the South African Government.

(6) Despatch of a delegation of Foreign Ministers to inform the Security Council of the explosive situation existing in South Africa.

(7) Coordination of concrete measures of sanction against the Government of South Africa.

(8) Appeal to all states, and more particularly to those which have traditional relations and cooperate with the Government of South Africa, strictly to apply U.N. resolution 1761 of 6 November 1962, concerning apartheid.

(9) Appeal to all governments who still have diplomatic, consular, and economic relations with the Government of South Africa to break off those relations and to cease any other form of encouragement for the policy of apartheid.

(10) Stress the great responsibility incurred by the colonial authorities of territories neighbouring of South Africa for the pursuit of the policy of apartheid.

(11) Condemnation of racial discrimination in all its forms in Africa and all over the world.

(12) Expression of the deep concern aroused in all African peoples and governments by the measures of racial discrimination taken against communities of African origin living outside the continent and particularly in the United States of America. Expression of appreciation for the efforts of the Federal Government of the United States of America to put an end to these intolerable malpractices which are likely seriously to deteriorate relations between the African peoples and governments on the one hand and the people and government of the United States of America on the other.

III. *Africa, Non-Alignment, and the United Nations*

The Summit Conference, *believing* that the United Nations is an important instrument for the maintenance of peace and security among nations and for the promotion of the economic and social advancement of all peoples; *reiterating* its desire to strengthen and support the United Nations; *noting* with regret that Africa as a region is not equitably represented in the principal organs of the United Nations; *convinced* of the need for closer cooperation and coordination among the African states members of the United Nations:

(1) *Reaffirms* its dedication to the purposes and principles of the United Nations Charter, and its acceptance of all obligations contained in the Charter, including financial obligations;

(2) *Insists* that Africa as a geographical region should have equitable representation in the principal organs of the United Nations, particularly the Security Council and the Economic and Social Council and its Specialized Agencies;

(3) *Invites* African governments to instruct their representatives in the United Nations to take all possible steps to achieve a more equitable representation of the African region;

(4) *Further invites* African governments to instruct their representatives in the United Nations, without prejudice to their membership in and collaboration with the African-Asian group, to constitute a more effective African Group to bring about closer cooperation and better coordination in matters of common concern.

IV. *General Disarmament*

The Summit Conference, *having considered* all aspects of the question of general disarmament; *unanimously convinced* of the imperious and urgent necessity of coordinating and intensifying their efforts to contribute to the achievement of a realistic disarmament programme through the signing, by all states concerned, of a Treaty on general and complete disarmament under strict and effective international control; *have agreed* unanimously to concert and coordinate their efforts and action in these various fields, and to this end have decided on the following measures:

(1) To declare and accept Africa as a denuclearized zone, the banning of nuclear and thermonuclear tests; the peaceful use of nuclear energy and the banning of the manufacture of nuclear weapons.

(2) The destruction of existing nuclear weapons.

(3) The removal of military bases from Africa and disentanglement of African countries from military pacts with foreign powers.

(4) To appeal to the great powers to: (a) reduce conventional weapons; (b) put an end to the arms race; and (c) sign a general and complete disarmament agreement under strict and effective international control.

(5) To appeal to the great powers, in particular to the Soviet Union and the United States of America, to use their best endeavours to secure the objectives stated above.

(6) To undertake to bring about by means of negotiation the end of military occupation in the African continent, the elimination of military bases and nuclear tests which constitute an essential element of African independence and unity.

V. *Economic Problems*

The Summit Conference, *concerned* with the active share of the developing countries in world trade and at the persistent deterioration of the terms of trade in these external commercial relationships; *conscious* of the fact that owing to its extreme dependence on the export of primary products, Africa and Madagascar more than any other developing region are adversely affected by persistent deteriorations in export earnings; *convinced* of the necessity for concerted action by the African countries and Madagascar in order to ensure a much more remunerative price from the sale of their primary products; *mindful* of the need to eliminate the barriers to trade between the African states and thereby to strengthen their economies; *considering* that economic development, including the expansion of trade on the basis of fair and remunerative prices, should tend to eliminate the need for external economic aid, and that such external economic aid should be unconditional and should not prejudice the independence of African states; *considering* the imperative necessity for African countries to pool their resources and harmonize their activities in the economic field; *aware of* the necessity for the joint utilization of river basin resources, the study of the use of

Saharan zones, the coordination of means of transport and communication systems, and the provision of research facilities, all of which serve to stimulate economic growth and expansion of trade, both regionally and inter-regionally; *convinced* that the acceleration of the rate of economic and social development of the various African countries lies in the industrialization of these countries and the diversification of their production; *considering* the serious problems arising from the great shortage of trained and skilled personnel, the lack of qualified staff, scarce capital resources, grossly inadequate infra-structure, limited outlets for industrial products and the far too inadequate participation of Africans in the economic construction of their countries; *desiring* to explore the effects of regional economic groupings of the African economy; *noting* with satisfaction that the Executive Secretary of the Economic Commission for Africa has decided to convene a Conference of African Ministers of Finance, to be held in Khartoum (Sudan) in July 1963, with a view to setting up an African Development Bank; *resolves to*:

(1) Appoint a preparatory economic committee to study, in collaboration with governments and in consultation with the Economic Commission for Africa, *inter alia*, the following questions and submit their findings to member states: (a) the possibility of establishing a free trade area between the various African countries; (b) the establishment of a common external tariff to protect the emergent industries and the setting up of a raw material price stabilization fund; (c) the restructuralization of international trade; (d) means for developing trade between African countries by the organization of and participation in African trade fairs and exhibitions and by the granting of transport and transit facilities; (e) the coordination of means of transport and the establishment of road, air, and maritime companies; (f) the establishment of an African Payments and Clearing Union; (g) a progressive freeing of national currencies from all non-technical external attachments and the establishment of a Pan-African monetary zone; (h) ways and means of effecting the harmonization of existing and future national development plans;

(2) Invite the Economic Commission for Africa to request their Executive Secretary to give the Commission of Experts all the necessary support and assistance which it may require in the fulfilment of its assignment;

(3) Welcome the forthcoming Conference of African Ministers of Finance and give the respective Ministers of Finance instructions to take the necessary measures for the rapid establishment of the African Development Bank;

(4) The Summit Conference of Independent African States note with satisfaction the progress achieved by the Economic Commission for Africa in establishing the Dakar Institute of Economic Development and Planning and affirm their profound interest in that Institute and their intention of giving it appropriate financial and other support;

(5) Welcome the forthcoming World Conference on Trade and Development which is to examine international trade problems in relation to the economic development of emerging countries;

(6) *Urge* all states concerned to conduct negotiations, in concert, with a view to obtaining from the consumer countries real price stabilization and guaranteed outlets on the world market so that the developing countries may derive considerably greater revenue from international trade.

VI. *The future of the CCTA*

The Summit Conference, *considering* that at the last CCTA session in Dar-es-Salaam in January to February 1963, the final adoption of the new CCTA convention was deferred until the Heads of African States had had an opportunity to consider and direct on the role of the CCTA within the overall context of Pan-African cooperation; *and in view* of the fact that Article 23 of this new convention lays down as follows: 'Pending the signature and the ratification of this convention as provided in Article 16, the Parties having initialled this convention agree to apply it provisionally as if it had entered into force as from the date of initialling, subject to any decision which may be taken by the Heads of African States at the Conference at Addis Ababa or at any subsequent conference on the role of the CCTA within the overall context of Pan-African cooperation'; decides to reconsider its role in order to bring it eventually within the scope of the organization of African states which will have, as one of its arms, an organ for technical, scientific, and cultural cooperation.

References

1 *Fighting Talk*, Johannesburg, August 1961.

2 Mr Henry Hopkinson when Minister of State at the Colonial Office, quoted in Patrick Keatley: *The Politics of Partnership*, Penguin African Library, London, 1963, p. 389.

3 Thomas Hodgkin in *African Political Parties*, London, 1961, lists 239 leading parties, congresses, and movements.

4 Roland Oliver and J. D. Fage, *A Short History of Africa*, Penguin African Library, London, 1962, rev. edn. 1970, p 49.

5 Jean Leclant, 'Égypte pharaonique et Afrique Noire', in *Revue Historique*, April–June 1962, p. 329.

6 Lucy Mair, *Primitive Government*, Penguin Books, London, 1962, repr. 1970, p. 15.

7 G. W. B. Huntingford, 'The Peopling of the Interior of East Africa by its Modern Inhabitants' in *History of East Africa* (ed. R. Oliver and C. Mathew), Oxford, 1963, p. 66.

8 See for example J. Goody, 'Feudalism in Africa?' in *The Journal of African History*, 1963, No. 1.

9 In Rattray, *Ashanti Law and Constitution*, Oxford, 1929, p. 82. See Davidson, *The Africans*, London, 1969; Boston, 1970.

10 Mair, op. cit., p. 47.

11 J. C. Anene in the *Journal of the Historical Society of Nigeria*, December 1961, p. 289.

12 G. Fortune, 'The Contribution of Linguistics to Ethnohistory' in the *Proceedings* of the Tropical Africa History Conference of September 1960, Salisbury, 1962, p. 17.

13 J. Greenberg, 'Langues et histoire en Afrique' in *Présence Africaine*, 1963, No. 1, p. 35.

14 Audrey I. Richards, 'The Political System of the Bemba Tribe' in *African Political Systems* (ed. M. Fortes and E. E. Evans-Pritchard), Oxford, 1940, p. 82.

15 T. Olawale Elias, *The Nature of African Customary Law*, Manchester, 1956, p. 162.

References

16 *Ntu*, 3 Collingham Gardens, London, SW5, January 1962.

17 In G. Stinglhamber and P. Dresse, *Léopold II au travail*, Brussels, 1945, p. 52; quoted in Jean Stengers, 'Études historiques', *Tome I du Livre Blanc de l'Académie Royale etc.*, Brussels, 1962, p. 125.

18 G. S. P. Freeman-Grenville, 'The German Sphere 1884–98' in *History of East Africa*, p. 444.

19 In Basil Davidson, *Report on Southern Africa*, London, 1962, p. 62.

20 In *Report of Central African Council* (Migrant Labour), Salisbury, 1947.

21 In Basil Davidson, *The African Awakening*, London, 1955, p. 204.

22 *Colonial Students in Britain*, Political and Economic Planning, London, 1955, p. 55.

23 In Davidson, op. cit., p. 236.

24 *The Educated African*, ed. R. Sloan and H. Kitchen, London, 1962.

25 In Christopher Fyfe, *A History of Sierra Leone*, Oxford, 1962, p. 87.

26 In David Kimble, *A Political History of Ghana*, Oxford, 1963, p. 545.

27 op. cit., p. 537.

28 R. C. Haw, *No Other Home*, Bulawayo, 1962, p. 7.

29 Adriano Moreira, *Portugal's Stand in Africa*, New York, 1962, p. vi.

30 In G. Shepperson and T. Price, *Independent African*, Edinburgh, 1958, p. 163.

31 Mentioned by T. O. Ranger in the introduction to *Proceedings* of the Tropical Africa History Conference, 1960, *supra*.

32 In Fritz-Ferdinand Müller, *Deutschland-Zanzibar-Ostafrika*, Berlin, 1959, p. 455, drawing on archives of Reichskolonialamt, Deutschen Zentralarchiv, Potsdam.

33 Petöfi Sándor: *Eszkesünk, eszkesünk,*
   Rovák tovább nem leszünk!

34 Ndabaningi Sithole, *African Nationalism*, Oxford, 1959, p. 100.

35 Sir A. B. Ellis, *The Ewe-Speaking Peoples of the Slave Coast of West Africa*, London, 1890, p. 9.

36 J. Mensah Sarbah, *The Fanti Constitution*, London, 1906, in Kimble, op. cit., p. 540.

37 J. E. Caseley Hayford, *West African Leadership* (collected speeches), Stockwell, 1949.

38 Martin R. Delany, *The Condition, Elevation, Emigration, and Destiny of the Colored People of the United States, Politically Considered*, Philadelphia, 1852, p. 210, in G. Shepperson, 'Notes

on Negro American Influences on the Emergence of African Nationalism' in the *Journal of African History*, 1960, No. 2, p. 299.

39 Sithole, op. cit., p. 20.

40 In Thomas Hodgkin, 'A Note on the Language of African Nationalism', *St Anthony's Papers*, No. 10 (ed. Kenneth Kirkwood), London, 1961, p. 24.

41 loc. cit., p. 25.

42 In Colin Legum, *Pan-Africanism*, London, 1962, p. 15.

43 In *Spark*, Accra, 26 April 1963.

44 See especially Shepperson and Price, op. cit.

45 In Legum, op. cit., p. 28.

46 Summarized by Legum, p. 133.

47 Kwame Nkrumah, *Africa Must Unite*, London, 1963, p. 141.

48 op. cit., p. 142.

49 *Daily Express*, 14 January 1960.

50 In Kimble, p. 548.

51 Translated by Marjorie Grene in Janheinz Jahn, *Muntu*, London, 1961, p. 238.

52 In Ezekiel Mphahlele, *The African Image*, London, 1962, p. 26.

53 loc. cit., p. 27.

54 In Langston Hughes, *An African Treasury*, London, 1961, p. 185.

55 In Basil Davidson, 'The African Personality', *Africa, Handbook* (ed. Colin Legum), Penguin Books, London, 1969, p. 539.

56 In *Black Mother*, translation by Basil Davidson, London, 1961, p. 233. Original in M. de Andrade, *Antologia*, Paris, 1958.

57 Ulli Beier, *Art in Nigeria 1960*, Cambridge, 1960, p. 9.

58 Mphahlele, op. cit., p. 24.

59 In Keatley, op. cit., p. 222.

60 Haw, op. cit., p. 1.

61 Geoffrey Parrinder, *West African Religion*, London, 1961, p. 9.

62 Placide Tempels, *La Philosophie bantou*, Paris, 1948, p. 112.

63 *Nru* editorials, London, 1962.

64 Margaret Field, *Search for Security*, London, 1960, p. 29.

65 In Jack Woddis, *The Roots of Revolt*, London, 1960, p. 30.

66 In Davidson, *Report on Southern Africa*, p. 62.

67 ibid., p. 66.

68 *Report* of the East Africa Royal Commission 1953–5, Cmd. 9475, p. 37.

69 In Marvin Harris, *Portugal's African 'Wards'*, New York, 1958, p. 33.

70 L. Marquet in the *Bulletin* of the Centre d'Études des Problèmes Sociaux Indigènes, Elisabethville, 1946, No. 2, p. 16.

71 In Basil Davidson, *Report on Southern Africa,* p. 98.

72 ibid., p. 93.

73 C. W. de Kiewiet, *A History of South Africa,* Oxford, 1941, p. 161.

74 *Voice of Africa,* Accra, 6 March 1963.

75 Report of Debates, Legislative Assembly, Salisbury, 30 November 1944.

76 B. Gussman in Woddis, op. cit., p. 140.

77 ibid., p. 234.

78 *Report* of the East Africa Royal Commission, pp. 45 and 206.

79 In Woddis, ibid., p. 209.

80 Quoted by E. Dhanis in *Zaire,* May 1953, p. 489.

81 K. A. Busia, *A Report on a Social Survey of Sekondi-Takoradi,* Crown Agents, 1950, p. 93.

82 Georges Balandier, 'Sociological Survey of the African Town of Brazzaville' in *Social Implications of Industrialization etc. ... South of the Sahara,* UNESCO for International African Institute, 1956, p. 108.

83 *Report* of the East Africa Royal Commission, p. 50.

84 ibid., p. 214.

85 N. de Cleene, *Le Clan matrilinéal dans la societé indigène,* Inst. Roy. Col. Belge, 1946, p. 70.

86 In Conor Cruise O'Brien, *To Katanga and Back,* London, 1962, p. 85, footnote.

87 O'Brien, p. 238.

88 U.N. Mission *Report on Ruanda Urundi,* 1960, vol. 1, p. 131.

89 Ayo Ogunsheye, 'Whither West Africa?', *Listener,* 8 October 1959.

90 *Flash,* Durban, 11 November 1952.

91 Thomas Hodgkin and Ruth Schachter, *French-Speaking West Africa in Transition,* Carnegie Endowment, May 1960, p. 405.

92 In Davidson, *The African Awakening,* p. 135.

93 René Dumont, *L'Afrique noire est mal partie,* Paris, 1962, p. 34.

94 G. M. Carstairs, *This Island Now* (B.B.C. Reith Lectures), London, 1963, p. 55.

95 André Blanchet: in Gwendolen M. Carter (ed,) *African One-Party States,* New York, 1962, p. 275.

96 Margery Perham, 'Britain and Africa in 1963', *Listener,* 4 April 1963.

97 Julius K. Nyerere, *Democracy and the Party System,* Dar-es-Salaam, 1963, p. 15.

98 In *Spark,* Accra, 15 March 1963.

99 Nyerere, *Democracy and the Party System*, p. 15.
100 Lord Hailey, *Native Administration in the British African Territories*, London, H.M.S.O., 1951, part 4, p. 2.
101 In G. M. Childs, *Umbundu Kinship and Character*, London, 1949, p. 23.
102 Rattray, op. cit., p. 82.
103 Field, op. cit., p. 26.
104 See, for example, Sithole, op. cit., p. 97.
105 Senator A. J. Ellender quoted in *Africa Today*, New York, May 1963, p. 4.
106 R. N. Donaldson, 'Tanganyika's Economy', *Venture*, London, January 1960, p. 5.
107 Kimble, op. cit., p. 22.
108 See especially Nkrumah, *Building a Socialist State*, Accra, 1961.
109 Kwame Nkrumah, *Autobiography*, London, 1957, appendix A.
110 Hodgkin and Schachter, op. cit., p. 387.
111 Julius K. Nyerere, '*Ujamaa*': *The Basis of African Socialism*, Dar-es-Salaam, 1962, p. 3.
112 J. S. Kasambala, statement at opening of All-African Conference on Cooperatives, Moshi, November 1962.
113 Mamadou Dia, *The African Nations and Worlds Solidarity* (trans. Mercer Cook), London, 1962, p. 29.
114 Alhaji Sir Ahmadu Bello, Sardauna of Sokoto, *My Life*, in *West Africa*, 1 December 1962.
115 Kwame Nkrumah, *Sunday Times*, 9 January 1960.
116 Kwame Nkrumah, *Africa Must Unite*, London, 1963, p. 173.
117 Sékou Touré, *La Planification économique*, Conakry, 1960, p. 77.
118 Guy Hunter, *The New Societies of Tropical Africa*, Oxford, 1962, p. 186.
119 Woddis, op. cit., p. 227.
120 *Memorandum on Mining in the Gold Coast*, Government Printing Department, Accra (marked *Confidential, Limited Circulation*), 1951, esp. p. 25.
121 *Central Africa in Business*, Voice and Vision Ltd, 1962, p. 18.
122 In Davidson, *Tomorrow's Africa*, London, 1962, p. 8.
123 *Frankfurter Allgemeine Zeitung*, 12 September 1958.
124 *Die Welt*, 14 March 1959.
125 *Der Spiegel*, 7 February 1962.
126 In Davidson, 'Jacobins in Africa', *History Today*, February 1959.
127 *Daily Mail*, 12 June 1963.
128 Dumont, op. cit., p. 70.
129 ibid., p. 65.

References

130 *Report of the Coker Commission of Inquiry into the Affairs of Certain Statutory Corporations in Western Nigeria*, Federal Ministry of Information, Lagos, 1962, vol. 1, p. 37.

131 ibid., p. 3.

132 *Révolution Africaine*, Algiers, No. 1, 2 February 1963.

133 Tom Stacey, *Sunday Times*, 19 May 1963.

134 Dumont, op. cit., p. 119.

135 Colin Legum (ed.), *Africa Handbook*, p. 234.

136 North-Western University Press, *Growth Without Development*, quoted in *West Africa* 10 February 1969.

137 Samir Amin, *Le Développement du Capitalisme en Côte d'Ivoire*, Paris, 1967, quoted in *West Africa* 4 November 1967.

138 ibid.

139 *Tunisia Works*, Secretariat of State for Information, Tunis, 1960, p. 130.

140 Anouar Abdel-Malek, *Égypte, société militaire*, Paris, 1962, p. 75.

141 In André Mandouze, *La Révolution algèrienne par les textes*, Paris, 1961, p. 126.

142 ibid., p. 115.

143 *El Moudjahid*, 21 December 1961.

144 Figures given to me by Si Abdulazziz, Director of the Office National de la Réforme Agraire, Algiers, in October 1963.

145 H. L. Bretton, *Power and Stability in Nigeria*, New York, 1963, quoted in *West Africa*, 23 March 1963.

146 Sir Ahmadu Bello, Sardauna of Sokoto, *My Life*, in *West Africa*, 17 November 1962.

147 Tai Solarin, 'A View of Nigerian Independence', in *African Independence* (ed. Peter Judd), New York, 1963, p. 246.

148 *West Africa* editorial, 23 March 1963.

149 *The Economic Development of Nigeria*, Report of a Mission Organized by the International Bank for Reconstruction and Development, Baltimore and Oxford, 1955, p. 14.

150 *Economic Rehabilitation of Eastern Nigeria*, Report of the Economic Mission to Europe and North America, Government Printer, Enugu, 1955, p. 4.

151 *West Africa*, 7 April 1962.

152 *Guardian*, 26 April 1969.

153 Oginga Odinga, *Not Yet Uhuru*, London, 1967, pp. 302–3, 250–51.

154 quoted in *Africa Digest*, London, December 1969, p. 103.

155 ibid.

156 *Observer*, 23 November 1969.

157 *Time*, 3 August 1962.

158 *Atlantic Monthly*, November 1962.

159 Dunduza K. Chisiza, *Africa – What Lies Ahead*, New York, 1962, p. 28.

160 *Arusha Declaration: Answers to Questions*, Government Printer, Dar-es-Salaam, 1967. Nyerere's previous thinking can be studied to some extent in a selection of writings and speeches up to 1965; J. K. Nyerere, *Freedom and Unity: Uhuru na Umoja*, Oxford U.P., Dar-es-Salaam, 1967.

161 J. K. Nyerere, *After the Arusha Declaration*, Government Printer, Dar-es-Salaam, 16 October 1967.

162 ibid.

163 J. K. Nyerere, *Socialism and Rural Development*, Government Printer, Dar-es-Salaam, September 1967.

164 ibid.

165 J. K. Nyerere, *Education for Self-Reliance*, Government Printer, Dar-es-Salaam, March 1967.

166 Nkrumah, *Africa Must Unite*, p. 54.

167 *The Times*, 8 May 1963.

168 Nkrumah, *Building a Socialist State*, speech of 22 April 1961.

169 F. M. Bourret, *The Gold Coast*, Oxford, 1949, p. 135.

170 Nkrumah, *Daily Graphic* (Accra), 26 March 1963.

171 Walter Schwarz, *Daily Graphic*, 5 March 1962.

172 Nkrumah, speech of 24 March 1962.

173 loc. cit.

174 M. A. Ribeiro, *Daily Graphic*, 1 July 1963.

175 *Daily Graphic*, 1 July 1963.

176 Details in *West Africa*, 8 February 1969.

177 Jacques Charrière, 'Une Expérience de planification', *Cahiers internationaux*, Paris, March–April 1961, p. 82.

178 N. S. Hopkins, 'Socialism and Social Change in Rural Mali', *Journal of Modern African Studies*, Cambridge, 3 of vol. 7, 1969, p. 467.

179 *West Africa*, 7 December 1968; see also articles in *Africa Report*, Washington D.C., March–April 1969.

180 See a key statement of Kaunda's position: 'A Guide to the Implementation of Humanism in Zambia', address by Dr K. D. Kaunda to the Mulungushi Conference of the United National Independence Party, 14–20 August 1967; and, for further background, letters written by Kenneth D. Kaunda to Colin M. Morris, in *A Humanist in Africa*, London, 1966: e.g. p. 115, 'Realism demands that we face unflinchingly the enemies of

African unity. Neo-colonialism, though often waved like a banner in the faces of the people by unscrupulous leaders to divert attention from their own short-comings, remains the greatest threat to Africa's unity.... It is all too possible for an African country to emerge from the colonial prison to find itself enmeshed in a net of financial, diplomatic and ideological obligations which effectively destroy its freedom of action.'

181 Brian Bunting, *The Rise of the South African Reich*, Penguin African Library, London, rev. edn. 1969, p. 209.

182 H. J. and R. E. Simons, *Class and Colour Conflict in South Africa 1850–1950*, Penguin African Library, London, 1969, p. 618.

183 U.N. Report (ST/PSCA/SER.A·6) 'Foreign Investment in the Republic of South Africa', 1968, p. 21.

184 ibid. See also a valuable study by Sean Gervasi, 'Industrialization, Foreign Capital and Forced Labour in South Africa', U.N. Report (ST/PSCA/SER.A.10), 1970.

185 Ronald Segal (ed.), *Sanctions Against South Africa*, Penguin Books, London, 1964.

186 Henry Nevinson, *More Changes, More Chances*, London, 1925, p. 76.

187 Bunting, op. cit., p. 429.

188 *The Nationalist*, Dar-es-Salaam, 17 June 1968.

189 *Guardian*, London, 25 April 1969.

190 loc. cit.

191 Previously difficult of access or beyond public reach, documentation of the national independence movements in the Portuguese African empire considerably improved in 1969. The following are important, and also point the way to further reading:

Angola: Origins discussed by D. L. Wheeler, 'Early Stirrings of Angolan Nationalism and Protest, 1822–1910', in *African Historical Studies*, 1 of vol. 2, Boston, 1969, a paper of pioneering value; see also Mario de Andrade, *La Poésie africaine d'Expression portugaise*, Paris, 1969. On the development and progress of the MPLA, see a pamphlet, *L'Angola*, with an introduction of Agostinho Neto, published by CONCP, 18 rue Dirah, Algiers, 1969; also, Robert Davezies, *La Guerre d'Angola*, Bordeaux, 1968. For a recent eye-witness description of GRAE/UPA, P. P. Rossi, *Pour Une Guerre Oubliée*, Paris, 1969: though sympathetic to GRAE/UPA, this book delineates their essentially *attentiste* posture. Consult also D. L. Wheeler, 'The Portuguese Army in Angola', *Journal of Modern African Studies*, 3 of vol. 7, 1969; and, especially in its early chapters, John Marcum, *The Angolan Revo-*

lution, M.I.T. Press, Camb., Mass., vol. 1, 1969. For the military situation in 1970, see Basil Davidson, 'Advance in Angola', *Sunday Times* (London), 16 August 1970; ibid., 'Dans la Brousse de l'Angola', *Le Monde Diplomatique*, September 1970; ibid., 'Angola: Seeing for Oneself', *West Africa*, 29 August and 5 September 1970. *Guiné (Guinea-Bissau, Portuguese West Africa)*: See Basil Davidson, *The Liberation of Guiné: Aspects of an African Revolution*, introduction by Amilcar Cabral, and bibliography, Penguin African Library, London, 1969; and E. Handyside (ed.), *Revolution in Guinea: An African People's Struggle*, selected texts by Amilcar Cabral, Stage One, 21 Theobalds Road, London WC1, 1969. *Moçambique*: See Eduardo Mondlane, *The Struggle for Mozambique*, Penguin African Library, London, 1969. For the 2nd congress of FRELIMO, July 1968, Basil Davidson, 'La Guérilla africaine à l'Assaut des Bastions blancs', *Le Monde Diplomatique*, November 1968. For the dependence of Portugal on arms supplies from NATO countries, see S. J. Bosgra and Chr. van Krimpen, *Portugal and NATO*; Klarenburg 253, Amsterdam, 1969.

192 Mondlane op. cit., p. 125.

193 J. M. Kariuki, '*Mau Mau' Detainee*, with a foreword by Margery Perham, Oxford, 1963, p. 181.

194 Bello, *My Life*, in *West Africa*, 24 November 1962.

195 Modibo Kéita, 'Democracy and the One Party State', *Fighting Talk*, March 1962.

196 *Report of the Nyasaland Commission of Inquiry*. Cmd. 814, 1959.

197 *Observer*, 8 October 1961.

198 *Guardian*, 27 May 1963.

199 Kariuki and Perham, pp. 137 and xii respectively.

200 E. H. Carr, 'The Russian Revolution and the Peasant', *Listener*, 30 May 1963 (abridgement of British Academy Raleigh Lecture, 1963).

201 T. Mboya, statement at the 8th session of Economic Commission for Africa, Lagos, 13–25 February 1967.

202 ibid.

203 The comparison between Africa and Latin America is in fact distant and imprecise: among other reasons, because 'the crystallization of ruling strata of a capitalist type in Latin America was greatly assisted by social, ethnic and political factors which are generally not present in Africa.' For a discussion of this point, see Basil Davidson, 'The African Prospect', *The Socialist Register*, London, 1970.

Index

Abidjan, 120, 135

Accra, and Ghana central government, 187
and diamond dealing, 190
Conference of African students (1963), 63–4
All-African People's Conference (1958), 68

Addis Ababa, African Unity Conference (1963), 68, 70, 71

Aderibigbe, Nigerian historian, and resistance to colonialism, 52

Africa, state of revolutionary change, 11–14
emergence from foreign domination, 16
strangeness to Europeans, 19
increasing knowledge of its past, 20–22
multiplicity of political and social patterns, 21, 22–3, 29
movement into states and kingdoms, 23–5, 27–8, 30–31
primitive systems of government, 26–8, 114–16
adjustment to environment, 27, 28, 31
forces of political change, 28
European denial of its historical identity, 30

its basic unities, 30–32, 33, 78, 79, 80
knowledge of outside world, 34
renewed by outside ideas and techniques, 35
cultural gap between Europe and, 35–6
five phases of European experience, 37–8
effect of economic intervention by invaders, 39–42
impoverishment of rural life, 42, 87–8
postwar economic development, 43
movements towards self-government, 47ff., 55, 58–63, 102
'great year' of independence, 66
prospect of unified civilization, 66–70, 73, 133, 215, 217
acknowledgement of historical past, 78–9
analysis of philosophical systems, 81
land measures, 86–7
maladjustment in urban life, 95–6, 103
reassessment of Europeanization, 104
search for a modern framework, 107, 116
one-party states, 111–16

Africa – *contd.*
 absence of class interest, 112–13
 central 'problem of power', 112,
  116ff., 214
 irrelevance of democratic government, 113–14
 need for economic freedom from
  the West, 123
 right of choice, 124
 danger from neo-colonialism,
  126
 movement towards domination
  by state capitalism, 131–2
 ideal of unity, 133
 government by oligarchical élite,
  137
 battle between tribe and state,
  139
 main directions of change, 149ff.
 military *coups*, 216–17
 search for progress in stability,
  217
 limitations of foreign aid, 218–
  19
 see also Colonialism
Africa, East, 22
 traffic with Eastern world, 34
 impact of Islam, 35
 Germany and, 39
 friendship with Europe, 216
Africa, North, state-forming process, 23
 gold and salt trade, 25
 Arab invasion, 30
 Muslim traffic with the East,
  34
 use of force to achieve independence, 66
 former French Empire, 143–5
Africa, South, state of racism, 12,
  19, 203, 204, 215
 sale of arms to, 20, 205

exploration of, 37
Great Britain and, 39
land enclosure, 40
'Native Reserves', 40, 85
Rand mining industry, 42, 89,
 112
and nationalism, 51
Africa's common enemy, 69
terms of acceptance of Africans,
 77
attitude to Négritude, 77
position of the artist, 77–8
impoverishment of rural population, 84–5
migrant labour system, 88
multi-party government, 114
British capital and, 128, 204
and Biafra, 171, 206
and Smith régime, 207
threat to African advancement,
 202
Sharpeville and Langa, 203
foreign investment, 204, 205
production for export, 205
loan to Malawi, 206
neo-imperialism, 205–6
aggressive aims, 206–7
military expenditure, 207 and n.
and Rhodesia, 207–9
Africa, West, political organization in grasslands, 24–5
traffic with the East, 34
loyalty to Islam, 34–5
exploration of, 37
and nationalism, 58, 74
and Pan-Africanism, 64
and 'fetishism', 80
rate of impoverishment, 84–5
absence of class interest, 112
democratic government, 114
socialist programme, 116
efforts at private enterprise, 117

emergence of new model states, 131

employment of Whites, 216

'Africa for the Africans', 64

African, the, memories of pre-colonial ideas, 17, 47

foolish myths concerning, 19, 20

devaluation in slave trade, 19

movement across land masses, 28, 31

development in skills, 28, 31

denial of his historical identity, 30

religious and metaphysical systems, 32

effect of land enclosure on, 40–41

migrant labour and, 40–43

increased access to higher education, 43–6

memory of resistance to colonialism, 52–3

desire for emancipation, 55ff.

relegated to position of inferiority, 58

restricted by European ideological boundaries, 60 61

growing sense of 'one-ness', 73

his personality, 73, 78–9, 82, 104

artistic dilemma, 77–8

terms of 'acceptance' offered to, 77

and urban employment, 88–93

need for equality of status as citizen, 97

ideas of a new Africa, 101ff.

need to solve 'problem of power', 112, 116ff.

imbued with socialist ideas, 119–24

desire for ethnic identity, 140

need to activate and enthuse, 217

African Common Market, 72

African National Congress of S. Africa, and Luthuli, 101

African student unions, demands of London conference (1963), 67–8

African Unity Conference, Charter, 68–9

Nkrumah and, 68, 71–2

condemns atomic explosions, 125–6

Africanization, by élites, 135–6

Afrikaner National Party, 188

creation of 'Bantustans', 85, 142

Aggrey, Dr J. E. K., 73–4

Aguiyi–Ironsi, General, 167, 194n.

Akintola, Chief Samuel, at 6th Pan-African Congress, 65–6

Premier of W. Nigeria, 166–7

rigs the elections, 167

assassination, 167

Akosombo, Volta dam project, 191n.

Al Bakri, on W. Sudan, 24, 25

Al Mas'udi, on typical kingship (*Meadows of Gold and Mines of Gems*), 23–4

Algeria, effects of land enclosure, 40

production of wine for export, 40, 88

Front de Libération (FLN), 69, 145, 154

migrant labour in France, 88

colonial occupation, 145–6, 145n., 154, 155

policy of land reform, 154–5, 156

education, 156

'state capitalism', 156–7

Algerian rebellion, 40, 145, 216
  nature of, 154, 156
Algiers Charter (1964), 157
All-African People's Conference (1958), 69
Americas, the, import of slaves, 37, 39
Anene, J. C., on moral assumption in political organizations, 30
Angola, 37, 76, 85, 86, 205, 206, 209, 210
  forced labour policy, 42–3
  numbers of African school-children, 44
  a dictatorship, 114
  democratic government, 115
  export of armaments to, 131
  repression of revolts, 209, 210
Ankrah, General J. A., National Liberation Council, 194, 195
Anuak, the, 29
Apartheid, offers permanent deprivation, 77
  and African artists and writers, 77–8
Arabs, invasion of N. Africa, 30
  and slave trade, 45
Arendt, Hannah, and 'tribal nationalism', 55, 180
Ashanti, and the 'Golden Stool', 24, 29
  democratic constitution, 115
  and independence, 187
Atlantic Monthly, on Ghana's socialism, 178
Atomic explosions, condemned by African states, 125
Awolowo, Chief Obafemi, imprisonment, 166
Azikiwe, Nnamdi, 78
  and Nigerian self-government, 61–2

Baganda separatism, 133, 172
Bakary, Djibo, Sawaba Party, 142
Balandier, Georges, and Brazzaville, 96
Balewa, Sir Abubakar Tafawa, and African Unity, 70
  and neutralism, 124
  assassination, 167
Balkanization, of Kenya, 99, 139, 141
  instrument of neo-colonialism, 126
  post-independence reaction to, 140
Balum Naba, 101
Bamako, the author and, 108–10, 120, 125
  becomes Mali, 125
Banda, Dr Hastings, accusations against his Malawi Party, 215–16
  on friendship with S. Africa, 206
Bantu, the, language variations, 32
  political organization, 32
  effect of Kaffir wars, 39
'Bantustans', creation and purpose, 85, 142
Basutoland, problems of migrant labour, 87
Basutos, the, form a nation, 29
Beier, Ulli, on artistic dilemma of the African, 76–7
Beira, Bishop of, on cotton production, 86
Belgium, domination in Africa, 16, 43, 44–5
  and African education, 44
  see also Congo
Bello, Sir Ahmadu, and old Emirates, 99n.

and African neutrality, 124–5
and independence, 159–60
domination of Nigerian Federal Government, 166–7
assassination, 167
and one-party state, 214
My Life, 99n., 124–5, 159–60
Ben Arafa, Sultan, 143
Ben Barka, Mehdi, and UNFP, 144
assassination, 144
Ben Bella, Ahmed, 145, 156
and land reform, 155
Benue Plateau States, 169
Berbers, 144
Biafra, 168–72, 210
Black Moslems, 77, 82
Bobo-Dioulasso, 120
Boers, 37
regard Africans as slaves, 41
Booth, Charles, and London poor, 96
Botsio, Kojo, 118 and n.
Boumédienne, Colonel, 156
deposes Ben Bella, 145, 156
Bourghiba, President, 145
Brazza, Pierre Savorgnian de, 39
Brazzaville, intervention of French troops, 71
competition for women, 96
Brazzaville Bloc, 67, 69, 70
Bretton, Professor, *Power and Stability in Nigeria*, 160, 161
British East Africa, African education in, 46
regional unity, 70
wage levels, 92
British South Africa Company, 50
British West Africa, 53
demand for self-government, 59–60

Bruce, James, exploration of Ethiopia, 37
Buganda, the *Kabaka* and, 133, 140
Burton, Sir Richard, and African inferiority, 57
Bushmen, primitive government, 27
Busia, K. A., and youthful crime, 95
opponent of CPP, 194
and Progress Party, 195

Cape Province, 12
Capitalism, the African and its meaning, 17, 178
rejected in favour of socialism, 116
Ghana and, 117–18, 178
result of its choice, 118–19
condemned by Pan-Africanism, 119
a 'middle class solution', 219
Carr, E. H., *The Russian Revolution*, 217–18
Casablanca Bloc, 67, 69, 70
meeting of states (1961), 69
Central African Federation, 15, 129–30
Césaire, Aimé, Martinique poet, 63
and Négritude, 74
Notes on Going Home, 74
Chad, 71
Cheng-Ho, Admiral, in Ma-lin, 34
Chiefs, the, changes in their rule, 99–100
attitude to political change, 99–101
see also Tribalism
China, trade with Africa, 34

China – *contd.*
  halt in technological achievement, 36
Chisiza, Dundunza, 178
Christianity, 49, 51–2
Class interest, absence from Africa, 112–13
Classe, Mgr, Bishop of Ruanda, and Tutsi caste, 100
Cloete, Stuart, on black hatred of white, 56
  denigration of the African, 56–7
Cocoa production, poverty caused by, 83–4, 86
  collapse in world price, 179, 193–4
  rise in income from, 189
  and loan repayments, 191
Coker Commission of Inquiry, and Marketing Board finances, 137, 161
Colonial Development and Welfare Scheme, 162
Colonialism, destructive impact, 16, 35, 37, 38, 83
  contribution to Africa, 36, 83
  social dislocation caused by economic interference, 39ff.
  use of forced labour, 41–3, 87ff.
  inter-wars standstill, 43, 47, 61, 84
  compared with Industrial Revolution, 46–7
  African resistance to, 52–3
  based on white supremacy, 56–8
  denial of Africa's historical past, 79–80
  caused poverty and malnutrition, 81ff.

emphasis on production for export, 86
  ignorance of political activity, 108
  results of itsdis integration, 110–11, 112, 134–5
  fate of its 'leading élites', 135
Commission for the Protection of the Natives (Belgian), estimation of Congo population, 38
Commonwealth, African attitude to, 124
Communism, the African and its meaning, 17
Communist bloc, neutralism and, 124
Communists, credited with nationalist manifestations, 15, 51, 108
  African leaders and, 103, 106
  in French W. Africa, 120
Conakry, 120, 134, 198
Congo, the (formerly Belgian), 38, 131
  exploitation by concession companies, 39
  use of forced labour, 41 and n.
  'armed operations' against Africans, 43
  and African education, 44
  call for national union, 62
  French intervention, 71
  concentration on export, 86
  decline of rural life, 87–8
  child malnutrition, 91–2
  breaking of tribal ties, 97–8
  chaos following colonial withdrawal, 98, 141, 172–3
  Conakat party, 98–9
  shift of chiefly control, 99–100

Africanization by élites, 136–7
collapse of nationalist morale, 136
Congolese, idea of a nation, 67
positions of 'occupying salaries', 136
Congress resistance movement, 12, 203
Consolidated Gold Fields, record profit, 90
Cotton production, occupation of farm land, 86
Creech-Jones, Arthur, 165–6, 166n.
Czechoslovakia, 125

d'Arboussier, Gabriel, 132
Dahomey, 104
Dakar, 120
William Ponty *lycée*, 73
Damas, Léon, 75
Dar-es-Salaam, 179
African living conditions, 96
Dartmouth, William Legge, Earl of, on profit motive in slave trade, 19–20
de Freitas, Sir Geoffrey, and Ghana, 193
de Gaulle, President, proferred referendum (1958), 142
Dei-Anang, Ghanaian poet, 75–6
Delany, Martin R., on need for *national* claims, 60
Deschamps, Professor Hubert, and French practice in Africa, 142n.
Dia, Mamadou, on economic freedom, 123
Diallou, Abdoulaye, the author and, 108–10
Dinka, primitive government, 26–7

Disease, in mining industry, 89–90
Djenne, its scholarship, 35
Dogon, philosophy of, 81
Drakensbergs, 29
DuBois, W. E. B., and Pan-Africanism, 64, 65
Dumont, René, on African 'élites', 135–6

East African Royal Commission (1955), Report on land use, 85–6
on cash earnings and housing, 92–3, 96
on breakdown of old social order, 96
Eboh, Okotie, Finance Minister, 167
assassination, 167
Economic planning, emphasis on, 122–4
and drain of wealth, 129
Education, increase in University students, 43–4
Portuguese and, 44
Great Britain and, 45–6
progress in Nigeria, 164–5
in Ghana, 193
Egypt, 69, 153–4
switch from food to cotton, 86
semi-colonial state, 152
reforms of Nasser, 152–4
and Arab socialism, 153
Egypt, Ancient, and Africa's history, 21
Negro government, 49–50
El Glaoui, Pasha of Marrakesh, 144
El Moudjahid, and land reform, 154
Elias, T. O., 32

Ellender, Senator, and private enterprise system, 116

Engels, Friedrich, report on British working classes (1844), 95–6

Ethiopia, 29, 49
Bruce and, 37
and African Unity, 69
progress in, 149

Europe, denial of African historical identity, 30
expansive civilization, 35
cultural gap between Africa and, 35–6
exploration and partition of Africa, 37–8
land enclosure by, 40–41, 84
and forced labour, 40–43, 84
increase in African students, 43–4
opinion of 'nationalism', 55
and seizure by force, 57–8
denial of African cultural unity, 78–9
contribution to Africa, 83
results of mass industrialization, 95–6
efforts to balkanize African states, 98–9, 141
irrelevance of her parliamentary system, 113ff.
and 'divide and rule' in Africa, 140, 141–2
and African commitment to socialism, 179
criticism of Nkrumah, 188
irritation with independent Africa, 216

Fagbure, Gabriel, on Nigeria's misgovernment, 161
Fanti, the, 59

Feudalism, African type, 23

Field, Margaret, on results of cocoa cultivation, 83–4
and democracy in W. Africa, 115

Fighting Talk, its suppression, 12–13

Firearms, impact on African society, 28, 29, 35

Flash, on Luthuli, 101

Fouta Djallon, pro-French chiefs, 142

Frafra Youngsters' Union, 16

France, domination in Africa, 16, 39, 42
efforts to shape new Africa, 16–17
policy in Algeria, 40
withdraws political control from W. and Equatorial Africa, 62
Loi Cadre and Federation, 62n.
defence agreement with African territories, 71
Algerian migrant labour in, 88
election of African deputies to National Assembly, 120
Communist Party, 120
economic aid mission, 125
its *interlocuteurs valables*, 135
supply of arms to Biafra, 171
supply of arms to S. Africa, 207 and n.

Freeman-Grenville, G. S. P., on Peters in Africa, 39

French Africa, use of forced labour, 41
higher education for Africans, 43–4
influence of the Revolution on, 47–8
and self-government, 59, 62

failure to achieve federation, 62 and n.
semi-colonial states, 70
presence of French troops, 70–71
import of alcohol, 103–4
failure of Union Française, 108
nationalist movements, 108ff.
aftermath of colonialism, 112, 139
Marxist study groups, 120
neo-colonialism in, 126
treatment of old hierarchies, 142ff.
policy in N. Africa, 143–5
equatorial ex-colonies, 158

Gabon, 136
Gale, Dr, and disease in mining industry, 89
Gao, Spanish tombs, 35
Garvey, Marcus, 77
Germany, colonial behaviour, 39
  investment in Africa, 130–31
Ghana, 113, 158
  political organization, 24–5, 59
  manipulation of gold and salt trades, 24–5
  and African Unity, 69, 70
  import of food, 86
  use of migrant labour, 87
  efforts at private enterprise, 117–18, 191–2
  choice and form of socialism, 119–20, 122, 168
  borrowings from U.S. and U.S.S.R., 131
  outburst of luxury living, 137, 186
  Western criticism of, 178

position of leadership, 185
achievements of industrial and social programmes, 185 ff.
attains sovereignty, 186
attitude of chiefs to independence, 187
wave of terror-bombing, 188
post-school employment problem, 189
purchase of gold-mining concerns, 190
transfer of diamond dealing, 190
and private investment, 191–2
Preventive Detention Act, 193
and collapse of cocoa prices 193–4
army *coup*, 194 and n.
attempt at 'middle class solution', 194–5
elections, September 1969, 195; *see also* Nkrumah
Ghana Convention People's Party, 104
  six-point programme, 119–20
  Nkrumah and, 186, 189
  degeneration into interest groups, 193
Ghana Guinea Union, 69
Ghana-Guinea-Mali Union, 69
Ghana Workers' Brigade, 190
Gillman, J. and L., on malnutrition in Transkei, 85
Gogo, the, Peters and, 39
Gold Coast, 58, 65
  recognition of British criminal law, 59
  development of self-government, 59
  regions of increasing poverty, 83–4, 86
  and youthful crime, 95

Gold Coast – *contd.*
  private enterprise ventures,
    117–18
  fight for independence, 119
  earnings from gold export, 128
  Nkrumah and, 186
Gold Coast Independent, 49
Gold Coast Regiment, in World
    War 1, 49
Gold trade, in Ghana, 25, 190
  Europe and, 37
Gowon, General, 167–8, 169
Great Britain, and Central Afri-
    can Federation, 15
  domination in Africa, 16
  efforts to shape new Africa, 16
  attitude to slave trade, 19–20
  sale of arms to S. Africa, 21
  import of Guinea gold, 25
  exploration of Africa, 37
  use of forced labour, 41
  her coloured students, 43–4, 45
  and self-government, 59, 71
  aftermath of colonialism, 112
  and W. African democracy,
    115
  criticism of Nkrumah, 125
  investment in Africa, 128, 204
  and rebel government in
    Rhodesia, 207ff.
  arms for Nigerian Federal
    Government, 210
Griaule, Marcel, 80, 81
Guardian, and African leaders,
    216
Guinea, 142, 195ff.
  state-forming process, 23
  choice of socialism, 119, 195–6
  civil service frauds, 138
  suppression of pro-French
    chiefs, 142
  bauxite deposits, 197–8

  achievement of independence,
    195–6
  links with Ghana and U.S.S.R.,
    196

Haile Selassie, Emperor, 149
Hailey, Lord, and pre-colonial
    government, 115
Hassan II, King, his royal auto-
    cracy, 144
Hayford, Joseph E. Caseley, 48
  and African self-government,
    59–60
Herodotus, and Egyptians, 50
Hertzog, Dr Albert, 206
Horton, J. Africanus, 48
  on Africa's place in history,
    49–50
  efforts to float gold mine
    syndicate, 117
Houphouët-Boigny, President
    Felix, 69, 150–51
  opposed by Balum Naba, 101
  veneration of, 111
  and Marxism in Europe, 120
Huggins, Sir Godfrey (Lord
    Malvern), and cheap African
    labour, 91
Hughes, Langston, 43
Hungary, and nationalism, 55
Hunter, Guy, 127–8
Huntingford, G. W. B., use of
    the word 'tribe', 22

Imperialism, internecine rival-
    ries, 37
India, movement towards inde-
    pendence, 66
  and neutralism, 106, 124
Industrial Revolution, 37
  compared with colonialism,
    46–7

Industry, African worker and, 88ff.

Investment, overseas, foreign companies and, 127–8
  influence of foreign shareholders, 129
  warnings of 'boycott', 129, 131
  and industrial development, 130
  and social services, 130
  preference for government-to-government process, 131
  Ghana and, 192

Iron Age, 13
  African development in, 19, 23, 26ff.
  origins of political history, 26–7

Islam, penetrating influence, 34–5
  power of Muridite Brotherhood, 143

Israel, capital investment partnership with Africa, 121–2 and n.

Istiqlal, the, 143, 144

Italy, colonial rule, 43

Ivory Coast, 69, 70, 150–51
  migrant labour in, 87
  import of alcohol, 103–4
  importance of Houphouët-Boigny, 111, 150–51
  its plantocracy, 113
  development of Abidjan, 199

Ivory trade, 25, 37

Johnson, at Pan-African Congress, 66

Juvenile delinquency, causes of, 95
  symptom of maladjusted society, 95

Kariuki, J. M., 'Mau Mau' Detainee, 98n., 216

Kasai, the Baluba and Lulua, 99

Kasambala, J. S., 122–3

Katanga, 99

Kaunda, President, 201

Kéita, President Modibo, and Mali, 69, 199, 200
  and one-party government, 215
  and coup of 1968, 200

Kenya, 16, 65, 85, 173ff.
  land enclosure, 40
  Britain and African education, 45, 46
  and independence, 67
  and regional unity, 70
  Committee on African Wages, 92–3
  manifestations of tribalism, 98 and n., 139, 141, 180
  result of parliamentary system, 98
  proposal to balkanize, 99, 139, 141
  first election expenses, 139
  problems of unification, 173–7

Kenya African Democratic Union, 139

Kenya African National Union, 173–5, 177
  and 'African socialism', 173–4

Kenya People's Union, 175, 176

Kenyatta, Jomo, 173, 175, 176
  at 6th Pan-African Congress, 65
  government refusal to recognize, 98n.
  and chiefly opposition, 187

Kikuyu, 98n., 173, 175, 176

Kinshasa (Congo), 206

Konaté, Mamadou, the author and, 108–10

Labour, forced and migrant, 40ff., 87ff.
  migrants 'on contract', 88–9
Labour Party (British), 66
  and Ghana's independence, 187 and n.
Lagos, 59
Land, African belief in its universality, 32
  enclosure by colonial invaders, 40, 84
  African demands, 65
  alienation powers, 101
Language, basic unity in Africa, 31, 32
Latin America, and private enterprise, 117, 220
Law, basic unity of traditional ideas, 32
Lennox-Boyd, Alan, 187 and n.
Leopold II, King of the Belgians, and the Congo, 38, 39
  and forced labour, 41n.
Liberia, unity discussions, 69
  True Whig Party, 111
  colonial stagnation, 117
  under Tubman, 149–50
Libya, 69
Lumumba, Patrice, 173
Luthuli, Chief, Nobel prizewinner, 101

McKay, Claud, 63
Madagascar, 70, 71
Mair, Lucy, on the word 'tribe', 21–2
  on the Nuer, 27
Makakulu Tseke, 94
Makerere University College, 46
Malawi, 178
  migrant labour, 87

accusations against Congress Party, 215
  loan from S. Africa, 206
Ma-lin, E. African city-state, 34
Mali, 35, 69, 108, 110, 142, 214–15
  failure to achieve federation, 69, 143, 199
  choice of socialism, 119, 122, 195–6
  and neutralism, 125
  achievement of independence, 199
  devaluation of Mali franc, 200
  army *coup*, 200
Malnutrition caused by colonialism, 83–4
  among children, 84, 92
Marxism, independence leaders and, 103, 120
  in post-colonial transition period, 120
Masai, the, 13–14
Mau Mau, 98n., 216
Mboya, Tom, on limitations of foreign aid, 218–19
  assassination, 175
Mbulu, 14
Mbundu, 76
Mineral deposits, profits-export from, 128–9
Mining industry, use of forced and migrant labour, 40–41, 42, 87
  medical services, 89–90
  incidence of disease, 89
  wage levels, 90–91
  effect of federation, 91
  1913 Rand disturbances, 112
  remittances abroad, 128–9

Ghana and, 190

Missionaries, Christian Negro, and Pan-Africanism, 64

Moçambique, 37, 85, 209, 210, 212
  numbers of African school-children, 44
  cotton production, 86
  migrant labour, 87
  a dictatorship, 114
  anti-colonial revolt, 209–10

Mombasa riots, 92

Mondlane, Eduardo, 211, 212

Monrovia Bloc, 66–7, 69, 70

Morocco, 68, 69
  invasion of W. Sudan, 24
  traffic with the East, 34
  French policy in, 143–4
  domestic stagnation, 154

Mouvement Autonome de Casa-mance, 16

Mphahlele, Ezekial, on Négri-tude, 77

Muhammad ben Youssef, Sul-tan, and the Istiqlal, 140, 143–4, 145

Musi, E., and *Fighting Talk*, 12–13

Muslims, of W. Africa, 21, 155
  trade with the East, 34–5

Nairobi, 46, 98, 171
  African housing conditions, 92
  wage levels, 92

Nasser, Colonel Gamal, revolu-tionary reforms, 152–4
  and Arab socialism, 153

Natal Indian Congress, 101

National Congress of British West Africa, 59–60

Nationalism, African, credited with Communist origins, 15, 51–2
  rise of, 43
  ideas and aspirations, 47–8, 49–50, 53–4, 55ff., 102–3
  not a minority phenomenon, 50–51
  political and religious origins, 51–2
  and resistance to colonialism, 52–3
  regional characteristics, 53, 58
  appearance in World War I, 59–60
  essential framework to freedom demands, 60ff.
  comes of age in World War II, 61
  and federal structures, 62–3, 66–7
  prospect of African unity, 66–7
  and continental integration, 72–3
  poets of, 74–6, 103
  and a new social order, 97, 108
  personal careerists, 103
  emphasis on material change, 103ff.
  neurotic declarations, 104
  and choice between West and East, 106
  chooses neutralism and non-alignment, 106
  nest-featherers, 110–11
  and need for economic free-dom, 122–3
  transition into economic plan-ning, 123
  and exports by foreign com-panies, 127–8
  movement towards humanism, 132

Nationalism – *contd.*
underground of prickly suspicion, 134
reaction to balkanization, 140–41
'Native', a word of contempt, 58
Négritude, characteristic writings, 74ff.
poets of, 74–6
denial of assimilation, 77
Africans and, 77–8
Negroes, and government of Egypt, 49–50
Negroes, American, and Pan-Africanism, 63–4
loss of ethnic loyalties, etc., 64 and n.
Neo-colonialism, 54, 145, 148, 198, 201
defiintion of, 126
and capitalism, 126–7
its dangers, 128, 129–30
its stereotype, 130
Neto, Agostinho, *Black Mother*, 76
Neutralism, 54, 68, 79, 131
choice of independence, 106, 124, 215
and NATO, 124
a diplomatic device, 125–6
Ghana and, 191
New York Age, 63
Ngorongoro, 13
Nicol, Abioseh, 75
Niger, the, 35
Niger Delta, and slave trade, 29
sovereign history, 159
Niger Territory, survival of chiefly power, 142
Nigeria, 66, 113, 178, 214
movement towards independence, 59, 61–2, 159

a multi-national reality, 61, 159, 161–2
need for national framework, 62
and African Unity, 69–70
dilemma of the artist, 76–7
rate of impoverishment, 84–5
chiefly rule in, 99 and n., 100–101, 141
period of corruption, 137, 161
its unresolved state, 159ff., 168
breakdown of Federation (1966), 161, 166–7
lack of ideology in independence, 159
Western disappointment with, 160
source of its troubles, 152, 160–63
criticisms of its government, 161–2
ideas on planning for development, 162ff.
failure of 'middle class solution', 163–5, 166–7, 168, 181
achievements in education, 164–5
dilemma of the young, 165
use of state accumulated reserves, 165–6
army *coup*, 167–8, 194n.
reshaping of Federation, 169
Tiv people's autonomy, 169, 170, 171
Nigeria, East, the Ibo, 159, 167, 168
education in, 164–5
secessionist state, 168ff.
Nigeria, North, Hausa, Bornu and Fulani states, 159, 160
south fears its domination, 166
under military leader, 167

massacre of Ibo, 168
Nigeria, West (Yoruba), chiefly
    authority, 160
  and political responsibility, 164
  and education, 164
  state of uproar, 166
  mutiny of Northern troops,
    167–8
Nile, Upper, 31
  Iron Age in, 26
  exploration of, 37
Nkrumah, Kwame, at sixth Pan-
    African Congress, 65–6
  and cause of African Unity,
    68–9, 71–2
  on United Africa Company, 72
  on primary need of a 'political
    kingdom', 97
  early aims, 102–3
  on Ghana's development plan,
    117, 189
  and Gold Coast independence,
    119
  on the Commonwealth, 125
  defines neo-colonialism, 126
  condemns luxury living, 138
  Western criticism of, 178
  and chiefly opposition, 187
  achieves unity, 188–9
  socialist convictions, 189, 190
  gains under his leadership, 193
    in Peking, 194
  blackening of his reputation,
    194n.
  overthrown, 194
Non-alignment, independence
    leaders and, 106
North Atlantic Treaty Organiza-
    tion (NATO), 124, 210
Ntu Ntu-ism, philosophy of, 81–2
Nuer, the, primitive government,
    27–8

adjustment to environment,
    27–8
  obedience to 'tribal life', 27, 28
Nyasaland, 15
  effect of migrant labour on,
    42–3
  Malawi Party Congress, 215
Nyerere, President Julius, on the
    acquisitive society, 105–6
  on the irrelevance of European
    political systems, 114
  and African Socialism, 120–22,
    179, 180, 181
  cuts extravagant spending,
    138–9
  Western expectation of, 179
  and TANU, 180, 181–3
  and foreign aid, 219
  on future development of Tan-
    zania, 184–5
  and education, 185
  and democratization, 201
  on repressive regimes, 213

Obote, Milton, his measure of
    success, 133, 172
Odinga, Oginga, 175, 176
Ogotommeli, and Dogon phil-
    osophy, 81
Ojukwu, Colonel, 168, 171, 172
Organization of African Unity,
    133, 201
  formation, 68, 69

Padmore, George, 103
Pan-African Congress (1900), 64
  (1919), 64–5
  (1945), 65
Pan-African Freedom Movement
    for East and Central Africa
    (PAFMECA), Charter,
    102–3

Pan-Africanism, 53–4, 63ff.
  diaspora of American Negro, 63–4
  ignored by imperialists, 64
  and threat of force, 66
  and coming of independence, 66
  and African Unity, 66–8, 73
  acquires a philosophical justification, 78
  condemns capitalism, 119
Park, Mungo, explores W. Sudan, 37
Parrinder, Geoffrey, *West African Religion*, 80
Pepper trade, 37
Perham, Margery, and 'problem of power', 112
  and Kariuki, 216
Peters, Carl, behaviour in E. Africa, 39
Pondoland, 12
Portuguese, attitude to nationalist manifestations, 15, 51
  introduction of new foodstuffs, 31
  trading partnership with Africa, 37
  Salazar regime, 51, 70, 209n., 210
  support for Biafra, 170–71
Portuguese Africa, 158
  use of forced labour, 41, 42–3
  higher education for Africans, 44
  its isolation, 53
  and use of force, 66
  enforced cotton production, 86
  suppression of revolts, 209–13
Portuguese Guinea, 209n., 210, 212
Poverty, in Kenya, 67

  eve of independence state, 83
  worsened by poor wages, 90
  in Latin America, 117
Prostitution, symptom of a maladjusted society, 95, 96
Public opinion, its existence in Africa, 14–16
  eagerness for change, 147, 214
  dominant trends, 215
Pygmies, primitive government, 27

Rassemblement Démocratique Africaine (R D A), 120
Rattray, R. S., 80
  and Ashanti 'enstoolment', 24
  and its democratic constitution, 115
Religion, African, basic unity, 32–3
  systems of, 32–3
  spiritual respectability, 50
  common ground with other systems, 80
Révolution Africaine, 138
Rhodesia, Northern, forced labour in Copperbelt, 42
  African education, 46, 128
  profits-export from mines, 128
Rhodesia, Southern, 69–70, 85, 147, 158
  White rebellion of 1965, 12, 207ff.
  land enclosure, 40
  African education, 46
  and communism, 51
  effort to prove black inferiority, 56
  land used in tobacco production, 86
  cheap migrant labour system, 90–91

multi-party system, 114
police repression, 147
Rhodesias, the, 15
changes in imperial structure, 29
federation with Nyasaland, 91
Richards, Dr Audrey, 32
Ruanda, 87, 99
rise of Hutu against Tutsi, 100
Russia, emancipation of Serfs, 217–18

Sahara, 31
salt deposits, 25
Salt trade, Ghana and, 24–5
Sandór, Petöfi, Hungarian revolutionist, 55
Saniquellie, 69
Sarbah, Mensah, on use of word 'native', 58
Sekondi, 95
Senegal, the French and, 39, 143
achieves independence, 66
nationalist/chiefly struggle, 143
and Federation of Mali, 143, 199
Senghor, Léopold, compares Harlem with Manhattan (in poem *New York*), 74–5, 104
Seton-Watson, Professor H., criticism of Ghana government, 188
Shamshama, Mr, and TANU, 14
Sierra Leone, 20, 47–8, 66, 160
and representative gvt, 59
military *coup*, 217
Sithole, Ndabaningi, 61
on Black/White hatred, 56
on seizure by force, 57–8

Slave trade, 52
devaluation of Africans, 19
profitability, 19–20, 37
in Niger Delta, 29
Europe and, 37
abolition, 37
the Americas and, 37, 39
end of Arab–Swahili traffic, 45
Smith, Ian, 147, 148, 151–2, 207–9
Socialism, African, 54, 79, 177
and European values, 104–7
choice against capitalism, 116–17, 119–20, 178–9, 215
a political complex, 120
Nyerere and its ideology, 120–22
and cooperative production, 121
and the Extended Family, 122
importance of Arusha Declaration, 181–2, 218, 219
and foreign aid, 219
as a solution for the future, 177–8, 220
Sokoto, 99n., 159–60
Soudan (Sudan), 69, 108
state-forming process, 23
achieves independence, 66
Union Soudanaise, 142
and Federation of Mali, 142
South-West Africa, a colony of S. Africa, 209
Soviet Union, economic aid mission, 125
rate of lending money, 131
loan to Volta dam project, 191
links with Guinea, 201
industrial collaboration in Algeria, 156

aid to nationalists in Portuguese colonies, 210n.
Spanish colonial rule, 43, 44
Stone Age, 30
Sudan, Western, 37
political organization, 24, 29
law and order in, 35

Tanganyika (Tanzania), Iron Age
site, 13
acquisition of chiefs, 29
education under British, 45
and regional unity, 70, 179–80
migrant labour, 87
colonial heritage, 117
poverty at independence, 118,
179–80
chooses socialism, 119, 179,
181
marketing cooperatives, 121
evidence of 'Ujamaa', 122
cuts extravagant spending,
138–9
absence of tribalism, 141
union with Zanzibar, 179n.
state trading corporation, 182
Tanzania African National Union
(TANU), village offices,
13–14
its purpose, 113
first article of creed, 122
becomes the whole government, 179–80
dangers and advantages, 180–81
problems of total involvement,
181
Arusha Declaration, 181ff.
Tawney, R. H., *Acquisitive Society*, 105
Taxation, and forced labour, 41,
87

Tempels, Placide, *Bantu Philosophy*, 80–81
Timbuktu, scholarship, 35
Times, The, 171, 172, 176, 188
Togo, 68
Touré, Sékou, President, 127,
134, 196–7
Nkrumah and, 68–9
and civil service frauds, 138
suppression of pro-French
chiefs, 142
and Guinea's independence,
195–6
Townships, African, urban employment in, 88
maladjusted society, 95–6,
103–4, 120
'free enterprise phenomena',
105
Trade Unions, 16
and independence campaigns,
102–3
Tribalism and tribal systems,
114–15
and breakdown of old social
order, 96ff.
post-independence survival,
139ff., 175
France and, 142–6
Tribe, a, use of the term, 21–2
Tshombe, Moise, his Conakat
party, 99
Tubman, President, 69
policy in Liberia, 149–50
Tunisia, Néo-Destour Party, 145
reorganization, 152 and n.

Uganda, 172
African education, 45
and regional unity, 70, 132–3
and tribalism, 140
Uganda People's Congress, 133

'Ujamaa', describes African Socialism, 122

Underdeveloped countries, foreign investors and, 127ff.

Unemployment, in Kenya, 67

UNESCO, report on children in Leopoldville, 92, 94

Union Nationale des Forces Populaire (UNFP), 144

Union of African States, formation, 68–9

Union of Tanzania, 179n.

Unions des Populations Camerounaises, *comités de village*, 16

United Africa Company, 190

Unilever Ghana plant, 72, 192

United Gold Coast Convention, 186

United National Independence Party of Northern Rhodesia, 102

United Nations, investigation into miners' wages, 91
   applies sanctions to Rhodesia, 208–9

United States, its Black Moslems, 77, 82
   criticisms of one-party systems, 114
   economic aid mission, 125
   private investment in Africa, 130, 197–8, 204
   loans to Ghana, 131, 191
   aid to Africa, 150, 164
   and Africa's socialism, 178, 179
   criticism of Ghana, 188

United States Agency for International Development, 150

Upper Volta, 69, 136
   migrant labour from, 87

Urundi, 87

Venereal disease, in mining industry, 89–90

Verwoerd, Dr, National Party, 69, 188

Volta Republic, 152

Volta dam project, 191 and n.

Vorster, Balthazar, 206, 208

Wages, in urban employment, 88, 90ff.
   and worsening poverty, 90–93

Welensky, Sir Roy, Federal Prime Minister, 215–16
   and 'communist' nature of nationalism, 51

West Africa, on French agreements with ex-colonies, 71

West African Lands Committee, 32

West African Railroad, Tramways and Canal Co., 118

West European Common Market, and Brazzaville states, 70, 71, 72–3
   absorption of French colonies, 130

West Indies, 103
   and Pan-Africanism, 63
   and Négritude, 74

Western Region Marketing Board, dissipation of public funds, 137

Wilberforce, William, on Sierra Leone colonists, 47–8

Williams, H. Sylvester, 64

Winterbottom, Dr Thomas, 20

Wissmann, Hermann von, in E. Africa, 52

World War I, African troops in, 49
   appearance of nationalism, 59

Index

World War II, aftermath in Africa, 43, 49
  African nationalism in, 61

Yaoundé, 135
Yoruba, the, 21, 22, 170
Yorubaland, 100, 159, 160
Youlou, President (Abbé), 111–12

Yugoslavia, 125

Zambesi River, 23, 37
Zambia, 16, 201, 206, 209
Zanzibar, Union with Tanganyika, 179n., 181
  revolutionary activities, 181
Zimbabwe Labour News, 102
Zulus, 29, 115

*Other books by Basil Davidson are
described overleaf.*

Basil Davidson

The Liberation of Guiné
Aspects of an African Revolution

The revolutionary struggle in Portuguese Guiné began in
earnest in September 1956, when six Africans formed
the African Independence Party of Guiné and the Cape
Verde Islands (P A I G C). It sharpened after the Pidgiguiti
massacre of August 1959, when fifty lives were lost as dock
workers were forced back to work at gun-point by police.
By 1963 the P A I G C had finally taken to armed
resistance: five years later it had liberated two thirds of
the country.

This volume of the Penguin African Library is an important
new field-study of guerrilla warfare in an African context.
In it Basil Davidson tells the remarkable story of the
liberation of Guiné and discusses its wider significance.

The African Past*
Chronicles from Antiquity to Modern Times

Africa can no longer be denied her place in the past. In this
anthology Basil Davidson shows that, contrary to popular
belief, Africa was not a country of chaos and stagnation
when the first European traders and explorers arrived.
He proves this by presenting us with a fascinating collection
of records which bear witness to Africa's long tradition and
through which we trace Africa's history from its beginnings
in Egypt, through the important Nok culture and on into
the tragic and cruel period of the slave trade.

'A most exciting, scholarly, and timely book, of deep
significance and importance to the understanding of
present-day Africa and Africans' – *Glasgow Herald*

*Not for sale in the U.S.A.